THE GREEN GUIDE TO SPECIFICATION
An Environmental Profiling System
for Building Materials and Components

Fourth edition

Jane Anderson
BRE Global

David Shiers
Oxford Brookes University

Kristian Steele
BRE Global

IHS

bre press    WILEY-BLACKWELL   breglobal
A John Wiley & Sons, Ltd., Publication

BRE, Garston, Watford WD25 9XX
Tel: 01923 664000
enquiries@bre.co.uk
www.bre.co.uk

BRE publications are available from
www.ihsbrepress.com
or
IHS BRE Press
Willoughby Road
Bracknell RG12 8FB
Tel: 01344 328038
Fax: 01344 328005
Email: brepress@ihs.com

Requests to copy any part of this publication should be made to the publisher:
IHS BRE Press
Garston, Watford WD25 9XX
Tel: 01923 664761
Email: brepress@ihs.com

Front cover photographs:
Left: *Innovate* Green Office, Thorpe Park, Leeds
          (*BREEAM* Offices award-winner 2007)
          Architect: Rio architects, Cardiff
          Environmental Engineer: King Shaw Associates
Right: Code for Sustainable Homes rated houses on
          the BRE Innovation Park:
          Top: Lighthouse™, Kingspan Offsite
          Middle: Ecohouse™, Hanson
          Bottom: Organics™ house, ecoTECH

Printed on paper sourced from
responsibly managed forests

This edition first published 2009
© 2009 BRE and Oxford Brookes University

Blackwell Publishing was acquired by John Wiley & Sons in February 2007. Blackwell's publishing programme has been merged with Wiley's global Scientific, Technical, and Medical business to form Wiley-Blackwell.

Registered office
John Wiley & Sons Ltd, The Atrium, Southern Gate, Chic
West Sussex, PO19 8SQ, United Kingdom

Editorial offices
9600 Garsington Road, Oxford, OX4 2DQ,
United Kingdom
2121 State Avenue, Ames, Iowa 50014-8300, USA

Set in 9pt ZapfHumnst by IHS BRE Press
Printed and bound in Great Britain by TJ International Ltd, Padstow, Cornwall

BR 501
© Copyright BRE and Oxford Brookes University 2009
First published 2009
IHS BRE Press ISBN 978-1-84806-071-5

1 2009

Wiley-Blackwell ISBN 978-1-40511-961-0

CONTENTS

FOREWORD

The relationship between the built and the natural environments has received an unprecedented level of coverage in the media in recent years as well as driving much new scientific research. Concerns regarding our ability to meet our present economic and social requirements without compromising the needs of future generations, have also been responsible for recent extensive and far-reaching environmental legislation introduced in many countries, including the UK.

This has happened for good reasons; the use of energy in buildings, in industrial processes and in our transport systems, and the consequent release of carbon dioxide and other emissions into the earth's atmosphere, has raised very real fears of global climate change. At the same time, the increasing rates of deforestation, the extensive use of many of our natural but finite resources and the production and management of waste materials, are just some of the environmental issues that point to the unsustainable nature of many human systems.

There are no guarantees that even with an immediate and concerted effort on the part of politicians and industry, the future will be better than it might otherwise have been or that the predicted environmental and economic problems will be avoided. However, a new and more responsible approach to the natural environment is surely our best chance of, at the very least, reducing the scale of these impacts to hopefully more manageable proportions. It is also self-evident that less pollution and less profligate use of resources can offer many financial and quality-of-life advantages now.

Many organisations in both the public and private sectors are finding that 'greener' property can lead to lower running costs, reduced enviro-legal risks, greater occupier satisfaction (through better working environments) and enhanced PR and marketing benefits. The numbers of businesses now signing up to Corporate Social Responsibility programmes is evidence of this growth in environmental and social awareness. Better, more environmentally responsible choices regarding the types of materials that we put into our buildings are therefore central to reducing the global environmental impact of the property sector.

In this book, building materials and components are assessed in terms of their environmental impact across their entire life cycle – 'from cradle-to-grave', within comparable specifications. Such accessible and reliable information will be of great assistance to all those involved in the design, construction and management of buildings as they work to reduce the environmental impact of their properties.

We are sure that this book will help to ensure that in the future, property professionals will be able to make the soundest possible environmentally responsible choices in their materials selection.

Neville Simms
Chairman
BRE Trust

Jonathon Porritt
Chairman
Sustainable Development Commission

ACKNOWLEDGEMENTS

The authors wish to acknowledge the contribution made and the support given by the following individuals and organisations. Particular thanks are due to the Construction Products Association and their members for helping the team with information capture and constructive criticism. A special thank you is given to Jane Thornback, without whose hard work and support *The Green Guide* would not be possible.

BRE Global Project Team
Kim Allbury
Tim Allan
Julia Barnard
Victoria Blake
Andrew Dutfield
Sue Fakes
Emma Franklin
Katie Halls
Jo Mundy
Kavita Ramchandra
Bridget Randall
Paul Thistlethwaite

BRE Global
David Crowhurst
Richard Hardy

BRE
Peter Bonfield
Mike Clift
Martin Cook
Angus Jack
Chris Watson

Oxford Brookes University
Professor Martin Avis
Richard Grover

Others
John Bowdidge
Kathryn Bourke — *Faithful+Gould*
Suzy Edwards
Professor Anthony Heath — *University of Oxford*
Dr Karen Kearley — *University of Oxford*
Miles Keeping — *GVA Grimley*
Professor Anthony Lavers — *White & Case*
Professor Paul McNamara — *PruPIM*
Alan Pearman — *Centre for Decision Research, University of Leeds*
Eva Schmincke — *Five Winds, Germany*
Jane Thornback — *Construction Products Association*
Wayne Trusty — *Athena Sustainable Materials Institute, Canada*

PROJECT SPONSORS

bre

bretrust

BERR | Department for Business
Enterprise & Regulatory Reform

department for
children, schools and families

energy saving trust®

**Homes &
Communities**
Agency

HSBC ◆X◆

NHBC

oGc buying.solutions

OXFORD
BROOKES
UNIVERSITY

POST
OFFICE®

RBS
The Royal Bank of Scotland Group

WILLMOTT DIXON
CONSTRUCTION

wrap **Material change for
a better environment**

THE AUTHORS

Jane Anderson BA MSc DipLCM FRSA
BREEAM Materials, BRE Global

Jane is an expert in the development and application of Life Cycle Assessment (LCA) methodology for building construction and materials. She is Technical Manager of the BREEAM Materials Group where she has been a key member since 1998. She co-authored *The Green Guide to Housing Specification* and the third edition of *The Green Guide to Specification*. She gained a distinction in her master's degree in Architecture at the University of East London.

David Shiers BA BArchHons CertHEduc RIBA
Department of Real Estate,
Oxford Brookes University

A qualified architect and teacher and environmental consultant with AEA Technology, David has written extensively on many property-related environmental issues and was co-author and designer of the methodology underpinning the original version of *The Green Guide to Specification*. David has co-edited a special Property and the Environment edition of the journal *Construction Management and Economics* with Professor Anthony Lavers and has contributed to other publications including *Property Management, The Journal of Property Investment and Finance,* and *Property Review*. He has also advised and collaborated with many organisations on green issues including the Housing Corporation, the GLA, Urban Buzz, DTZ, and King Sturge. He was a Visiting Research Scholar at the University of Oxford in 2002 and is a member of the CIB International Working Commission on Sustainable Construction.

Kristian Steele MEng EngD
BREEAM Materials, BRE Global

A civil engineer by training, Kristian has a history in infrastructure management, environmental assessment and sustainability. Kristian joined BRE in 2002 following completion of an EngD in Environmental Technology with the University of Surrey and Surrey County Council. Kristian is currently group leader of the BREEAM Materials team. The BREEAM Materials team provides advice, training and information on the environmental performance of building systems and is responsible for the development of *The Green Guide to Specification* and Envest. It also manages the BRE Certification scheme for Environmental Product Declarations.

PART 1 INTRODUCTION

1   BACKGROUND

The purpose of this 4th edition of *The Green Guide to Specification* is to provide designers and specifiers with easy-to-use guidance on how to make the best environmental choices when selecting construction materials and components. It is more comprehensive than its predecessors and contains more than 1200 specifications used in various types of buildings.

Developing the content has involved the widest possible consultation with industrial partners, manufacturers and trade associations, academics and researchers, and reference to a wide range of other reliable sources of environmental data and information.

The whole process has also been the subject of more rigorous peer review procedures than its predecessors and, as a result, both the methodologies used and the findings made are as robust and dependable as they can be at the present time in the field of environmental impact assessment and life cycle assessment of construction products.

1.1 ENVIRONMENTAL CONSERVATION

Many in the property sector are becoming more aware of the need to reduce exposure to 'environmental risk'. While the most common construction and development-related risks have been associated with polluting activities or the failure of specialists to deal with specific environmental hazards, the future scope of environmental liability may have far-reaching implications for the construction industry. The impact of the construction process and the associated impact from materials extraction and manufacture in terms of energy and resource use or levels of emissions on global conditions could be identified as a major 'indirect' environmental hazard. As such, it is possible that these issues will become potential legal liability flashpoints and that designers, specifiers and materials manufacturers will be obliged to take this into account in the design and construction process.

Environmental impacts come in many different forms. It is widely accepted that there is mounting evidence to suggest that the concentrations of carbon dioxide (CO_2) and other 'greenhouse' gases (such as methane) in the atmosphere are increasing. This, it is argued, is leading to global warming and climate change. As the main source of these greenhouse gases is the burning of fossil fuels for energy, a reduction in the energy levels required in the manufacture of building materials represents an opportunity for producers of materials to minimise the environmental impact of their products. The release of chemicals into the atmosphere from manufacturing processes has been linked to damage to the ozone layer and to other effects that are harmful to the environment and human health. Volatile organic compound (VOC) emissions may be irritant or toxic. Nitrogen dioxide and nitrogen oxide (NOx), released in combustion processes, are both contributors to acid rain and react with VOCs in sunlight to produce photochemical smog. This smog is implicated in an increased incidence in asthma and respiratory illness. Sulfur dioxide (SO_2), also released from the combustion of oil and coal products, is a main contributor to acid rain. All these impacts are relevant and present in building product manufacture. Suppliers and producers have a responsibility to understand the relative impacts of manufacture and to work towards impact mitigation. Designers and specifiers can assist in this process through making more environmentally responsible choices.

Similar responsibilities are evident in other parts of the construction value chain. Property investors and funding institutions, under pressure from shareholders and insurers, are also seeking a 'greener' and more 'socially responsible' approach to the design and procurement of buildings, and many property-owning organisations are signing up to Corporate Social Responsibility (CSR) initiatives. A more carefully considered, environmentally aware approach to the specification of materials is important in being able to demonstrate that projects are well managed and are protecting shareholders' interests through minimising the risks associated with environmental impact. Across all these issues, *The Green Guide* is designed to provide robust information to assist in decision-making processes.

1.2 THE PURPOSE OF THE GREEN GUIDE

Before the publication of the first edition of *The Green Guide* in 1996[1], there was little accessible, reliable or methodologically robust guidance available for specifiers seeking to minimise the environmental impacts of building materials. Much of the relevant research and information at that time offered either generalised guidance, usually unsupported by quantitative data, or, alternatively, complex numerical assessments that proved difficult for designers and clients to interpret. The first edition of this publication therefore aimed to provide a simple 'green guide' to the environmental impacts of building materials which was both easy for busy professionals to use and soundly based on numerical data. This ethos was maintained through the publication of subsequent *Green Guides*, and has remained as an aim and purpose for developing this 4th edition.

The Green Guide is intended for use with whole building assessment tools such as BREEAM, The Code for Sustainable Homes and EcoHomes rather than as a stand alone tool. Material choice and specification has an impact on the overall environmental, social and economic impact of a building which *The Green Guide* cannot take into account. For this reason, BRE Global does not recommend that targets based on *The Green Guide* ratings are set independently, for example by Planning Authorities.

1.3 THE DEVELOPMENT OF THE GREEN GUIDE

The success of the Environmental Profiling system used in *The Green Guide* is demonstrated by the continuing demand for successive, updated editions. The 2nd edition was launched by the Minister for Construction in 1998, and contained over 200 specifications[2]. Since that time, *The Green Guide* has been part of the BRE Environmental Assessment Method (BREEAM)[3], EcoHomes[4], and more recently The Code for Sustainable Homes[5], becoming the UK's leading construction-embodied impact assessment tool. A version developed specifically to appraise the materials used in housing was released in 2000[6]. The 3rd edition, profiling around 300 different commercial specifications, was published in 2002[7].

Information on the relative environmental performance of materials and components is continually advancing, reflecting changes in manufacturing practices, the way materials are used in buildings, and our evolving environmental knowledge. This developing context has led to the compilation of this 4th edition of *The Green Guide*.

1.4 CONTENT AND LAYOUT OF THE GREEN GUIDE

The scope of this book examines the relative environmental impacts of the construction materials commonly used in six different generic types of building including:
* commercial buildings, such as offices,
* educational buildings, such as schools and universities,
* healthcare buildings, such as hospitals,
* retail,
* residential,
* industrial.

Materials and components are arranged on an elemental basis: external wall construction, internal walls, landscaping, etc., so that the reader can compare and select from comparable systems or materials. Furthermore, it is meaningless to compare the environmental profiles of, say, concrete floors and a particular type of paint; ratings are therefore based only on product performance within each respective element group. The principal

building elements covered in this edition of *The Green Guide* include:
* ground floors,
* upper floors,
* roofs,
* external walls,
* windows,
* internal walls and partitions,
* insulation,
* landscaping.

Across these building element categories *The Green Guide* provides an extensive, but not complete, catalogue of building specifications covering most common building materials. It is therefore intended that the number of products profiled will continue to increase with subsequent editions and through updates to the online version of *The Green Guide to Specification*[8]. It is also fully expected that other building element categories will be added in time.

Materials and components are presented in their typical, as-built, elemental form. They are compared on a like-for-like basis, for 1 m² of construction, as components that fulfil the same or very similar functions; important variables such as the mass of a material required to fulfil a particular function are therefore taken into account. For example, a direct comparison between the Environmental Profile of 1 tonne of structural steel and 1 tonne of structural concrete would be misleading, as less steel is required to achieve the same structural performance.

It should be noted that *The Green Guide* does not take operational performance into account in terms of the potential energy-saving benefits of materials with high insulation values or high thermal mass. Because *The Green Guide* is intended for use within overall building assessment tools such as BREEAM[3] and The Code for Sustainable Homes[5], which already reward the minimisation of operational impacts, it would be double counting to also include these benefits within *The Green Guide*. All relevant specifications are compared on the basis of a common U-value and therefore equivalent heat loss.

1.5 ENVIRONMENTAL IMPACTS

The environmental ratings in this publication are based on life cycle assessment (LCA), an environmental impact assessment method for products and materials that is described in *Chapter 3*. The LCAs that underpin the ratings take into account the environmental impacts of the winning of the raw materials, manufacture, transport, assembly, maintenance, repair and replacement, demolition and waste management at the end of life.

LCA also takes into consideration a wide number of environmental issues. The environmental issues covered by *The Green Guide* ratings reflect the generally accepted areas of concern related to the production of building materials used in the UK and were arrived at through an industry consultation and consensus process that took place during *The Green Guide*'s development work. The issues included are listed in Box 1.1.

**Box 1.1: Environmental issues covered by
The Green Guide**

- Climate change
- Water extraction
- Mineral resource extraction
- Stratospheric ozone depletion
- Human toxicity
- Ecotoxicity to freshwater
- Nuclear waste (higher level)
- Ecotoxicity to land
- Waste disposal
- Fossil fuel depletion
- Eutrophication
- Photochemical ozone creation
- Acidification

1.6 THE GREEN GUIDE RATING SYSTEM

Although the environmental ratings in this publication are underpinned by extensive quantitative LCA data, it was felt that these numerical values and comparisons would be of interest only to specialists rather than those involved in the day-to-day procurement of building projects.

To assist decision making, *The Green Guide* translates the numerical LCA data into a simple environmental rating system to enable specifiers to make meaningful comparisons between materials and components. As a means to this end, an A+ to E ranking system is used, where 'A+' equals good environmental performance, ie least environmental impact, with A, B, C, D and E ratings increasing as environmental impact increases. Every specification included in *The Green Guide* is rated using this scale for each of the 13 categories of environmental impact, together with an overall Summary Rating. This is explained in more detail in *Chapter 4*.

1.7 STATUS OF SPECIFICATIONS

The specifications shown throughout this publication are generic and are used to illustrate a range of typical materials and are not intended to be used to specify construction. Although every effort has been made to ensure that the information given here is accurate, knowledge and understanding in this new field is still evolving. The ratings shown here represent our best efforts to provide objective, helpful guidance to enable the specifier to make more informed choices, based on the data and methodologies available at this present time.

1.8 BALANCING THE GREEN GUIDE WITH OTHER REQUIREMENTS

Designers will be aware of the view among many environmental researchers that operational impacts of buildings normally outweigh the embodied impacts arising from materials production and construction, by a factor in the region of 9:1. There may therefore be circumstances under which a less than environmentally ideal specification choice can be justified in the interests of better long-term operational environmental performance. This is not to say, however, that embodied impacts presented here in *The Green Guide* are inconsequential. For example, the materials sector still consumes around 30% of total UK industrial energy and approximately 10% of all UK energy. The Environmental Profile (ie LCA) of a building material is only one of many factors which needs to be taken into consideration when compiling a specification. Other important and potentially decisive issues are:

- cost,
- durability,
- appearance,
- development control issues,
- buildability,
- function and operational issues (including the benefits of using high thermal mass materials),
- maintenance,
- availability.

It must also be recognised that the scientific understanding of what is best environmental practice is subject to change. Designers will be aware of the ongoing debate concerning the merits of recycling and how recycling may not always represent best environmental practice, especially where high value and polluting energy resources are consumed to recycle low-value material. The merits of recycling should be judged on a case-by-case basis, looking particularly at key issues for each individual material and location. For example, the relatively low impacts of some reclaimed materials can be adversely affected if they have to be transported over long distances when compared with new materials that may be produced more locally.

The most successful approach for establishing the appropriate balance between conflicting requirements is to establish the underlying objectives and priorities in the early stages of a project.

Even in the best buildings, compromise is an inevitable part of design and specification; 'green' considerations will no doubt be subject to this same process of trade-off in achieving the right balance of priorities for a particular project. It is hoped that, by thoughtful consideration and the careful use of this book, designers and client organisations will at the very least begin to 'move in the right direction' towards reducing the environmental impacts of construction projects.

2 THE GREEN GUIDE AND RELATED BRE PUBLICATIONS AND TOOLS

Like its predecessors, this edition of *The Green Guide to Specification* is intended for use within BREEAM[3], EcoHomes[4] and The Code for Sustainable Homes[5] to assess the credits for materials specification. It is one of a suite of tools produced by BRE which provides guidance to designers and specifiers on the environmental impacts of buildings and their construction materials. This chapter explains how this edition and the work that went into it relate to other BRE publications and tools.

2.1 THE ENVIRONMENTAL PROFILES METHODOLOGY AND DATABASE

The Environmental Profiles Methodology enables environmental assessment of construction materials by applying a consistent life cycle assessment (LCA) calculation that is designed to provide a 'level playing field'. The method allows direct comparison of the environmental impacts of functionally equivalent products and building specifications, and, as a method, has been uniformly applied to all data included in *The Green Guide*.

BRE developed the first edition of the Environmental Profiles Methodology and its associated database in 1998[9,10]. This was the culmination of a three-year project funded by a former UK Government Department [Department of the Environment, Transport and the Regions (DETR)] with the partnership of 24 construction manufacturing trade associations. The development and publication of the methodology was a significant achievement, providing the UK with a single agreed approach to the environmental LCA of all types of construction materials. This methodology received the approval of all partner trade associations, many of whom provided data on their own manufacturing processes to allow the production of a database of environmental LCA information. This was used to underpin the 3rd edition of *The Green Guide to Specification*[7] and *The Green Guide to Housing Specification*[6].

In developing this 4th edition of *The Green Guide*, BRE also undertook work to update the Environmental Profiles Methodology and its associated database, and this research programme culminated in the publication of a 2nd edition of the Environmental Profiles Methodology (2009)[11]. The project was made possible through funding from the BRE Trust together with support from a further 13 research sponsors. This group, along with a further five members (to provide fuller construction sector

representation) formed the project steering group (PSG). The full membership listing can be found in the *Appendix*.

An aim of the project was to achieve the widest possible consultation with industry stakeholders, and wherever possible, to ensure consensus in decision making. In this way a true 'level playing field' could be maintained. The project was led from the immediate PSG, but also benefited from a series of detailed industry critical reviews, peer reviews and formal dialogues. The full scope of these is illustrated in Figure 2.1.

In addition to the PSG, the project was undertaken under the auspices of the BRE Global* governance body, the Sustainability Board (see Figure 2.1). This board is an independent group established under a UKAS-accredited structure to oversee BRE Global's sustainability work. On a wider level, consultation on the project involved industrial partners, manufacturers and trade associations, academics and researchers. The terms of the review included all aspects of the Environmental Profiles Methodology and its application to *The Green Guide*, including:

* *The Green Guide* format and content,
* Environmental Profiles: LCA methodology,
  * Characterisation,
  * Normalisation,
  * Weightings,
* Specifications,
* Energy models,
* Service life methodology,
* End-of-life and waste models,
* Existing LCA data and update requirements.

On each aspect, BRE Global articulated its intentions in a public briefing note to which responses were invited. An open forum with trade associations and manufacturers was commonly held to review content. This was managed through the Construction Products Association Manufacturers' Advisory Group (MAG). On conclusion of the public consultation, BRE answered feedback by issuing a document giving responses and summarising its intended way forward. The project briefing note and response document process involved all groups under the Sustainability Board as represented in Figure 2.1. This process established a common way forward based on consensus. The full extent of this work can be found on *The Green Guide to Specification* website[8].

---

* BRE Global is the BRE Group's certification business.

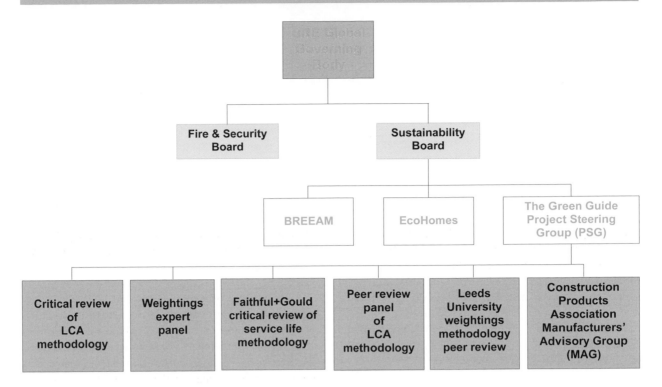

Figure 2.1: Governance structure under which *The Green Guide to Specification* and the Environmental Profiles Methodology update project were undertaken

The whole process was subject to a rigorous critical review in which four internationally established LCA practitioners commented on the project briefing notes to provide advice towards the Environmental Profiles LCA methodology. A listing of these practitioners can be found in the Appendix.

A goal of the project was to ensure that the second edition of the Environmental Profiles Methodology was compliant with relevant ISO standards. This was achieved and formalised through an independent third-party peer review of the methodology. The panel established that the Environmental Profiles Methodology was developed in accordance with the ISO 14040 series of standards[12], as well as ISO 14025[13] and ISO 21930[14]. These standards have been developed to standardise and define the manner in which LCA should be undertaken and also applied to the built environment.

As a result, the methodology used and the findings made and presented in this edition of *The Green Guide* are as robust and dependable as they can be at present in the field of environmental impact assessment and life cycle assessment of construction products.

Because the work to update the Environmental Profiles Methodology was undertaken so closely with industry, there was also real impetus from trade associations to capture and provide new LCA data. Therefore, this *Green Guide to Specification* also benefits from comprehensive industry data and much of the material information used in the publication is based on UK-specific data on the supply and manufacture of construction materials.

2.2 PREVIOUS EDITIONS OF THE GREEN GUIDE TO SPECIFICATION

The first edition of *The Green Guide*[1] was developed as an in-house publication for the Post Office and their design consultants. Published in 1996, it was intended to provide guidance on the environmental impacts of common building specifications, including those being considered for use in Post Office properties such as offices, warehouses, sorting offices and post offices. Following great interest in the first edition, which had been circulated widely amongst the Post Office's design consultants, a second edition for elements and materials was published by BRE in conjunction with the Post Office and Oxford Brookes University in September 1998[2]. This version was linked to *BREEAM '98 for Offices*[15], and was used to assess credits for materials specification. In 2000 BRE produced *The Green Guide to Housing Specification*[6] which for the first time was based on the Environmental Profiles LCA methodology. This publication focused on domestic construction. A third edition of *The Green Guide* which focused on commercial buildings followed in 2002[7].

2.3 WEB UPDATES AND THE GREEN GUIDE TO SPECIFICATION ONLINE[8]

As the base information and the ways in which it is interpreted become more sophisticated and reliable over time, the advice given in publications of this type may be modified. For this reason and in parallel with the publication of this book, BRE is also publishing *The Green Guide to Specification Online*[8].

The Green Guide to Specification Online has been developed along with this printed publication and in its first iteration is founded on the same information and underlying data. However, the web-based version will be updated when new information becomes available. For this reason the reader should consult *The Green Guide to Specification Online*[8] for the latest updates and guidance on the use of *The Green Guide* ratings.

2.4 BREEAM AND ECOHOMES

The BRE Environmental Assessment Method (BREEAM)[3] is an assessment tool that provides a credible, transparent environmental label for buildings based on encouraging best practice. Its holistic structure and multi-criteria approach mean that it preserves the design team's flexibility to provide overall value through the design process. BREEAM is now widely used to specify overall environmental performance for buildings in the UK and internationally. EcoHomes is the BREEAM scheme for housing.

One of the aims of BREEAM is to encourage the use of materials that have a lower impact on the environment, taking account of their full life cycle. For this reason in all BREEAM schemes a proportion of the total score available is for the specification of low-embodied impact materials. This makes the selection and reuse of materials an important factor in determining the building's overall score. The assessment can be applied at the design stage in new build and refurbishment schemes as well as in existing buildings.

BREEAM uses *The Green Guide to Specification* to consider the embodied environmental impacts of different specification options and awards credits for using specifications that minimise environmental impact.

Using *The Green Guide to Specification* to assess materials specification in this manner allows BREEAM to address a number of environmental impacts of major building elements, such as embodied energy, emissions, consumption of resources, recycling issues and toxicity in a comprehensive, quick and easy way.

2.4.1   The Code for Sustainable Homes[5]

The Code for Sustainable Homes[5] is owned by the UK Government's Department for Communities and Local Government (CLG), was developed by BRE in conjunction with CLG and is based on EcoHomes. As with BREEAM, The Code for Sustainable Homes uses *The Green Guide to Specification* to consider the embodied environmental impacts of different specification options and awards credits for using specifications that minimise environmental impact. The Code includes a mandatory materials credit, requiring E-rated specifications to be used for no more than two of the major building elements within any assessed dwelling.

2.5 ENVEST[16]

The Green Guide to Specification is aimed at providing designers and specifiers with the straightforward information they require to produce buildings with lower embodied impacts. However, for designers who wish to consider their materials specification in more depth, and understand their choice of materials in the context of the operational aspects of a building (eg its heating, lighting

and air-conditioning), BRE has developed a software tool called *Envest*[16]. Intended for use at the initial design stage, *Envest* allows designers to enter their designs and identify those elements with the most impact. *Envest* also includes an indication of the operational energy demands to allow designers to investigate the trade-off between the life cycle impacts of their design structure and operational impacts arising from building use.

Envest modelling is based on the same Ecopoints data and weighting system as *The Green Guide to Specification*.

2.6 GREEN PROCUREMENT AND RESPONSIBLE SOURCING

Two important decisions affect the procurement of building products and their impact on the environment:
* *what to buy*, and
* *who to buy it from.*

The Green Guide to Specification provides assistance to specifiers with the first decision. They may also find it useful to distinguish between manufacturers once the type of product has been chosen, and this can be achieved in a variety of ways.
* Certification to ISO 14001 or an EMAS environmental management system can be used as an indicator of good performance by a supplier.
* Evidence of their use of specific measures such as use of raw materials with lower impacts or from local sources or low-emission technologies may also be useful.
* Evidence from an Environmental Product Declaration (EPD) based on LCA can be used for comparison with other products.

As well as the publication of *The Green Guide to Specification*, BRE has developed two product certification schemes (namely, the *Environmental Profiles Certification Scheme* and the *Responsible Sourcing of Materials Certification Scheme*, described below) aimed at improving the environmental sustainability of construction products and materials.

2.6.1   The Environmental Profiles Certification scheme

Neither an EMS nor evidence of a 'single-issue' approach to environmental impact will help to determine how a particular manufacturer's product compares with the typical UK product for the wide range of issues used in *The Green Guide to Specification*. Across Europe, many manufacturers are turning to Environmental Product Declarations (EPDs) to communicate their own environmental performance to their customers. In the UK, the BRE Environmental Profiles Certification scheme provides this option. The scheme is based on the same common rules [Product Category Rules (PCR)] defined in the Environmental Profiles Methodology[11] and provides a basis for manufacturers independently to demonstrate their performance against generic products using *The Green Guide to Specification* as the backdrop. This scheme allows manufacturers to make claims about their individual product performance as well as allowing trade associations to provide generic information on 'typical UK performance'. Significantly, in the future, *The Green Guide to Specification Online*[8] will allow the inclusion of specifications with manufacturer-specific data for products generated through Certificated Environmental Profiles which will enable comparison between the generic and proprietary products.

BRE advises specifiers to ask for EPDs from their suppliers and to use them to satisfy themselves that the company they are using takes a responsible attitude to the management of their environmental performance.

The creation of Environmental Profiles for manufacturers is offered as a service by BRE Global[17] and other licensed certification bodies. This enables product manufacturers to calculate the environmental impact of their products using Ecopoints and to compare them within building elements as shown in *The Green Guide to Specification*.

2.6.2   Responsible Sourcing of Materials (RSM) Certification Scheme

Responsible sourcing is demonstrated through an ethos of supply chain management and product stewardship. The scope of RSM is broad and encompasses the social and economic aspects of sustainability as well as the environmental. RSM addresses aspects such as stakeholder engagement, labour practices and the management of supply chains serving materials sectors upstream of the manufacturer. Product stewardship is demonstrated by continued engagement with the use of the product beyond the factory gate and a commitment to improve its life cycle performance. The idea behind RSM is that it provides a holistic approach to managing these criteria from the point at which a material is mined or harvested in its raw state, through manufacture and processing, through use, reuse and recycling, until its final disposal as waste with no further value.

BES 6001: Responsible Sourcing of Materials

The scope of Responsible Sourcing of Materials (RSM) and the criteria it covers are detailed in a BRE Global Certification Standard BES 6001[18]. The aim of BES 6001 is to provide a platform from which industry sectors and companies can seek to determine performance against RSM. Assessment against the standard is to be realised through the establishment of a certification scheme through BRE Global, or other licensed certification bodies. Direct certification of product and material manufacture against BES 6001 will be possible.

The standard considers a number of environmental issues such as global warming emissions, resource efficiency and minimisation of raw material usage, transport and biodiversity. It also takes account of embodied environmental impact as assessed in *The Green Guide to Specification*. Good RSM with regard to embodied impact can be demonstrated through a commitment to identify the significant environmental impacts of a supply chain and manufacturing process through the use of LCA methods such as the Environmental Profiles Certification scheme.

Building designers and specifiers should look for responsibly supplied products as well as ensuring that they have a low embodied environmental impact.

3 LIFE CYCLE ASSESSMENT (LCA) IN THE GREEN GUIDE

This chapter examines how life cycle assessment (LCA) in the form of the Environmental Profiles Methodology was applied in *The Green Guide to Specification*.

3.1 LIFE CYCLE ASSESSMENT (LCA)

The environmental information at the centre of *The Green Guide* is generated using LCA. LCA is a method of evaluating the environmental impacts of a system taking into account its full life cycle, 'from the cradle to the grave'. This means taking into consideration all the impacts associated with the production and use of a system, from the first time that mankind has an impact on the environment until the last. This approach is conceptualised in Figure 3.1.

At a specific level, if the manufacture and use of a brick wall is taken as an example, then in using LCA, we would aim to consider the environmental impacts associated with:

- the extraction and transport of clay to the brickworks,
- manufacture and transport of ancillary materials,
- the extraction and distribution of natural gas for the brick kiln,
- the mining, refining and transport of fuels for the generation of electricity for use in the factory,
- the production and transport of raw materials for the packaging,
- the manufacture and transport of packaging materials for the bricks,
- the manufacture of the brick in the brickworks,
- the transport of the bricks to the building site,
- the extraction of sand and production of cement for the mortar,
- the building of the brick wall,
- the disposal of waste materials and packaging,
- the maintenance of the wall, such as painting or repointing,

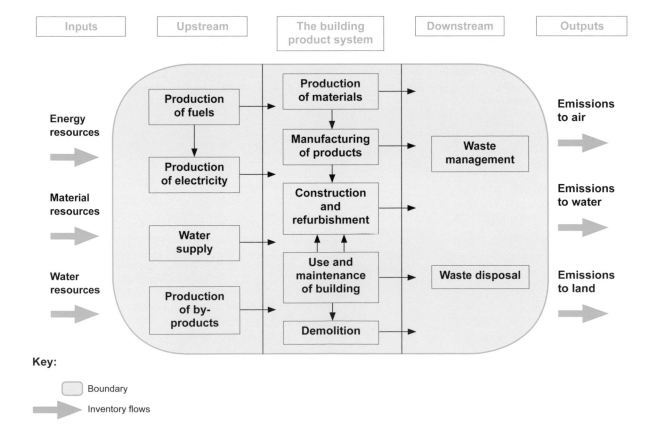

Key:

▢ Boundary

➜ Inventory flows

Figure 3.1: An example life cycle system of a building and its interventions with the physical environment. LCA can be used to model these scenarios and measure environmental impacts

- the demolition of the wall,
- the fate of the materials in the waste stream.

Undertaking an LCA study of a system like this is a detailed and complex process involving many modelling decisions. In common with many of BRE's embodied impact assessment tools, this edition of *The Green Guide to Specification* uses the Environmental Profiles Methodology as its LCA method.

3.2 THE ENVIRONMENTAL PROFILES METHODOLOGY

The Environmental Profiles Methodology is a set of product category rules (PCR) developed specifically for applying LCA to built environment life cycle scenarios. An LCA methodology or PCR is a record of the rules that need to be followed to ensure that the LCA is fair, consistently applied, and that the results can be used comparatively.

The Environmental Profiles Methodology has been developed to provide a 'level playing field' approach for applying LCA. Within it are full descriptions of aspects like the goal and scope of the method and how it should be applied, including details on system boundaries, cut-off rules, allocation methods, energy, waste and transport models, and characterisation and normalisation factors amongst much additional detail. Full documentation on the methodology can be found in BES 6050[11].

3.2.1 Turning emissions into environmental impacts

When using LCA to study a system like a brick wall, environmental interventions will be observed. These come from the use of resources, the release of atmospheric or aqueous emissions, or due to the occurrence of solid wastes. Almost all stages of a studied system will contribute, whether exhaust emissions from its road transport, or water effluent from a manufacturing process. In an LCA study, a detailed numerical record, known as an Inventory, is made of these different interventions. The Inventory is derived through the identification and quantification of the environmental inputs and outputs (inventory flows) of the system under investigation (Figure 3.1). The impact of these inventory flows is assessed and interpreted by linking them to environmental impacts through a step known as 'characterisation'. This is founded on environmental science where fate and impact models underpin the assessment of environmental damage that an inventory flow will create. *The Green Guide*, through its use of the Environmental Profiles Methodology, assesses impact using the 13 categories of environmental damage shown in Box 3.1.

Environmental impacts in one category can be caused by many different emission substances (inventory flows), and one substance can contribute to several impact categories. The step of characterisation assesses all the different substances contributing to an impact category relative to one another to give an overall measure of the level of environmental damage in that category.

This is undertaken by using a reference substance or unit, where the contribution of each measured emission is calculated by converting the amount of emission into the equivalent amount of the reference substance or unit. This conversion is done by using what are called characterisation factors. For example, for the impact category of climate change, the reference substance carbon dioxide (CO_2) is used.

The use of a characterisation factor can be examined by taking methane as an example (Figure 3.2). Methane contributes to climate change, but is measured to be 23 times more damaging than CO_2 over a 100-year timescale. So, through the step of characterisation, the effects of, for example, 1 kg of methane emission are converted into the amount of CO_2 needed to cause the same effect. This equates to applying the climate

Box 3.1: The environmental impact categories used by the Environmental Profiles Methodology and the issues that they represent

Environmental impact category	Environmental issue measured
Climate change	Global warming or greenhouse gas emission
Water extraction	Mains, surface and groundwater consumption
Mineral resource extraction	Metal ore, mineral and aggregate consumption
Stratospheric ozone depletion	Emissions of gases that destroy the ozone layer
Human toxicity	Pollutants that are toxic to humans
Ecotoxicity to freshwater	Pollutants that are toxic to fresh water ecosystems
Nuclear waste (higher level)	High- and intermediate-level radioactive waste from the nuclear energy industry
Ecotoxicity to land	Pollutants that are toxic to terrestrial ecosystems
Waste disposal	Material sent to landfill or incineration
Fossil fuel depletion	Depletion of coal, oil or gas reserves
Eutrophication	Water pollutants that promote algal blooms
Photochemical ozone creation	Air pollutants that react with sunlight and NOx to produce low-level ozone
Acidification	Emissions that cause acid rain

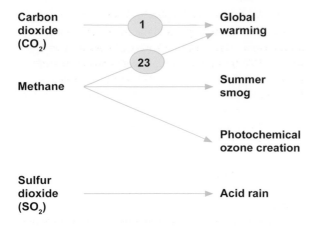

Figure 3.2: The step of characterisation in LCA measures the environmental impact of different emissions such as methane and CO_2

change characterisation factor of 23 to the measured methane amount of 1 kg which gives a figure of 23 kg CO_2 equivalent (100 years). Methane also contributes to Photochemical Ozone Creation, where a 1 kg methane emission has the same impact as the emission of 0.006 kg of ethane (C_2H_2).

The Environmental Profiles Methodology uses similar characterisation factors to cover the full range of emissions and environmental impacts caused by the manufacture, use and disposal of construction materials examined in this publication.

A summary of each of the environmental impact categories and what they address is provided below.

3.2.1   Climate change: kg CO_2 eq. (100 yr)

Climate change refers to the change in global temperature caused via the greenhouse effect by the release of 'greenhouse gases' such as CO_2. There is now scientific consensus that the increase in these emissions is having a noticeable effect on climate. Raised global temperature is expected to cause climatic disturbance, desertification, rising sea levels and spread of disease.

The Environmental Profiles characterisation model is based on factors developed by the United Nation's Intergovernmental Panel on Climate Change (IPCC). Factors are expressed as Global Warming Potential over the time horizon of 100 years (GWP100), measured in the reference unit, kg CO_2 equivalent.

3.2.2   Water extraction: m³ water extracted

Around the world, water is becoming an increasingly scarce resource, due to increased demand, and changes in patterns of rainfall. To recognise the value of water as a resource, and the damage that over-extraction from rivers and aquifers can cause, this category, established by BRE, includes all water extraction, except:
* seawater,
* water extracted for cooling or power generation and then returned to the same source with no change in water quality (water lost through evaporation would be included in the impact category),

* water stored in holding lakes on site for recirculation ('top-up' water from other sources would be included),
* rainwater collected for storage on site.

This category is measured using m³ of water extracted.

3.2.3   Mineral resource extraction: tonne of minerals extracted

This impact category is related to the consumption of all virgin mineral material (eg the extraction of aggregates, metal ores and minerals). The consumption of these substances can mean that they are unavailable for use by future generations. This indicator relates purely to resource use, with no coverage of other environmental impacts that might be associated with mining or quarrying, or the relative scarcity of different resources.

The indicator is based on the Total Material Requirement (TMR) indicators used by the EU and developed by the Wuppertal Institute, based on earlier work for the World Resources Institute. However, the indicators covering fossil fuel, biomass (mainly agricultural product) and soil erosion (only covered for agriculture, not forestry) are not included. Further details can be obtained in the Eurostat working papers[19].

The indicator calculates the total resource use associated with any use of any non-energy, abiotic materials within the EU, wherever the resource use occurs. For example, for steel use, it traces back to tonnes of iron ore extraction wherever this occurs. The TMR indicator includes material that is extracted as a result of economic activities, but not used as input for production or consumption activities, for example mining overburden, tailings or spoil. Excavated and dredged material is also included. For normalisation purposes, the Eurostat data provide relevant figures covering imports of materials as well as resource use within Europe.

This category is measured using tonnes of mineral extracted.

3.2.4   Stratospheric ozone depletion: kg CFC-11 eq.

Ozone-depleting gases cause damage to stratospheric ozone or the 'ozone layer'. There is great uncertainty about the combined effects of different gases in the stratosphere, and all chlorinated and brominated compounds that are stable enough to reach the stratosphere can have an effect. CFCs, Halons and HCFCs are the major causes of ozone depletion. Damage to the ozone layer reduces its ability to prevent ultraviolet (UV) light entering the earth's atmosphere, increasing the amount of carcinogenic UVB light hitting the earth's surface.

The characterisation model has been developed by the World Meteorological Organization (WMO) and defines the ozone depletion potential of different gases relative to the reference substance chlorofluorocarbon-11 (CFC-11), expressed in kg CFC-11 equivalent.

3.2.5   Human toxicity: kg 1,4 dichlorobenzene (1,4-DB) eq.*

The emission of some substances (such as heavy metals) can have impacts on human health. Assessments of toxicity are based on tolerable concentrations in air, water, air quality guidelines, tolerable daily intake and acceptable daily intake for human toxicity. Impacts to air and water have been combined in the ratings tables.

Characterisation factors, expressed as Human Toxicity Potentials (HTP), are calculated using USES-LCA[20], which is based on EUSES[21], the EU's toxicity model. This provides a method that describes fate, exposure and effects of toxic substances on the environment for an infinite time horizon. For each toxic substance HTPs are expressed using the reference unit, kg 1,4-dichlorobenzene (1,4-DB) eq.

Indoor air quality and its effect on human health is not covered by this category.

3.2.6   Ecotoxicity to freshwater and land: kg 1,4 dichlorobenzene (1,4-DB) eq.*

Ecosystem toxicity is measured as two separate impact categories which examine freshwater and land, respectively.

The emission of some substances can have impacts on the ecosystem. Assessment of toxicity has been based on maximum tolerable concentrations in water and land for ecosystems.

Ecotoxicity Potentials are calculated with the USES-LCA[20], as with Human Toxicity which describes fate, exposure and the effects of toxic substances on the environment. Characterisation factors are expressed using the reference unit, kg 1,4-dichlorobenzene eq. (1,4-DB), and are measured separately for impacts of toxic substances on:

- fresh-water aquatic ecosystems,
- terrestrial ecosystems.

BRE believes that toxicity is a key issue that must be addressed by Environmental Profiles and in *The Green Guide* has attempted to find the most relevant models to assess this impact category. It is recognised that toxicity models are still developing.

3.2.7   Nuclear waste: mm³ (higher level waste)

Radioactivity can cause serious damage to human health, and as yet, no treatment or permanently secure storage solution exists for higher level radioactive wastes, such as that generated by the nuclear power industry and from decommissioning nuclear power stations. Such wastes need to be stored for periods of 10,000 years or more before their radioactivity reaches safe levels.

The World Nuclear Association states that higher level nuclear waste (high- and intermediate-level waste) accounts for a very low percentage of nuclear waste, around 10% by volume, but 99% of its radioactivity[22]. Other characterisation methods, such as the Swiss Ecopoints[23], use the volume of highly active radioactive waste as a category.

The characterisation factor for the category is measured in mm³ of spent fuel, and high- and intermediate-level radioactive waste. All of these wastes:

- are highly radioactive, accounting in total for more than 99% of the radioactivity attributed to the nuclear industry,
- have no agreed form of permanent disposal anywhere in the world,
- require storage for at least 10,000 years before they may be safe.

All higher level nuclear waste impacts recorded within Environmental Profiles and *The Green Guide* arise from the use of nuclear electricity.

3.2.8   Waste disposal: tonne solid waste

This category represents the environmental issues associated with the loss of resource implied by the final disposal of waste. BRE uses an absolute measure based on the mass of any waste that is disposed of in landfill or incinerated. This aspect is also used in other characterisation methodologies, for example the Dutch EcoIndicator[24] and the Swiss Ecopoints[23] methods. The characterisation factor is based on the mass of solid waste. Key points for this characterisation factor are:

- it reflects the loss of resource resulting from waste disposal (in contrast to recycling or reuse),
- it does not include any other impacts associated with landfill or incineration – emissions from decomposition, burning and associated transport and other machinery are included in the relevant categories,
- the mass of waste is used as a proxy for the loss of resource,
- it includes waste sent to incineration and landfill or any other form of final disposal (eg dumping on land or in the sea),
- it does not differentiate between hazardous, non-hazardous, inert or organic wastes,
- different impacts from hazardous, non-hazardous, etc. waste will be included within the waste treatment models (landfill, incineration and composting) for these wastes.

Where heat recovery, energy recovery or other material recovery (eg recovery/recycling of ash, metal residues, etc.) are undertaken as part of incineration or landfill, then economic value is used to calculate the loss of resource.

---

* *Toxicity:* It should be noted that issues relating to toxicity generate much debate. Designers are advised to review carefully the material supplier's guidance, to note any relevant regulations, codes and standards appropriate to different industries and materials and to consider the context and application within which the materials are to be used. The results in *The Green Guide* do consider some toxic effects, but these should in no way be considered comprehensive for any of the material options considered. Many of the chemicals used in society in materials and products have not undergone a risk assessment, and assessment techniques are still developing.

3.2.9   Fossil fuel depletion: MJ

This impact category indicator is related to the use of fossil fuels. Fossil fuels provide a valuable source of energy and feedstock for materials such as plastics. Although there are alternatives, these are able to replace only a small proportion of our current use. Fossil fuels are a finite resource and their continued consumption will make them unavailable for use by future generations.

BRE uses an absolute measure based on the energy content of the fossil fuel. This does not take into account the relative scarcity of different fossil fuels, but in fact these vary by only 17% between coal (the most common) and gas (the most scarce). The characterisation factor is measured in mega joules (MJ).

3.2.10   Eutrophication: kg phosphate (PO_4) eq.

Nitrates and phosphates are essential for life, but increased concentrations in water can encourage excessive growth of algae and reduce the oxygen within the water available for other organisms. Eutrophication can therefore be classified as the over-enrichment of water courses. Its occurrence can lead to damage of ecosystems, increasing mortality of aquatic fauna and flora and to loss of species dependent on low-nutrient environments. Emissions of ammonia, nitrates, nitrogen oxides and phosphorus to air or water all have an impact on eutrophication.

Eutrophication potential is based on the work of Heijungs et al[25], and is expressed using the reference unit, kg PO_4 eq.

Direct and indirect impacts of fertilisers are included in the method. The direct impacts are from production of the fertilisers and the indirect ones are calculated using the IPCC method[26] to estimate emissions to water causing Eutrophication.

3.2.11   Photochemical ozone creation: kg ethene (C_2H_4) eq.

In atmospheres containing nitrogen oxides (NOx, a common pollutant) and volatile organic compounds (VOCs), ozone can be created in the presence of sunlight. Although ozone is critical in the high atmosphere to protect against ultraviolet (UV) light, low-level ozone is implicated in impacts as diverse as crop damage and increased incidence of asthma and other respiratory complaints. Photochemical ozone creation potential (also known as summer smog) for emission of substances to air is calculated with the United Nations Economic Commission for Europe (UNECE)[27a,b] trajectory model (including fate) and expressed using the reference unit, kg ethene (C_2H_4) eq.

3.2.12   Acidification: kg sulfur dioxide (SO_2) eq.

Acidic gases such as sulfur dioxide (SO_2) react with water in the atmosphere to form 'acid rain', a process known as acid deposition. When this rain falls, often a considerable distance from the original source of the gas, it causes ecosystem impairment of varying degrees, depending on the nature of the landscape ecosystems. Gases that cause acid deposition include ammonia, nitrogen oxides and sulfur oxides.

Acidification potential is expressed using the reference unit, kg SO_2 eq. The model does not take account of regional differences in terms of which areas are more or less susceptible to acidification. It accounts only for acidification caused by SO_2 and NOx. This includes acidification due to fertiliser use, according to the method developed by the Intergovernmental Panel on Climate Change (IPCC)[26]. The Institute for Environment, Leiden University (CML) has based the characterisation factor on the RAINS model developed by the University of Amsterdam[28].

3.2.13   Further information

Further information on these issues, and the way they have been measured and assessed, is included in the *Environmental Profiles Methodology*[11]. Users may note that these issues have altered from the previous edition of *The Green Guide to Specification*[7].

3.3   CREATING A SINGLE SCORE: ECOPOINTS AND WEIGHTING

Life cycle assessments provide information to users by quantifying the impacts of the studied system. The Environmental Profiles Methodology does this through examining performance using the 13 environmental impact categories described above. *The Green Guide* takes this approach and applies it in studies which focus on construction materials and building specifications.

An experienced practitioner with a background in environmental assessment might be able to use discrete LCA impact category information easily, but for the majority of users within the construction industry, an easier method of dissemination is desirable. For this reason, BRE developed Ecopoints.

The application of the Environmental Profiles Methodology to any specific material or building specification will always produce an Environmental Profile of 13 environmental impact categories. An Ecopoint is a single score that measures the overall environmental impact of these 13 impact categories.

An Ecopoint is not calculated by simply adding the impact categories together. This is not possible because each impact category is measured using different units (eg tonnes of waste, kg of toxicity, etc.), and also the environmental impact categories are not of the same importance. To address these aspects, two further steps are undertaken before an Ecopoint can be calculated. These are called *normalisation* and *weighting*.

3.3.1   Normalisation

Before impact categories can be aggregated, it is first necessary to create a dataset with common units – achieved by applying normalisation. In the Environmental Profiles Methodology, characterised impacts of the studied system are normalised (to the impacts of an average European citizen (as measured over one year). This is a crucial point. As the Environmental Profiles Methodology now normalises against a European context, it means the methodology is transferable within that European context. This makes it well established for wider use in Europe over the next period. This is particularly important as European LCA practitioners move towards harmonised methods for applying LCA to the built environment.

Normalisation also has the added benefit of providing the environmental impact category data with a perspective of 'significance'. However, ascertaining the relative 'importance' of the different environmental impacts is what is required if the datasets are to be aggregated fairly. This final step is complex but necessary, if we are to identify environmental priorities and improve decisions on product specification.

3.3.2   Weighting

Since people have different views and different levels of understanding of environmental issues, a standardised procedure for assigning relative importance to different environmental impacts is required if there is to be a consistent basis for decision making. This procedure is known as weighting*.

The weightings used in *The Green Guide* have been obtained through a panel of 10 European experts. The panel was able to provide an authoritative overview and judge the relative importance of the 13 environmental issues covered in the Environmental Profiles Methodology. To substantiate the study, an expert and independent peer reviewer was retained for the exercise.

The weightings study was undertaken through the internet and participants were provided with simple objective summary information on each of the environmental impact categories. Individual expert perspectives were obtained by asking each participant to judge the comparative importance of the environmental impact categories against one another. BRE then aggregated the responses to create a single set of environmental weightings which were further normalised to sum to 100 (so as to provide percentage weightings for each environmental issue). The final calculated weightings can be seen in Table 3.1. BRE has also published two further publications on the study[29,30].

3.3.3   ECOPOINTS

The final step of the Ecopoint calculation process simply multiplies the dimensionless, normalised impact category data by its relevant weighting factor. It is then just a simple process of aggregating the 13 different numbers. The sum output is the Ecopoint. This metric is therefore a true single unit of environmental impact and represents the total environmental impact of the study system expressed in a single environmental measurement. In simple terms: the more Ecopoints, the higher the environmental impact of a material or building specification. Because of the use of a European citizen as the Norm, one citizen's share of Europe's impact will be equivalent to 100 Ecopoints.

Ecopoints are used as the basis for determining *The Green Guide* Summary Ratings listed in the tables in

---

* Weighting is also commonly referred to as 'valuation' where it is described in ISO 14040[12].

Table 3.1: The weightings of the 13 environmental impact categories used in *The Green Guide to Specification*

Environmental impact category	Weighting (%)
Climate change	21.6
Water extraction	11.7
Mineral resource extraction	9.8
Stratospheric ozone depletion	9.1
Human toxicity	8.6
Ecotoxicity to freshwater	8.6
Nuclear waste (higher level)	8.2
Ecotoxicity to land	8.0
Waste disposal	7.7
Fossil fuel depletion	3.3
Eutrophication	3.0
Photochemical ozone creation	0.20
Acidification	0.05

Chapter 6. The metric simplifies and standardises the process of comparing the environmental performance of building elements (eg 'brick and block walls' against 'timber frame walls') and further assists in comparison by providing the origin of the easy-to-use A+ to E Summary Ratings.

3.4   APPLYING THE ENVIRONMENTAL PROFILES METHODOLOGY TO CONSTRUCTION SYSTEMS IN THE GREEN GUIDE

One of the most important 'rules' of LCA is the definition of the functional unit, for example if we want to compare the environmental impacts of two internal walls:
* one constructed using aerated blockwork, and
* one constructed using timber studwork with timber panelling.

The Environmental Profiles database provides data on the environmental impacts associated with the production of a tonne of aerated blockwork and a tonne of UK-consumed kiln-dried softwood in the form of 'per tonne' Environmental Profiles. However, the comparison of the two internal walls cannot be made immediately on the basis of the two profiles. A tonne of each product would produce very different areas of wall. Instead, we need to define the functional unit we will use to compare the two internal walls.

Within the Environmental Profiles Methodology, and therefore in *The Green Guide*, the functional unit is commonly defined as one square metre of internal wall over a 60-year building study period. Included in this is any repair and maintenance over the 60-year period, and an assumed dismantling/demolition of the building at the end.

Therefore, to make the comparison of the two internal walls specifications, we need to calculate the mass of each material required to produce an average one square metre of internal wall, including mortar, plaster/plasterboard and paint (for the aerated blockwork) and timber, plasterboard and paint (for the timber partition). This will include the additional material which may be wasted during the construction process, and its disposal from site.

We also need to consider whether any components of the partitions will be repaired or replaced during the 60-year period. For an office building, we will need to take account of 'churn', the regular replacement of partitions as office layouts and tenants change. These 'replacement intervals' have to be assigned.

The final consideration is the fate of the two internal walls when they are replaced or demolished at the end of the building's life. The Environmental Profiles Methodology considers the amount of waste material going to landfill or incineration, and also considers the relative value of any material entering the recycling stream.

For an external wall or roof, the functional unit also takes into account the thermal resistance of the construction, to ensure that all the specifications are compared on a like-for-like basis for overall thermal resistance based on a common U-value.

Designers and specifiers who are seeking more detailed, numerical LCA data may find *The Green Guide to Specification Online*[8] provides them with the additional information that they require.

3.5 SOURCES OF LCA DATA IN THE GREEN GUIDE TO SPECIFICATION

In addition to the work to develop this edition of *The Green Guide to Specification* and to update the Environmental Profiles Methodology, there has also been a major initiative to develop and capture new LCA information representative of UK-supplied construction materials, products and specifications. This has come about through extensive LCA data development work with UK and international construction product trade associations and manufacturers.

The LCA models of materials (ie Environmental Profiles) have been produced by BRE using the Environmental Profiles Methodology. Many of the datasets were developed by working directly with UK trade associations. These data provided the most accurate and representative picture of products from the sector and were the preferred source of LCA data whenever they were available. If such data were not forthcoming, BRE was able to draw from a number of other sources. These included existing LCA studies undertaken by trade associations, and BRE encouraged industry to make them

available for review and inclusion where possible. In all such cases, BRE and the trade association maintained a dialogue to ensure that LCA data were being accurately adapted (where necessary) to be used within *The Green Guide*.

However, LCA data for some materials were not available through trade associations. Where assessment has not occurred, or permission to use Environmental Profiles has not been obtained, BRE has had to refer to other sources of data. These sources include LCA data in the public or private domain and overseas studies, or LCA databases including:

* *EcoInvent:* produced for the Swiss Government (www.ecoinvent.ch)
* *Boustead:* produced by a UK-based LCA consultancy (www.boustead-consulting.co.uk)
* *GaBi:* produced by PE Consulting (www.gabi-software.com)
* *Idemat:* produced by TU Delft (www.idemat.nl)
* *IVAM:* produced by the University of Amsterdam (www.ivam.nl)

When necessary, BRE has adapted these studies to take account of differences between UK and overseas practice, in energy mix and in methodology, and improvements in production techniques where older LCA studies have been used. In some cases, data were not available, and have therefore been inferred by analogy or assumption.

Environmental Profiles with data coming directly from UK trade associations are the most relevant and representative source of LCA data for the construction industry. Wherever permission to use Environmental Profiles has been given by manufacturers, BRE has used this data within *The Green Guide*. A summary of the LCA datasets derived directly from the UK industry is given in Table 3.2.

A further important contribution that trade associations gave throughout the project was to provide comment on the background data use for *The Green Guide* Environmental Profile models. These data included:

* building and material specification design details (including specific material and specification properties, dimensions and build-ups),
* material and component service-life information,
* material waste rates at installation/construction and during maintenance,
* relative waste disposal routes at material end-of-life.

Table 3.2 provides a listing of the organisations that contributed information to this exercise.

Table 3.2: **Trade associations which took part in provision of data for The Green Guide to Specification and in the review of specification design details and associated information**

Trade Association or Body	LCA Environmental Profile data	• Building and material specification design details • Material and component service life • Material site waste rates • Material waste disposal routes
Aircrete Products Association	✓	✓
Architectural Cladding Association		✓
Brick Development Association	✓	✓
British Cement Association	✓	✓
British Lime Association	✓	
British Plastics Federation, Plastics Europe	✓	✓
British Precast Concrete Federation		✓
British Ready Mixed Concrete Association	✓	✓
British Rigid Urethane Foam Manufacturers Association	✓	✓
British Woodworking Federation	✓	✓
Cementitious Slag Makers Association	✓	
Composites Processing Association		✓
Concrete Block Association	✓	✓
Concrete Tile Manufacturers Association	✓	
Copper Development Association, Deutsches Kupferinstitut	✓	✓
Council for Aluminium in Building, European Aluminium Association	✓	✓
Engineered Panels in Construction		✓
Eurisol	✓	✓
European Extruded Polystyrene Insulation Board Association	✓	
Flat Roofing Alliance		✓
GUT	✓	✓
Gypsum Products Development Association	✓	
Interpave	✓	✓
Precast Flooring Federation	✓	✓
Quarry Products Association	✓	✓
Single Ply Roofing Association	✓	✓
Steel Construction Institute, International Iron & Steel Institute, Corus	✓	✓
Steel Window Association		✓
Stone Federation Great Britain	✓	✓
The Concrete Centre		✓
UK Forest Products Association		✓
UK Quality Ash Association	✓	
UK Resilient Flooring Association, European Resilient Flooring Manufacturers Institute	✓	✓
Wood Panel Industries Federation	✓	✓

4   HOW THE GREEN GUIDE TO SPECIFICATION WAS COMPILED

The Green Guide to Specification has been compiled in five stages:
- choosing the building element categories,
- choosing the building specifications,
- creating the Environmental Profile for a specification,
- generating *The Green Guide* environmental impact ratings,
- generating *The Green Guide* summary ratings.

4.1   CHOOSING THE BUILDING ELEMENT CATEGORIES

The elements included in this edition of *The Green Guide to Specification* cover those parts of the building where the designer or specifier has the opportunity to make a significant difference to the embodied environmental impact of the building. This includes elements such as external walls which are fundamental to the appearance of the building, to those such as upper floor constructions which are often hidden but essential to its structure. Some elements, such as floor structure, are expected to last for the entire life of the building; others, such as partitions, may be changed regularly throughout the life of the building. *The Green Guide* also contains elements such as landscaping and boundary protection which are outside the building envelope.

Substructure and superstructure* elements have not been included within this fourth edition as it has not been possible to provide either representative functional units for these elements, or comparable specifications. The reader may also notice that this edition does not include some of the building elements (eg kitchen cupboards, suspended ceilings) included in previous editions. This is because it has not been feasible to establish the necessary LCA information to represent them with the same robustness as other elements.

In the future, BRE plans to work with industry to develop further LCA information so that additional elemental categories and ratings can be established. *The Green Guide to Specification Online*[8] offers a flexible medium in which to introduce information as and when it becomes available.

Despite the omissions, this *Green Guide* is considerably more comprehensive than any previous edition. Not only does it include specifications for six different building types (commercial buildings: offices, educational,

healthcare, retail, residential and industrial), but also a significantly greater number of specifications.

4.2   CHOOSING THE BUILDING SPECIFICATIONS

Specifications in *The Green Guide* are based on sub-categories of information recorded at component, assembly and material levels. From these, a listing of specifications has been compiled. This has been chosen to provide a representative range of commonly used UK specifications.

Each specification is based on UK construction practice which satisfies current Building Regulations in England and Wales. Care has been taken to ensure that each specification complies with the functional unit for the building element (see also *section 5.2*). This is particularly important because it defines the basis for ensuring fair comparison in the generation of the ratings.

A key goal in compiling *The Green Guide* has been to ensure that the specifications are representative of those being built and constructed by the industry. For this reason, throughout *The Green Guide's* development, extensive research and consultation across the construction industry took place. This included Boxall Sayer (a Quantity Surveying group) who provided an expert review of the specification listings used in this edition of *The Green Guide*. After this, an open consultation encouraged Trade Associations, the Project Steering Group and other relevant parties to add to or amend the list of possible specifications. This has resulted in a significant increase in the number of specifications from just over 300 in the third edition of *The Green Guide* to well over 1200 in this fourth edition. Subsequently, BRE has also worked with a number of independent architects who have helped to bring together the specification listings and have provided detailed design work.

These activities were further supported by a comprehensive construction product manufacturer review exercise. Working with trade associations who had expressed interest to take part in the review, BRE held dialogue with industry representatives to review in detail the information behind the building components and specifications relevant to their product category. The organisations which took part in this work are summarised in Table 3.2.

Consultation was detailed, covering all physical design parameters of each specification including material

---

* 'Superstructure' in this context is used to describe the vertical supporting structure of the building.

and product specifications (ie aspects such as product densities and dimensions) as well as component and specification details (eg design dimensions, materials quantities and relevant calculation methods). In this way, a common and agreed listing of specifications has been established.

4.3 CREATING THE ENVIRONMENTAL PROFILE FOR A SPECIFICATION

The environmental information presented in this edition of *The Green Guide to Specification* is for building specifications which have been assessed on the common basis of a per m² functional unit over a 60-year study period. This context provides the basic boundary to the LCA models from which the environmental impact ratings and summary ratings have been determined.

To calculate the environmental impact ratings, the first step is to take the specification design details and to assess the net quantity of material they represent (as discussed in *section 4.2*). This must take into account any replacement anticipated over the 60-year study period.

Data on replacement intervals are based on probability of failure or replacement and reference service life values are used (see *section 4.6.2*) for all specification components or materials. Net replacements over the 60-year study period are determined by using a replacement factor formula to allow for the distribution around any discrete reference service life. A fuller description of the performance and service life methodology can be found in BRE's *Information Paper* IP 1/09[31], and additional details are described in *section 4.6*.

Wastage of materials during construction or refurbishment is also considered and is based on wastage rates for materials in specific contexts from Laxton's Building Price Book[32]. Where appropriate, BRE has made adjustments to the original dataset based on either:

* evidence in the form of an established report which is representative of UK-wide practice provided by a trade association.
* best available BRE knowledge from the Centre for Resource Efficiency on waste practices (the centre has been active in the construction industry for 10 years), including data acquired from commercial in-confidence projects using the SMARTWaste™ System.

The numbers of replacements, together with the masses of material per m² of specification, are then factored to give a total mass of each material required over the 60-year study period.

The relevant LCA data on the embodied environmental impacts for manufacture of each material are collated from the Environmental Profiles database (see *section 3.6*). These data are derived for the manufacture of a tonne of each material, and cover the entire process from 'cradle to gate': that is all the environmental impacts associated with the extraction, processing and transport of raw materials, and the production and manufacturing processes undertaken until the product leaves the factory gate.

Data on environmental impacts from typical transport of materials from the factory gate to site were also produced, based on information provided from materials Trade Associations or in their absence the UK Goverment's Department for Transport from the *Continuing Survey of Road Goods Transport**.

The fate of 'end-of-life' material arising from site wastage, or replacement and demolition during or after the end of the 60-year study period is then assessed, and end-of-life profiles for each material covering the associated environmental impacts are produced.

The data on environmental impacts from manufacturing, transport and end-of-life for each material are then combined with the quantity of each material within each specification representing an LCA of the specification for the 60-year study period. The sum of each environmental impact for each specification is then calculated to give the Environmental Profile for the specification.

4.4 GENERATING THE GREEN GUIDE ENVIRONMENTAL IMPACT RATINGS

To calculate *The Green Guide* environmental impact ratings, the Environmental Profiles for all the specifications within each building element group are considered separately. For example, ratings for External walls are assessed separately from the ratings for other elements such as Windows.

Where necessary, for ease-of-use and presentation purposes, element groups have been divided into subsections; for example 'brick and block cavity walls' and 'cladding on masonry' are subsections within the External walls group. However, in these cases despite the presentational separation, all the specifications are still assessed together as a whole across the element group, irrespective of subsection.

Within each element group, the environmental impact results for each specification are then compared. For each environmental impact, there will be a range, with the lowest ('minimum') and highest ('maximum') impact identified across all the specifications. This range provides the basis from which the A+ to E ratings are determined.

The process works by evenly dividing the range into six equal parts. Each part forms a rating segment within the A+ to E scale. A specification gets an 'A+' rating when the impact result is within the sixth of the range with the lowest environmental impact, an 'A' rating when it is within the second sixth, and so on until an 'E' rating is attributed when it is within the last sixth of the range with the highest environmental impact. This approach is also applied to determine the Summary Ratings based on Ecopoints. Figure 4.1 shows how the concept is applied.

---

* Typical load and haul data for 2005 calculated for common commodities used in construction and product manufacture from an extract from the Continuing Survey of Road Goods Transport provided to BRE by the Department for Transport in a personal communication (21 November 2006).

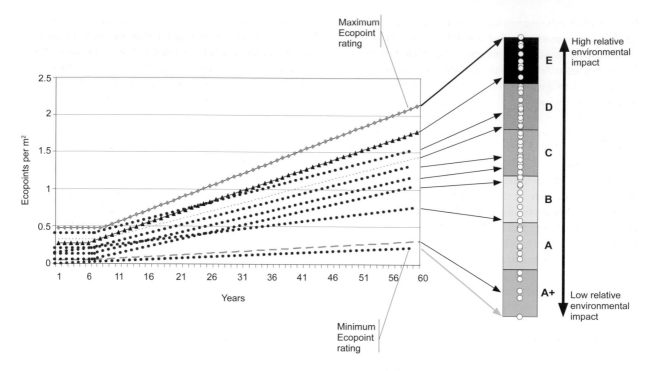

Figure 4.1: How *The Green Guide* ratings are determined for both the environmental impact categories and the Summary Rating based on Ecopoints

4.5 GENERATING THE GREEN GUIDE SUMMARY RATINGS

While some specifiers are happy to make a choice based on their own assessment of the importance of each environmental impact, there is also a demand for a Summary Rating, reflecting overall environmental performance.

The Green Guide Summary Ratings are created by the aggregation of the 13 individual impacts for each specification to determine an Ecopoint score as explained in *section 3.3.* Very simply, the individual environmental impacts are normalised so that they are measured in common units, weighted for their relative importance, and then added together. The summary Ecopoints are then assigned A+ to E ratings from their position within the range of summary results for each building elemental group. This is done in exactly the same way as the individual environmental impact ratings are calculated.

Figure 4.1 provides an illustration of the approach. The Ecopoints are calculated for each specification in the elemental group. The graph shows a group with 10 specifications plotted on the same x–y axis, running from low environmental impact at the bottom, to high environmental impact at the top of the axis. The study period is the standard 60 years shown across the y-axis.

Across the group of specifications there is a lowest and highest Ecopoint score as determined at the end of the defined 60-year study period. These two Ecopoint scores denote the environmental range of the assessment. Six equal segments are created across this range and the Ecopoint scores for the remaining specifications determine where they land within this segmented range, and therefore, the A+ to E rating they receive.

Note that in the Figure 4.1 range diagram, only a small number of specification Ecopoints are illustrated. An elemental group is commonly made up of an assessment of between 15 and 400+ different specifications.

4.6 OTHER INFORMATION

Although primarily a 'green' guide, this publication also provides data on maintenance, durability and recycling to ensure that environmental issues are considered within a wider context of specification choices. A summary of the additional data included in *The Green Guide* tables in *Chapter 6* is given in Table 4.1.

4.6.1 Replacement intervals

The specifications within *The Green Guide* are all assessed over a 60-year study period, and they take account of any maintenance, refurbishment or replacement within

Table 4.1: Summary of the other information recorded in *The Green Guide* tables	
Additional data	Scoring
Typical replacement interval	Years (for key component)
Embodied CO_2	kg CO_2 per m²
Recycled input	Recycled content by mass (kg per m²)
	Recycled content by mass (% per m²)
Recycled currently	Mass of element which is currently recycled at demolition, as % of total mass installed per m²

this period. In this respect, the 60-year period used for all elements in this *Green Guide* is not a statement of building life as many specifications are expected to be in use long after the end of the 60-year study period. Replacement intervals are set for each component or material in each specification and used to calculate the total amount of material used over the 60-year study period. Replacement intervals listed within this book indicate the typical service life of the key component(s) of each element.

It should be recognised that the replacement intervals are not always representative of durability, but may take account of other factors such as 'fashion', 'obsolescence' or 'churn' which may have a greater influence. For example, the replacement intervals for internal partitions frequently reflect fashion or a change of tenants in office accommodation and consequently the specification is replaced before it functionally requires replacement.

Replacement intervals used within this edition of *The Green Guide* have been provided by BRE's Centre for Whole Life Performance. This Centre at BRE has considerable expertise in the calculation and assessment of both durability and expected life of components within buildings. The data sources reviewed by the team in the assessment of service lives for *The Green Guide* were:
- HAPM Component life manual. 1992[33]*
- BLP Building fabric component life manual. 1999[34]*
- BLP Building services component life manual. 2000[35]*
- CIBSE Guide to ownership, operation and maintenance of building services. 2000[36]
- BCIS. BMI Life expectancy of building components. 2001[37]
- Property Services Agency (PSA). Costs-in-use tables. 1991[38].

Where differences between the data sets occurred, BRE derived average typical lives or lives based on its own experience.

A further step of reviewing this data with industry was undertaken. Working with those trade associations that had expressed interest in being part of the review, BRE held dialogue with industry representatives to examine the service-life values relevant to their product category. The organisations that took part in this work are summarised in Table 3.2. Through dialogue and where relevant evidence existed, BRE and industry representatives were able to arrive at a final set of reference service-life values.

As a final check, BRE commissioned Faithful+Gould as a third party to provide a peer review of the reference service lives that went into *The Green Guide*.

The replacement intervals used and listed in *The Green Guide* tables are given in years for the most frequently replaced major component. For example, for a masonry external wall with PVC weatherboarding, the replacement interval given is 35 years, based on the

PVC weatherboarding although the internal paint finish has been assumed to be reapplied at five-year intervals and the masonry wall is assumed to last for the life of the building (80 years). The replacement intervals shown are only an indication of the typical replacement interval: in practice, the replacement interval is expected to be distributed around this time period. This distribution is taken into account in the calculation of *The Green Guide* ratings through the use of a replacement factor formula.

The concept of the model is to spread the replacement period either side of the reference service-life value. This is done because the service life of materials, components or building elements, in the real world, is always a distribution of replacements around an 'average life period'.

The Green Guide distributes the service-life values equally over a period either side of the service-life reference value. This leads to its description as a fractional method based on the probability of replacement either side of the reference service-life value.

A summary of replacement factors for different reference service-life values can be seen in Table 4.2. The graphical trend lines for these different service-life periods are shown in Figure 4.2.

A benefit of the approach is that a definitive determination of reference service-life values is not necessary as a spread can be used; it also avoids the necessity to determine a reference service-life value in excess of 80 years for long-life components such as structure where it is inherently difficult to do so. To illustrate this, BRE has labelled long-life components in *The Green Guide* as having +60 years' service life.

Table 4.2: Replacement factors that a construction component will experience after initial installation within a study period of 60 years	
Service life (years)	Replacement factor
5	11.50
10	5.50
15	3.50
20	2.50
25	1.90
30	1.50
35	1.22
40	1.00
45	0.88
50	0.75
60	0.50
70	0.25
80	0
100	0

---

* The HAPM, BPG and BLP publications have now been updated and amalgamated into the BLP Construction Durability Database (www.blpinsurance.com: follow links to durability data); this was used as a central data record.

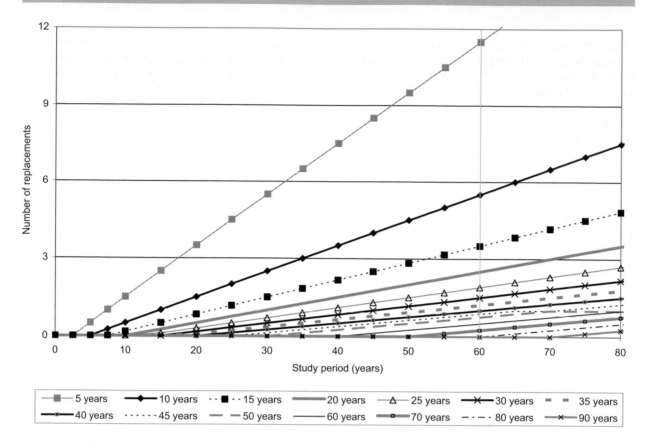

Figure 4.2: Replacement trends for all product-estimated service lives from 5 to 90 years as assessed in the Environmental Profiles 'cradle to grave' assessment

Once a replacement factor has been calculated it can be applied to determine the required material mass over the 60-year study period for the building element and its distinct material components. It should be noted that all specifications include impacts from disposal at demolition, be it at 60 years or any time after.

In calculating the material masses resulting from product replacement, only those items that require replacement and that are integral to the replaced item are included in the assessment. This means that in many instances material is retained.

Further information and detail on the performance and service life methodology used in *The Green Guide to Specification* can be found in BRE's *Information Paper* 1/09[31]. The reader should also recognise that the replacement intervals stated *The Green Guide* should be used as general guidance only.

4.6.2 Embodied CO_2

This metric has been included to reflect the importance of climate change. This refers to the change in global temperature caused via the greenhouse effect by the release of 'greenhouse gases' such as CO_2 by human activity. There is now scientific consensus that the increase in these emissions is having a noticeable effect on climate. Raised global temperature is expected to cause climatic disturbance, desertification, rising sea levels and spread of disease.

The amount, to two significant figures, provides the kilograms of CO_2 equivalent to the greenhouse gases arising from a square metre of specification over the 60-year study period, including manufacture, installation and final demolition. It is based on the climate change impact and calculated in exactly the same way (see *section 3.2.1*).

By multiplying the embodied CO_2 and the area of each specification, and summing the totals for the major building elements, an indication of the carbon footprint for the major building fabric (not operation) can be estimated.

In a very small number of specifications, the reader will find a small negative embodied CO_2 figure has been determined. This is due to what is called 'carbon sequestration' where, as part of the plant growth process, CO_2 is taken up and the carbon is locked into the cellular fabric of the timber or other biomass.

At the end of the defined 60-year study period used in *The Green Guide*, the majority of this carbon will be returned to the environment through the disposal process where the timber goes to landfill or incineration. However, due to the existence of end-of-life recycling and reclamation activity, and the fact that when timber is disposed of in landfill a portion of the sequestered carbon remains in the timber product at the end of the 100-year impact category time horizon (see *section 3.2.1*); in some cases where climate change impacts from manufacturing are low, this can result in a small net negative embodied CO_2 figure.

4.6.3   Recycled content

Improving resource efficiency and the drive to conserve and reuse materials has the potential to help us reduce the environmental impact of the construction materials we use. For this reason *The Green Guide* also presents a range of 'resource efficiency' indicators which focus on the issue of recycling. These include three metrics:
* recycled content by mass,
* recycled content by percentage mass,
* recycled currently.

Recycled content is based on the standard amount of recycled content in each material, and was based where listed on data used within WRAP's Recycled Content Toolkit, now replaced by their Net Waste tool[39]. For materials that were not included, BRE provided the figure based on data provided by industry or their own knowledge of the products. The metric is calculated by comparing the mass of recycled content in the installed specification with the total mass of the installed specification, expressed in kilograms (by mass) and as a percentage (by percentage mass). Note that the Standard Recycled Content as used by WRAP, based on the recycled content of the product commonly bought, may vary from the recycled content of a generic product as calculated by BRE, which is based on the average for the product sector.

4.6.4   Recycled currently

The 'Recycled currently' metric provides an indication of the amount of material that is recycled after demolition, based on current practice. The recycling rates were provided by BRE's Centre for Resource Management, based on their knowledge of the construction industry. As before, industry was given the opportunity to review and amend the rates where evidence could be provided. The metric is calculated by comparing the mass of material currently recycled at demolition of a specification, compared with the total mass of the specification immediately before demolition, expressed as a percentage.

It should be noted that the LCA data for the specifications takes account of:
* the generic recycled content of the materials, where this reduces environmental impact through reduced resource and energy use and associated emissions,
* end-of-life recycling, where this reduces impact through reduction in waste disposal, and
* reduction in manufacturing impact where the material available for recycling has a value based on the BRE Environmental Profiles Methodology.

PART 2 USING THE GREEN GUIDE

5 HOW TO USE THE GREEN GUIDE TO SPECIFICATION

5.1 LAYOUT OF THE ELEMENT SECTIONS

Each building element included in *The Green Guide to Specification* has its own section. Some of the elements have been subdivided into particular types of specification for ease of use. For example, the section on the element 'Internal walls' has been subdivided into three subsections:

* framed partitions,
* masonry partitions,
* demountable and proprietary partitions.

Additionally, some elements may be assessed separately for one or more different building types due to differences in the functional unit for each building type, and the type of specifications typically used for that building type.

Each section for a building element includes:

* a description of the functional unit for each building type, where relevant,
* a graph showing the range of A+ to E Summary Ratings for each building type, where relevant,
* a ratings table for each building type, and element subsection, where relevant.

5.2 FUNCTIONAL UNIT

At the start of each building elemental section, information is provided on the functional unit. For some elements, different functional units are provided for each building type. A functional unit provides essential information about the general attributes of each specification, including the unit of comparison and its performance characteristics. An example of the functional unit for solid and suspended ground floors is given below.

> **Functional unit for solid and suspended ground floors:**
> 1 m² ground floor of 40 m² area and exposed perimeter of 18 m to satisfy England & Wales Building Regulations and a U-value of 0.22 W/m²K. To include any repair, refurbishment or replacement over the 60-year study period.

The functional units were developed by BRE and put out to consultation to ensure they covered the relevant aspects and a typical situation for each element and building type.

All the specifications within each element section and building type, and any subsections, will have been chosen to comply with the functional unit.

All specifications included in *The Green Guide* comply with this functional unit to ensure fair comparison. While specifications are generally comparable, there are, inevitably, instances where comparisons are not exactly like for like: eg some partitioning systems have lower acoustic transmission than others. Specifiers are expected to use their expert judgement in such cases.

Where a specifier is looking at a building specification that has a different functional unit to the building element category presented in *The Green Guide*, then the ratings may be inappropriate if the rating is required for a BREEAM or Code assessment. In such a case, *The Green Guide to Specification Online*[8] should first be checked for any updated guidance. If none is available, the scheme assessor should ask the BREEAM or Code scheme operator for guidance.

5.3 SUMMARY RATINGS RANGES

Figure 6.1 shows the Summary Ratings ranges, based on housing and measured in Ecopoints/m², for all the elements included in *The Green Guide*. As can be seen, the ranges and minimum Summary Ratings for elements vary considerably.

External walls and Roofing elements have the greatest range of Summary Ratings, while the range for elements such as Insulation is much smaller. For elements with a very small range, the difference in impact between an A+ and an E rating is obviously much less than for those elements with a large range. Similarly, for elements such as Roofing, where the Summary Ratings are amongst the highest, the choice of a specification with an A+ Summary Rating will also have a greater benefit.

Where an element has separate ratings for more than one building type, the ranges for the different building types will be provided within that element section.

5.4 RATINGS TABLES

For each element, *The Green Guide* ratings are displayed by building type. Where separate ratings have been provided, then if the element group has been divided into sub-sections, the ratings are displayed alphabetically. The ratings are based on a range for the whole element group and building type, not the individual sub-sections. The layout of the tables is identical in each case. A sample table is illustrated in Figure 5.1.

Information on each specification is set out horizontally in rows starting with a brief description and the summary rating. For users wishing to look at a particular environmental impact (or understand the relative contributions to the Summary Rating), individual A+ to E ratings for each of the environmental impacts are given.

The replacement interval provides the typical number of years before the replacement of the key component of the specification (see *section 4.6.1*). The embodied CO_2 figures give kg CO_2 equivalent values for each specification (see *section 4.6.2*). Finally, information on recycling relating to the specification is given (see *section 4.6.3*).

5.5 USING THE RATINGS

A user looking for a straightforward answer as to which specifications within an element group have the lowest environmental impact, can review the summary ratings for the whole element group, including all subsections where relevant. Those with A+ ratings will have lower overall environmental impact than those with A or B ratings, and all will have lower environmental impact than those with E ratings. The summary rating takes account of the performance of the specification for each of the environmental impacts, and the fact that some impacts are assigned more importance than others.

Alternatively, users with an interest in a specific environmental impact may compare the different specifications for that impact rating and can therefore effectively choose to give it a 100% weighting.

When reviewing ratings, it is important to remember that the A+ to E ratings are relevant only within a specific element group. An A+ rating in one group is not equivalent to an A+ rating in another group.

The summary range graphs show that the A+ to E Summary Ratings for some elements span a much broader range of values than for other element groups. Hence, in some cases (eg Insulation), the difference between an A+ rated and an E rated specification may be relatively small, whereas for other elements it may be substantial.

For some environmental impacts, the range of values for an element group may be very small, or the values may all be very close to zero, even though different ratings have been given.

The number of A+ to E ratings are not equal for each environmental impact or element. This arises because the spread of results for a range of specifications is rarely evenly distributed within the A+ to E rating sub-ranges. Figure 4.1 shows how the number of A+ to E ratings depends on how many values lie in each rating range.

For borderline cases, products with a similar impact may have different ratings as they lie either side of a rating division. Equally, specifications with the same rating may have quite different levels of impact if one lies at the bottom of a rating range while the other lies at the top. In this respect, the summary rating is helpful since it is calculated according to the actual performance for each of the parameters.

Solid concrete ground floors	Element number	Summary Rating	Climate change	Water extraction	Mineral resource extraction	Stratospheric ozone depletion	Human toxicity	Ecotoxicity to freshwater	Nuclear waste (higher level)	Ecotoxicity to land	Waste disposal	Fossil fuel depletion	Eutrophication	Photochemical ozone creation	Acidification	Typical replacement interval	Embodied CO_2 (kg CO_2 eq.)	Recycled content (kg)	Recycled content (%)	Recycled currently at EOL (%)
Plywood (temperate, EN 636-2) decking on vapour control layer, on timber battens and insulation on:																			
in situ concrete floor on polyethylene DPM on blinded recycled aggregate sub-base	820100028	D	A	E	B	D	E	E	D	C	E	D	D	D	C	40	65	332	38	89
in situ concrete floor on polyethylene DPM on blinded virgin aggregate sub-base	820100027	E	A	E	D	D	E	E	E	C	E	D	D	D	C	40	65	2	0	89

Figure 5.1: Sample layout of *The Green Guide to Specification* tables

There is no implied weighting between the ratings for different environmental issues. The ratings simply indicate where each specification lies within the range of values found for each group. Only the Summary Rating has been weighted.

Most buildings will last much longer than the assumed 60-year study period and hence the value of low maintenance and design for longevity are potentially under-estimated in the ratings. In the typical replacement column in each table, a figure of +60 years is used to identify those specifications and components that have service lives that are greater than 60 years.

The ratings are assigned at the time of writing using the best of known available information. It is recognised that our knowledge of these issues is still evolving and the ratings will continue to be updated through *The Green Guide to Specification Online*[8]. Readers should consult *The Green Guide to Specification Online*[8] for the latest updates and guidance on the use of *The Green Guide* ratings.

PART 3 THE GREEN GUIDE RATINGS

6   THE GREEN GUIDE TABLES

The Green Guide specifications have been arranged into tabular form for common building elemental categories:
* Ground floors,
* Upper floors,
* Separating floors,
* Roofs,
* External walls,
* Windows and curtain walling,
* Internal walls,
* Separating walls,
* Insulation,
* Landscaping.

In some categories, elemental subsections are also used to provide tables specific to common types of specification (eg masonry partitions or framed partitions). For each elemental category the tables are also displayed by building type.

Each elemental category and subsection has been compiled based on a functional unit. This recognises the building type and defines technical performance requirements for each specification category. A full listing of the *Green Guide* functional units is shown in Table 6.1.

The functional unit ensures specifications are compared on a like-for-like basis against the identified performance criteria. The functional unit is based on a 60-year study period which includes the necessary manufacture and construction of materials, any repair and maintenance necessary during use, and finally disposal at end of life in the LCA assessment.

When using *The Green Guide to Specification* it is important to recognise that all specification choices are important. However, designers may wish to give particular attention to the elements of the building with the greatest environmental impact. An overview of this perspective is provided in Figure 5.1 where the full range of Ecopoint impacts across all elemental categories and building types is shown.

Designers and specifiers who are seeking more detailed numerical LCA data may find *The Green Guide to Specification Online*[8] provides them with the information that they require.

Table 6.1: The functional units used for The Green Guide to Specification ratings tables*

Element	Element sub-sections	Commercial	Domestic	Schools	Health	Retail	Industrial
Ground floors	• Solid • Suspended	N/A	1 m² ground floor of 40 m² area and exposed perimeter of 18 m to satisfy England and Wales Building Regulations and a U-value of 0.22 W/m²K.	N/A	N/A	N/A	N/A
Upper floors		1 m² of upper floor construction, to satisfy building regulations, capable of supporting a live floor load of 2.5 kN/m², including any additional beams to span a 7.5 m column grid and surface ready for addition of sub-structural floor system.	As Commercial but based on a 4 m span and area of 40 m², a live loading of 1.5 kN/m² and a surface ready for the addition of a sheet carpet and underlay.	As Commercial but based on a floor between classrooms with a 8 m span and a live loading of 3 kN/m², and a maximum weighted BB93[140] standardised impact sound pressure level 60 $L'_{nT(Tmf,max)w}$ (source: BB93[140]) and surface ready for the addition of a sheet flooring.	As Commercial but based on a 6 m span, a live loading of 2 kN/m² and surface ready for the addition of a sheet flooring.	As Commercial but based on a 6 m span, a live loading of 4 kN/m² and surface ready for addition of sub-structural floor system.	Where relevant, see Commercial.
Separating floors	• In situ concrete • Precast concrete • Timber • Composite	N/A	1 m² of upper floor with a live loading of 1.5 kN/m² to satisfy England and Wales Building Regulations, in particular a minimum airborne sound insulation D_{nTw} + C_x of 45 dB and impact sound insulation L'_{nTw} of 62 dB (source: Approved Document E 2003[141]) and a span of 5 m.	N/A	N/A	N/A	N/A
Roofs (flat or pitched)	• Flat • Low pitched (not exceeding 15°) • Pitched	1 m² of roof area, (measured horizontally), to satisfy building regulations and a U-value of 0.16 W/m²K (pitched) or 0.25 W/m²K (flat). Based on an overall span of 15 m with support at 7.5 m.	1 m² of roof area (measured horizontally), to satisfy England and Wales Building Regulations, particularly a U-value of 0.16 W/m²K (pitched) or 0.25 W/m²K (flat). Span of 8 m.	As Commercial and based on a span of 15 m with supports at a central corridor.	As Commercial with a span of 8 m.		As Commercial.

* These always include any repair, refurbishment or replacement over the 60-year study period.

Table 6.1: The functional units used for The Green Guide to Specification ratings tables* (cont'd)

Element	Element sub-sections	Commercial	Domestic	Schools	Health	Retail	Industrial
External walls		1 m² of external wall construction, to satisfy current building regulations, and a U-value of 0.3 W/m²K. Where relevant, the specification will also include an internal wall finish.					
Windows and curtain walling		1 m² of double glazed, fixed pane window or clear glazed curtain walling, to satisfy Building Regulations in England and Wales, and a U-value of 1.8 W/m²K.	Double-glazed window, based on the BFRC domestic window model (1.48 m high × 1.23 m wide with a central mullion and one opening light)[42], to satisfy Building Regulations in England and Wales, and a U-value of 1.8 W/m²K.	As Commercial for all windows in building.			
All Internal walls and Partitioning for buildings up to three storeys and non-loadbearing walls for buildings four storeys and more	• Framed • Masonry • Demountable and Proprietary	1 m² of internal wall or partitioning, to satisfy Building Regulations in England and Wales.		As Commercial for all walls except those for classrooms.	As Commercial.		
Internal walls and partitioning: additional for schools		N/A	N/A	1 m² of internal wall or partitioning between classrooms or classrooms and circulation; to satisfy building regulations, in particular minimum 45 $D_{nT\,(T_{mf,max}),w}$ (dB) airborne sound insulation (Source: BB93)[40], and mid-frequency reverberation time, T_{mf}, in classroom not to exceed 0.6 seconds (Source: BB93)[40]. Wall to be specified to Severe Duty (SD) as per BS 5234-2[43].	N/A	N/A	N/A

* These always include any repair, refurbishment or replacement over the 60-year study period.

Table 6.1: The functional units used for The Green Guide to Specification ratings tables* (cont'd)

Element	Element sub-sections	Commercial	Domestic	Schools	Health	Retail	Industrial
Separating walls	• Masonry • Steel • Timber	N/A	1 m² of party wall to satisfy England and Wales Building Regulations, in particular a minimum airborne sound insulation $D_{n\mathrm{Tw}} + C_x$ of 45 DB (Source: Approved Document E 2003[41]).	N/A	N/A	N/A	N/A
Insulation		1 m² of insulation with sufficient thickness to provide a thermal resistance value of 3 m²K/W, equivalent to approximately 100 mm of insulation with a conductivity (k value) of 0.034 W/mK.					
Landscaping: Hard surfacing	• Pedestrian only	1 m² of hard surfacing, suitable for pedestrian loading, informed by relevant British Standards and Industry consultation.					
	• Lightly trafficked areas	1 m² of hard surfacing, suitable for the parking of cars and light traffic loading, informed by relevant British Standards and Industry consultation.					
	• Heavily trafficked areas	1 m² of hard surfacing, suitable for heavier traffic loading, informed by relevant British Standards and Industry consultation.					
Landscaping: Boundary protection		1 m² of boundary protection or balustrading up to 2 m high, informed by relevant British Standards and Industry consultation.					

* These always include any repair, refurbishment or replacement over the 60-year study period.

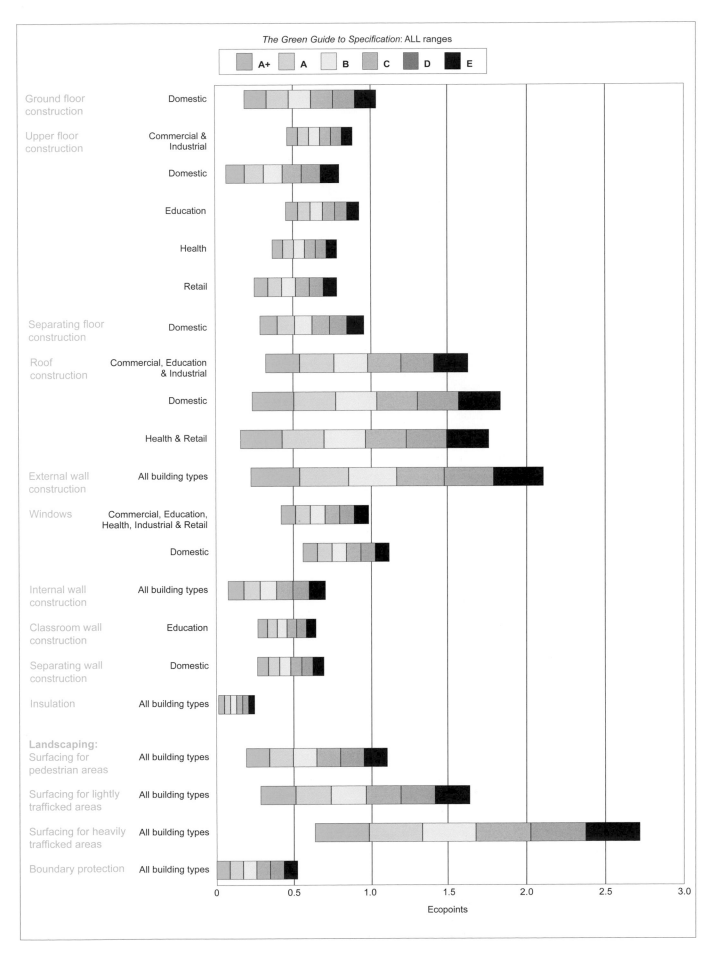

Figure 6.1: Summary Ecopoint ranges for all elemental categories included in The Green Guide to Specification

6.1 GROUND FLOORS

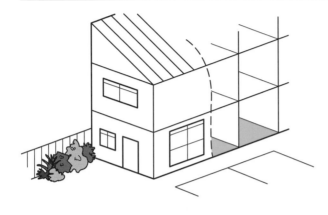

Ground floors are only examined within the context of domestic construction. This is because for non-domestic buildings, the ground floor construction is normally integrated with the foundations of the building and is much more dependent on the building design and ground condition.

Where a multi-residential building has car parking or commercial/retail use on the ground floor (or a basement floor in contact with the ground), then this floor does not need to be assessed. However, please refer to the latest guidance on application of the ratings on *The Green Guide to Specification Online*[8].

Functional unit for solid and suspended ground floors:
1 m² ground floor of 40 m² area and exposed perimeter of 18 m to satisfy England & Wales Building Regulations and a U-value of 0.22 W/m²K. To include any repair, refurbishment or replacement over the 60-year study period.

Division of ground floors into subsections
Ground floor specifications have been arranged into subsections for ease of use by designers. However, ratings have been arrived at through comparison of all ground floors shown across all subsections. The subsections are:
* Solid concrete ground floors,
* Suspended concrete ground floors,
* Suspended timber ground floors.

Note: where descriptions refer to, say 100% RCA, this refers to 100% of the coarse aggregate in the concrete being replaced with Recycled Concrete Aggregate (RCA).

Concrete block solid densities are as follows:
* Dense block/blockwork (≈ 1950 kg/m³),
* Medium density block/blockwork (≈ 1450 kg/m³),
* Lightweight blockwork (≈ 1100 kg/m³),
* Superlightweight block/blockwork (≈ 850 kg/m³).

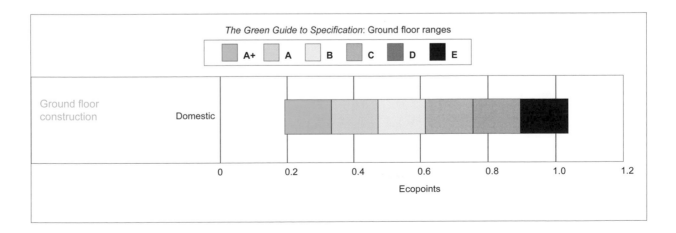

The Green Guide to Specification: Ground floor ranges

| A+ | A | B | C | D | E |

Ground floor construction — Domestic

Ecopoints: 0, 0.2, 0.4, 0.6, 0.8, 1.0, 1.2

Solid concrete ground floors

Domestic

	Element number	Summary Rating	Climate change	Water extraction	Mineral resource extraction	Stratospheric ozone depletion	Human toxicity	Ecotoxicity to freshwater	Nuclear waste (higher level)	Ecotoxicity to land	Waste disposal	Fossil fuel depletion	Eutrophication	Photochemical ozone creation	Acidification	Typical replacement interval	Embodied CO_2 (kg CO_2 eq.)	Recycled content (kg)	Recycled content (%)	Recycled currently at EOL (%)
Chipboard (P5) decking on vapour control layer, on timber battens and insulation on:																				
in situ 30% PFA concrete (100% RCA) floor on polyethylene DPM on blinded recycled aggregate sub-base	820100195	C	A	B	A	B	A	B	B	A	E	C	C	B	B	40	59	527	60	88
in situ 30% PFA concrete floor on polyethylene DPM on blinded recycled aggregate sub-base	820100197	C	A	C	B	B	A	B	B	A	E	C	C	B	B	40	59	350	40	88
in situ 30% PFA concrete floor on polyethylene DPM on blinded virgin aggregate sub-base	820100046	D	A	C	D	B	A	B	B	A	E	C	C	B	B	40	59	20	2	88
in situ 50% GGBS concrete (100% RCA) floor on polyethylene DPM on blinded recycled aggregate sub-base	820100199	C	A	B	A	B	A	A	B	A	E	C	C	B	B	40	50	532	60	88
in situ 50% GGBS concrete floor on polyethylene DPM on blinded recycled aggregate sub-base	820100053	C	A	C	B	B	A	A	B	A	E	C	C	B	B	40	50	354	40	88
in situ 50% GGBS concrete floor on polyethylene DPM on blinded virgin aggregate sub-base	820100052	D	A	C	D	B	A	A	B	A	E	C	C	B	B	40	50	23.8	3	88
in situ concrete (100% RCA) floor on polyethylene DPM on blinded recycled aggregate sub-base	820100056	C	A	B	A	B	A	B	B	A	E	C	C	B	C	40	66	517	58	88
in situ concrete floor on polyethylene DPM on blinded recycled aggregate sub-base	820100020	C	A	C	B	B	A	B	B	A	E	C	C	B	C	40	67	340	39	88
in situ concrete floor on polyethylene DPM on blinded virgin aggregate sub-base	820100016	D	A	C	D	B	A	B	B	A	E	C	C	B	C	40	67	9.6	1	88
OSB/3 decking on vapour control layer, on timber battens and insulation on:																				
in situ 30% PFA concrete (100% RCA) floor on polyethylene DPM on blinded recycled aggregate sub-base	820100084	B	A	C	A	B	A	A	A	A+	E	B	C	B	B	40	48	525	60	88
in situ 30% PFA concrete floor on polyethylene DPM on blinded recycled aggregate sub-base	820100196	A	A	C	B	B	A	A	A	A+	E	B	B	B	B	40	48	348	40	89
in situ 30% PFA concrete floor on polyethylene DPM on blinded virgin aggregate sub-base	820100081	D	A	C	D	B	A	A	B	A+	E	B	B	B	B	40	48	18	2	89
in situ 50% GGBS concrete (100% RCA) floor on polyethylene DPM on blinded recycled aggregate sub-base	820100087	B	A	C	A	B	A	A	A	A+	E	B	B	B	B	40	39	530	60	88

Cont'd . . . .

Solid concrete ground floors

Domestic

	Element number	Summary Rating	Climate change	Water extraction	Mineral resource extraction	Stratospheric ozone depletion	Human toxicity	Ecotoxicity to freshwater	Nuclear waste (higher level)	Ecotoxicity to land	Waste disposal	Fossil fuel depletion	Eutrophication	Photochemical ozone creation	Acidification	Typical replacement interval	Embodied CO2 (kg CO2 eq.)	Recycled content (kg)	Recycled content (%)	Recycled currently at EOL (%)
OSB/3 decking on vapour control layer, on timber battens and insulation on (cont'd):																				
in situ 50% GGBS concrete floor on polyethylene DPM on blinded recycled aggregate sub-base	820100047	C	A	C	B	B	A	A	A	A+	E	B	B	B	B	40	39	352	40	88
in situ 50% GGBS concrete floor on polyethylene DPM on blinded virgin aggregate sub-base	820100083	D	A	C	D	B	A	A	A	A+	E	B	B	A	B	40	39	21.8	2	88
in situ concrete (100% RCA) floor on polyethylene DPM on blinded recycled aggregate sub-base	820100086	C	A	C	A	B	A	A	A	A+	E	C	C	B	B	40	55	515	58	88
in situ concrete floor on polyethylene DPM on blinded recycled aggregate sub-base	820100085	C	A	C	B	B	A	B	B	A+	E	C	C	B	B	40	56	338	38	89
in situ concrete floor on polyethylene DPM on blinded virgin aggregate sub-base	820100023	D	A	C	D	B	A	B	B	A+	E	C	C	B	B	40	56	7.6	1	89
Plywood (temperate, EN 636-2) decking on vapour control layer, on timber battens and insulation on:																				
in situ 30% PFA concrete (100% RCA) floor on polyethylene DPM on blinded recycled aggregate sub-base	820100194	C	A	E	A	D	E	E	D	C	E	D	D	D	C	40	57	520	59	88
in situ 30% PFA concrete floor on polyethylene DPM on blinded recycled aggregate sub-base	820100089	D	A	E	B	D	E	E	D	C	E	D	D	D	C	40	57	342	39	89
in situ 30% PFA concrete floor on polyethylene DPM on blinded virgin aggregate sub-base	820100080	E	A	E	D	D	E	E	D	C	E	D	D	D	C	40	57	12	1	89
in situ 50% GGBS concrete (100% RCA) floor on polyethylene DPM on blinded recycled aggregate sub-base	820100051	C	A	E	A	D	E	D	D	C	E	C	C	D	C	40	48	524	59	88
in situ 50% GGBS concrete floor on polyethylene DPM on blinded recycled aggregate sub-base	820100057	D	A	E	B	D	E	D	D	C	E	C	C	C	C	40	48	346	39	88
in situ 50% GGBS concrete floor on polyethylene DPM on blinded virgin aggregate sub-base	820100198	E	A	E	D	D	E	D	D	C	E	C	C	C	C	40	48	16.2	2	88
in situ concrete (100% RCA) floor on polyethylene DPM on blinded recycled aggregate sub-base	820100090	C	A	E	A	D	E	E	D	C	E	D	D	D	C	40	64	509	58	88

Cont'd . . . .

Solid concrete ground floors

Domestic

	Element number	Summary Rating	Climate change	Water extraction	Mineral resource extraction	Stratospheric ozone depletion	Human toxicity	Ecotoxicity to freshwater	Nuclear waste (higher level)	Ecotoxicity to land	Waste disposal	Fossil fuel depletion	Eutrophication	Photochemical ozone creation	Acidification	Typical replacement interval	Embodied CO2 (kg CO2 eq.)	Recycled content (kg)	Recycled content (%)	Recycled currently at EOL (%)
Plywood (temperate, EN 636-2) decking on vapour control layer, on timber battens and insulation on (cont'd):																				
in situ concrete floor on polyethylene DPM on blinded recycled aggregate sub-base	820100028	D	A	E	B	D	E	E	D	C	E	D	D	D	C	40	65	332	38	89
in situ concrete floor on polyethylene DPM on blinded virgin aggregate sub-base	820100027	E	A	E	D	D	E	E	E	C	E	D	D	D	C	40	65	2.3	0	88
Powerfloated:																				
in situ 30% PFA concrete (100% RCA) slab, over insulation on polyethylene dpm laid on blinded recycled aggregate sub-base	820100208	B	A	A+	A	A+	A+	A+	A+	A+	D	A	A	A+	A	60+	56	519	60	90
in situ 30% PFA concrete slab, over insulation on polyethylene dpm laid on blinded recycled aggregate sub-base	820100203	B	A	A	B	A+	A+	A+	A+	A+	D	A	A	A+	A	60+	56	342	40	90
in situ 30% PFA concrete slab, over insulation on polyethylene dpm laid on blinded virgin aggregate sub-base	820100204	C	A	A	D	A+	A+	A+	A+	A+	D	A	A	A+	A	60+	55	12	1	90
in situ 50% GGBS concrete (100% RCA) slab, over insulation on polyethylene dpm laid on blinded recycled aggregate sub-base	820100207	B	A	A+	A	A+	A+	A+	A+	A+	D	A+	A	A+	A	60+	47	524	60	90
in situ 50% GGBS concrete slab, over insulation on polyethylene dpm laid on blinded recycled aggregate sub-base	820100205	B	A	A+	B	A+	A+	A+	A+	A+	D	A+	A	A+	A	60+	47	346	40	90
in situ 50% GGBS concrete slab, over insulation on polyethylene dpm laid on blinded virgin aggregate sub-base	820100206	C	A	A	D	A+	A+	A+	A+	A+	D	A+	A	A+	A	60+	46	16.2	2	90
in situ concrete (100% RCA) slab, over insulation on polyethylene dpm laid on blinded recycled aggregate sub-base	820100200	B	A	A+	A	A+	A+	A+	A+	A+	D	A	B	A+	A	60+	63	509	59	90
in situ concrete slab, over insulation on polyethylene dpm laid on blinded recycled aggregate sub-base	820100201	B	A	A	B	A+	A+	A+	A+	A+	D	A	A	A+	A	60+	63	332	38	90
in situ concrete slab, over insulation on polyethylene dpm laid on blinded virgin aggregate sub-base	820100202	C	A	A	D	A+	A+	A+	A+	A+	D	A	A	A+	A	60+	63	2.3	0	90

Solid concrete ground floors

Domestic

	Element number	Summary Rating	Climate change	Water extraction	Mineral resource extraction	Stratospheric ozone depletion	Human toxicity	Ecotoxicity to freshwater	Nuclear waste (higher level)	Ecotoxicity to land	Waste disposal	Fossil fuel depletion	Eutrophication	Photochemical ozone creation	Acidification	Typical replacement interval	Embodied CO2 (kg CO2 eq.)	Recycled content (kg)	Recycled content (%)	Recycled currently at EOL (%)
Screed on insulation laid on:																				
in situ concrete (100% RCA) floor on polyethylene DPM on blinded recycled aggregate sub-base	820100033	D	C	C	B	D	A	B	A	A	E	C	D	C	D	50	110	510	51	90
in situ concrete floor on polyethylene DPM on blinded virgin aggregate sub-base	820100009	E	C	C	E	D	A	B	B	A	E	C	D	C	D	50	110	2.9	0	90
in situ concrete on polyethylene dpm laid on blinded recycled aggregate sub-base	820100048	D	C	C	D	D	A	B	A	A	E	C	D	C	D	50	110	333	34	90
solid 30% PFA concrete (100% RCA) floor on polyethylene DPM on blinded recycled aggregate sub-base	820100043	D	C	C	B	D	A	A	A	A	E	C	D	C	C	50	100	520	53	90
solid 30% PFA concrete floor on polyethylene DPM on blinded recycled aggregate sub-base	820100034	D	C	C	C	D	A	A	A	A	E	C	D	C	C	50	100	343	35	90
solid 30% PFA concrete floor on polyethylene DPM on blinded virgin aggregate sub-base	820100035	E	C	C	E	C	A	A	A	A	E	C	D	C	C	50	100	13	1	90
solid 50% GGBS concrete (100% RCA) floor on polyethylene DPM on blinded recycled aggregate sub-base	820100036	D	B	C	B	D	A	A	A	A+	E	C	D	C	C	50	95	525	53	90
solid 50% GGBS concrete floor on polyethylene DPM on blinded recycled aggregate sub-base	820100037	D	B	C	C	D	A	A	A	A+	E	C	D	C	C	50	95	347	35	90
solid 50% GGBS concrete floor on polyethylene DPM on blinded virgin aggregate sub-base	820100038	E	B	C	E	C	A	A	A	A+	E	C	C	C	C	50	95	16.8	2	90
Screeded in situ:																				
30% PFA concrete (100% RCA) slab, over insulation on polyethylene dpm laid on blinded recycled aggregate sub-base	820100039	C	B	A	B	B	A	A	A+	A+	D	B	C	A	B	60+	79	520	53	90
30% PFA concrete slab, over insulation on polyethylene dpm laid on blinded recycled aggregate sub-base	820100041	C	B	A	C	B	A	A	A+	A+	D	B	C	A	B	60+	79	343	35	90
30% PFA concrete slab, over insulation on polyethylene dpm laid on blinded virgin aggregate sub-base	820100040	D	B	B	E	B	A	A	A+	A+	D	B	B	A	B	60+	78	13	1	90
50% GGBS concrete (100% RCA) slab, over insulation on polyethylene dpm laid on blinded recycled aggregate sub-base	820100042	C	B	A	B	B	A+	A+	A+	A+	D	B	B	A	B	60+	70	525	53	90

Cont'd . . . .

Solid concrete ground floors

Domestic

	Element number	Summary Rating	Climate change	Water extraction	Mineral resource extraction	Stratospheric ozone depletion	Human toxicity	Ecotoxicity to freshwater	Nuclear waste (higher level)	Ecotoxicity to land	Waste disposal	Fossil fuel depletion	Eutrophication	Photochemical ozone creation	Acidification	Typical replacement interval	Embodied CO_2 (kg CO_2 eq.)	Recycled content (kg)	Recycled content (%)	Recycled currently at EOL (%)
Screeded in situ (cont'd):																				
50% GGBS concrete slab, over insulation on polyethylene dpm laid on blinded recycled aggregate sub-base	820100045	C	B	A	C	B	A+	A+	A+	A+	D	B	B	A	B	60+	70	347	35	90
50% GGBS concrete slab, over insulation on polyethylene dpm laid on blinded virgin aggregate sub-base	820100044	D	B	B	E	B	A+	A+	A+	A+	D	B	B	A	B	60+	69	16.8	2	90
concrete (100% RCA) slab, over insulation on polyethylene dpm laid on blinded recycled aggregate sub-base	820100010	C	B	A	B	B	A	A	A+	A+	D	B	C	B	B	60+	86	510	51	90
concrete slab, over insulation on polyethylene dpm laid on blinded recycled aggregate sub-base	820100029	C	B	A	C	B	A	A	A+	A+	D	B	C	A	B	60+	86	333	34	90
concrete slab, over insulation on polyethylene dpm laid on blinded virgin aggregate sub-base	820100030	D	B	B	E	B	A	A	A	A+	D	B	C	A	B	60+	86	2.9	0	90

Suspended concrete ground floors

Domestic

	Element number	Summary Rating	Climate change	Water extraction	Mineral resource extraction	Stratospheric ozone depletion	Human toxicity	Ecotoxicity to freshwater	Nuclear waste (higher level)	Ecotoxicity to land	Waste disposal	Fossil fuel depletion	Eutrophication	Photochemical ozone creation	Acidification	Typical replacement interval	Embodied CO2 (kg CO2 eq.)	Recycled content (kg)	Recycled content (%)	Recycled currently at EOL (%)
Chipboard (P5) decking on timber battens with insulation on:																				
grouted hollow precast prestressed concrete planks	820140001	A	A	A	A+	B	A	B	B	B	B	C	C	B	B	40	60	10	4	85
grouted hollow precast reinforced concrete planks	820140017	C	C	C	A	D	B	B	C	D	C	E	E	D	E	40	110	42	10	87
grouted beam and aircrete block flooring	820140019	A+	A	A	A+	A	A	A	A	A	A	B	B	A	A	40	43	9.1	7	79
grouted beam and dense solid block flooring	820140002	A	A	A	A+	A	A	A	A	A	B	B	B	A	A	40	37	9.1	4	85
grouted beam and medium dense solid block flooring	820140018	A	A	A	A+	A	A	A	A	A	A	C	B	A	B	40	43	9.1	5	84
OSB/3 decking on timber battens on insulation on:																				
grouted hollow precast prestressed concrete planks	820144003	A	A	A	A+	A	A	A	B	A	B	B	B	B	B	40	49	7.9	3	86
grouted hollow precast reinforced concrete planks	820140021	C	C	C	A	C	B	B	C	C	C	D	D	D	D	40	100	40	10	88
grouted beam and aircrete block flooring	820140005	A+	A+	A	A+	A+	A	A	A	A+	A	A	A	A	A	40	32	6.8	5	82
grouted beam and cellular dense block flooring	820140023	A+	A+	A	A+	A	A	A	A	A+	A	A	A	A	A	40	22	7.1	4	85
grouted beam and dense solid block flooring	820140008	A	A+	A	A+	A	A	A	A	A+	A	A	A	A	A	40	26	7.1	3	86
grouted beam and medium dense solid block flooring	820140022	A+	A+	A	A+	A	A	A	A	A+	A	B	A	A	B	40	32	7.1	4	85
Plywood (temperate, EN636-2) decking on timber battens with insulation on:																				
grouted beam and aircrete block flooring	820140026	A	A	C	A+	B	D	D	D	C	A	C	B	C	B	40	41	1.5	1	79
grouted beam and dense solid block flooring	820140006	B	A	C	A+	C	D	D	D	C	B	C	C	C	B	40	35	1.8	1	84
grouted beam and medium dense solid block flooring	820140025	A	A	C	A+	C	D	D	D	C	A	C	C	C	B	40	41	1.8	1	83
grouted hollow precast prestressed concrete planks	820140004	B	A	C	A+	D	E	E	D	D	B	C	C	D	C	40	58	2.6	1	84
grouted hollow precast reinforced concrete planks	820140007	D	C	E	A	E	E	E	E	E	C	E	E	E	E	40	110	34	8	87

Solid concrete ground floors

Domestic

	Element number	Summary Rating	Climate change	Water extraction	Mineral resource extraction	Stratospheric ozone depletion	Human toxicity	Ecotoxicity to freshwater	Nuclear waste (higher level)	Ecotoxicity to land	Waste disposal	Fossil fuel depletion	Eutrophication	Photochemical ozone creation	Acidification	Typical replacement interval	Embodied CO₂ (kg CO₂ eq.)	Recycled content (kg)	Recycled content (%)	Recycled currently at EOL (%)
Screed on insulation laid on:																				
grouted beam and aircrete block flooring	820140014	B	B	A	A	B	A	A	A	A	A	B	B	B	B	50	88	2.1	1	89
grouted beam and dense solid block flooring	820140032	B	B	A	B	C	A	A	A	A	A	B	C	B	C	50	85	2.4	1	89
grouted beam and medium dense solid block flooring	820140031	B	B	A	A	C	A	A	A	A	A	C	C	B	C	50	88	2.4	1	89
grouted hollow precast reinforced concrete planks	820140046	D	D	C	C	E	B	B	C	C	C	E	E	E	E	50	160	35	7	90
grouted hollow prestressed precast concrete planks	820140012	C	C	A	B	C	A	B	A	A	A	C	C	C	C	50	110	3.2	1	89
Structural topping on:																				
beam and expanded polystyrene flooring	820140015	A+	A	A+	A+	A+	A+	A+	A+	A+	A+	A	A+	B	A	60+	50	4	2	87
beam and extruded polystyrene (CO₂ blown) block floor	820140051	A+	A	A+	A+	A+	A+	A+	A+	A+	A+	A	A+	A+	A	60+	51	4	2	88

Suspended timber ground floors

Domestic

Chipboard (P5) decking on timber joists with insulation over:	Element number	Summary Rating	Climate change	Water extraction	Mineral resource extraction	Stratospheric ozone depletion	Human toxicity	Ecotoxicity to freshwater	Nuclear waste (higher level)	Ecotoxicity to land	Waste disposal	Fossil fuel depletion	Eutrophication	Photochemical ozone creation	Acidification	Typical replacement interval	Embodied CO_2 (kg CO_2 eq.)	Recycled content (kg)	Recycled content (%)	Recycled currently at EOL (%)
100 mm 30% PFA oversite concrete	820470035	A	A+	B	A+	A	A	A	A	A	B	B	B	A	A	40	32	16	6	84
100 mm 30% PFA oversite concrete (100% RCA)	820470033	A	A+	B	A+	A	A	A	A	A	B	B	B	A	A	40	32	134	50	83
100 mm 50% GGBS oversite concrete	820470040	A	A+	B	A+	A	A	A	A	A	B	B	A	A	A	40	26	18.6	7	83
100 mm 50% GGBS oversite concrete (100% RCA)	820470037	A+	A+	B	A+	A	A	A	A	A	B	B	A	A	A	40	26	137	52	83
100 mm oversite concrete	820470017	A	A	B	A+	A	A	A	B	A	B	B	B	A	A	40	37	9.4	4	83
100 mm oversite concrete (100% RCA)	820470041	A	A	B	A+	A	A	A	B	A	B	B	B	A	B	40	38	127	48	83
50 mm 30% PFA concrete (100% RCA) on polyethylene membrane on 50 mm sand blinding	820470022	A	A+	B	A+	A	A	A	B	A	B	B	A	A	A	40	26	71.1	28	82
50 mm 30% PFA concrete on polyethylene dpm laid on sand blinding	820470126	A	A+	B	A+	A	A	A	B	A	B	B	A	A	A	40	26	12	5	83
50 mm 50% GGBS concrete (100% RCA) on polyethylene membrane on 50 mm sand blinding	820470027	A	A+	B	A+	A	A	A	A	A	B	B	A	A	A	40	23	72.6	28	82
50 mm 50% GGBS concrete on polyethylene membrane on 50 mm sand blinding	820470029	A	A+	B	A+	A	A	A	B	A	B	B	A	A	A	40	23	13.3	5	82
50 mm concrete (100% RCA) on polyethylene membrane on 50 mm sand blinding	820470031	A	A+	B	A+	A	A	A	B	A	B	B	A	A	A	40	28	67.6	26	82
50 mm concrete on polyethylene membrane on 50 mm sand blinding	820470018	A	A+	B	A+	A	A	A	B	A	B	B	A	A	A	40	28	8.3	3	83
50 mm fine aggregate on polyethylene dpm laid on 50 mm sand blinding	820470019	A	A+	A	A+	A	A+	A	A	A	B	B	A	A	A	40	18	7.7	4	82

Suspended timber ground floors

Domestic

	Element number	Summary Rating	Climate change	Water extraction	Mineral resource extraction	Stratospheric ozone depletion	Human toxicity	Ecotoxicity to freshwater	Nuclear waste (higher level)	Ecotoxicity to land	Waste disposal	Fossil fuel depletion	Eutrophication	Photochemical ozone creation	Acidification	Typical replacement interval	Embodied CO_2 (kg CO_2 eq.)	Recycled content (kg)	Recycled content (%)	Recycled currently at EOL (%)
OSB/3 decking on timber joists with insulation over:																				
100 mm 30% PFA oversite concrete	820470077	A	A+	B	A+	A+	A	A	A	A+	B	A	A	A	A	40	21	14	5	85
100 mm 30% PFA oversite concrete (100% RCA)	820470076	A+	A+	B	A+	A+	A	A	A	A+	B	A	A	A	A	40	21	132	50	83
100 mm 50% GGBS oversite concrete	820470079	A	A+	B	A+	A+	A	A	A	A+	B	A	A	A	A	40	15	16.6	6	83
100 mm 50% GGBS oversite concrete (100% RCA)	820470078	A+	A+	B	A+	A+	A	A	A	A+	B	A	A	A	A	40	15	135	51	83
100 mm oversite concrete	820470135	A	A+	B	A+	A+	A	A	A	A+	B	A	A	A	A	40	26	7	3	85
100 mm oversite concrete (100% RCA)	820470136	A+	A+	B	A+	A+	A	A	A	A+	B	A	A	A	A	40	26	125	48	83
50 mm 30% PFA concrete (100% RCA) on polyethylene dpm laid on sand blinding	820470059	A+	A+	B	A+	A	A	A	A	A+	B	A	A	A	A	40	14	69	27	83
50 mm 30% PFA concrete on polyethylene dpm laid on sand blinding	820470127	A	A+	B	A+	A+	A	A	A	A+	B	A	A	A	A	40	14	9.7	4	84
50 mm 50% GGBS concrete (100% RCA) on polyethylene dpm laid on sand blinding	820470066	A+	A+	B	A+	A	A	A	A	A+	B	A	A	A	A	40	11	70.6	28	83
50 mm 50% GGBS concrete on polyethylene dpm laid on sand blinding	820470073	A+	A+	B	A+	A+	A	A	A	A+	B	A	A	A	A	40	11	11.3	4	83
50 mm concrete (100% RCA) on polyethylene dpm laid on sand blinding	820470075	A+	A+	B	A+	A	A	A	A	A+	B	A	A	A	A	40	17	65.6	26	83
50 mm concrete on polyethylene dpm laid on sand blinding	820470014	A	A+	B	A+	A	A	A	A	A+	B	A	A	A	A	40	17	6.3	3	84
50 mm fine aggregate on polyethylene dpm laid on sand blinding	820470015	A+	A+	B	A+	A+	A	A	A	A+	A	A	A+	A	A+	40	7.1	5.6	3	83

Suspended timber ground floors

Domestic

Plywood (temperate, EN636-2) decking on timber joists with insulation over:	Element number	Summary Rating	Climate change	Water extraction	Mineral resource extraction	Stratospheric ozone depletion	Human toxicity	Ecotoxicity to freshwater	Nuclear waste (higher level)	Ecotoxicity to land	Waste disposal	Fossil fuel depletion	Eutrophication	Photochemical ozone creation	Acidification	Typical replacement interval	Embodied CO_2 (kg CO_2 eq.)	Recycled content (kg)	Recycled content (%)	Recycled currently at EOL (%)
100 mm 30% PFA oversite concrete	820470137	B	A+	D	A+	B	D	D	D	C	B	C	B	C	B	40	30	8.2	3	84
100 mm 30% PFA oversite concrete (100% RCA)	820470138	A	A+	D	A+	C	D	D	D	C	B	C	B	C	B	40	30	126	48	83
100 mm 50% GGBS oversite concrete	820470124	A	A+	D	A+	B	D	D	D	C	B	B	B	C	B	40	24	11	4	83
100 mm 50% GGBS oversite concrete (100% RCA)	820470125	A	A+	D	A+	C	D	D	D	C	B	B	B	C	B	40	24	130	49	83
100 mm oversite concrete	820470005	B	A	D	A	B	D	D	D	C	B	C	B	C	B	40	35	1.7	1	83
100 mm oversite concrete (100% RCA)	820470100	A	A	D	A+	C	D	D	D	C	B	C	B	C	B	40	35	120	45	83
50 mm 30% PFA concrete (100% RCA) on polyethylene dpm laid on sand blinding	820470096	A	A+	D	A+	C	D	D	D	C	B	B	B	C	B	40	23	63	25	82
50 mm 30% PFA concrete on polyethylene dpm laid on sand blinding	820470097	A	A+	D	A+	C	D	D	D	C	B	B	B	C	B	40	23	4.1	2	84
50 mm 50% GGBS concrete (100% RCA) on polyethylene dpm laid on sand blinding	820470098	A	A+	D	A+	C	D	D	D	C	B	B	B	C	B	40	20	65	25	82
50 mm 50% GGBS concrete on polyethylene dpm laid on sand blinding	820470099	A	A+	D	A+	C	D	D	D	C	B	B	B	C	A	40	20	5.7	2	82
50 mm concrete (100% RCA) on polyethylene dpm laid on sand blinding	820470095	A	A+	D	A+	C	D	D	D	C	B	C	B	C	B	40	26	60	23	82
50 mm concrete on polyethylene dpm laid on sand blinding	820470007	A	A+	D	A+	C	D	D	D	C	B	C	B	C	B	40	26	1.1	0	82
50 mm fine aggregate on polyethylene dpm laid on sand blinding	820470128	A	A+	D	A+	B	D	D	D	C	B	B	B	B	A	40	16	0.4	0	80

Suspended timber ground floors

Domestic

Reclaimed floorboards on timber joists with insulation over:	Element number	Summary Rating	Climate change	Water extraction	Mineral resource extraction	Stratospheric ozone depletion	Human toxicity	Ecotoxicity to freshwater	Nuclear waste (higher level)	Ecotoxicity to land	Waste disposal	Fossil fuel depletion	Eutrophication	Photochemical ozone creation	Acidification	Typical replacement interval	Embodied CO2 (kg CO2 eq.)	Recycled content (kg)	Recycled content (%)	Recycled currently at EOL (%)
100 mm 30% PFA concrete (100% RCA)	820470113	A+	A+	A+	A+	A+	A+	A+	A+	A+	A	A+	A+	A+	A+	50	12	134	51	85
100 mm 30% PFA oversite concrete	820470107	A+	A+	A+	A+	A+	A+	A+	A+	A+	A	A+	A+	A+	A+	50	12	16	6	86
100 mm 50% GGBS oversite concrete (100% RCA)	820470111	A+	A+	A+	A+	A+	A+	A+	A+	A+	A+	A+	A+	A+	A+	50	6.2	138	53	85
100 mm oversite concrete	820470103	A+	A+	A	A+	A+	A+	A+	A+	A+	A	A+	A+	A+	A+	50	17	9.3	4	86
100 mm oversite concrete (100% RCA)	820470105	A+	A+	A+	A+	A+	A+	A+	A+	A+	A	A+	A+	A+	A	50	17	128	49	85
50% GGBS oversite concrete	820470108	A+	A+	A+	A+	A+	A+	A+	A+	A+	A	A+	A+	A+	A+	50	6	18.9	7	85
50 mm 30% PFA concrete (100% RCA) on polyethylene dpm laid on sand blinding	820470112	A+	A+	A+	A+	A+	A+	A+	A+	A+	A	A+	A+	A+	A+	50	5.5	71.4	28	85
50 mm 30% PFA concrete on polyethylene dpm laid on sand blinding	820470109	A+	A+	A	A+	A+	A+	A+	A+	A+	A	A+	A+	A+	A+	50	5.5	12	5	86
50 mm 50% GGBS concrete (100% RCA) on polyethylene dpm laid on sand blinding	820470130	A+	A+	A+	A+	A+	A+	A+	A+	A+	A	A+	A+	A+	A+	50	2.5	72.9	29	85
50 mm 50% GGBS concrete on polyethylene dpm laid on sand blinding	820470131	A+	A+	A+	A+	A+	A+	A+	A+	A+	A	A+	A+	A+	A+	50	2.4	13.7	5	85
50 mm concrete (100% RCA) on polyethylene dpm laid on sand blinding	820470104	A+	A+	A+	A+	A+	A+	A+	A+	A+	A	A+	A+	A+	A+	50	8.1	67.9	27	85
50 mm concrete on polyethylene dpm laid on sand blinding	820470101	A+	A+	A	A+	A+	A+	A+	A+	A+	A	A+	A+	A+	A+	50	8	9	4	85
50 mm fine aggregate on polyethylene dpm laid on sand blinding	820470102	A+	A+	A+	A+	A+	A+	A+	A+	A	A	A+	A+	A+	A+	50	-2	8	4	85

Suspended timber ground floors

Domestic

t&g softwood boards on timber joists with insulation over:	Element number	Summary Rating	Climate change	Water extraction	Mineral resource extraction	Stratospheric ozone depletion	Human toxicity	Ecotoxicity to freshwater	Nuclear waste (higher level)	Ecotoxicity to land	Waste disposal	Fossil fuel depletion	Eutrophication	Photochemical ozone creation	Acidification	Typical replacement interval	Embodied CO2 (kg CO2 eq.)	Recycled content (kg)	Recycled content (%)	Recycled currently at EOL (%)
100 mm 30% PFA oversite concrete	820470120	A+	A+	A+	A+	A+	A+	A+	A+	A+	A+	A+	A+	A+	A+	60+	14	8.2	3	86
100 mm 30% PFA oversite concrete (100% RCA)	820470119	A+	A+	A+	A+	A+	A+	A+	A+	A+	A+	A+	A+	A+	A+	60+	14	126	48	85
100 mm 50% GGBS oversite concrete	820470122	A+	A+	A+	A+	A+	A+	A+	A+	A+	A	A+	A+	A+	A+	60+	7.9	11	4	85
100 mm 50% GGBS oversite concrete (100% RCA)	820470121	A+	A+	A+	A+	A+	A+	A+	A+	A+	A	A+	A+	A+	A+	60+	8	130	50	85
100 mm oversite concrete	820470009	A+	A+	A+	A+	A+	A+	A+	A+	A+	A+	A+	A+	A+	A+	60+	19	1.7	1	85
100 mm oversite concrete (100% RCA)	820470123	A+	A+	A+	A+	A+	A+	A+	A+	A+	A+	A+	A+	A+	A+	60+	19	120	46	85
50 mm 30% PFA concrete (100% RCA) on polyethylene dpm laid on sand blinding	820470114	A+	A+	A+	A+	A+	A+	A+	A+	A+	A+	A+	A+	A+	A+	60+	7.4	63.4	25	85
50 mm 30% PFA concrete on polyethylene dpm laid on sand blinding	820470115	A+	A+	A+	A+	A+	A+	A+	A+	A+	A+	A+	A+	A+	A+	60+	7.3	4.1	2	86
50 mm 50% GGBS concrete (100% RCA) on polyethylene dpm laid on sand blinding	820470116	A+	A+	A+	A+	A+	A+	A+	A+	A+	A+	A+	A+	A+	A+	60+	4.3	65	26	85
50 mm 50% GGBS concrete on polyethylene dpm laid on sand blinding	820470117	A+	A+	A+	A+	A+	A+	A+	A+	A+	A+	A+	A+	A+	A+	60+	4.3	5.7	2	85
50 mm concrete (100% RCA) on polyethylene dpm laid on sand blinding	820470134	A+	A+	A+	A+	A+	A+	A+	A+	A+	A+	A+	A+	A+	A+	60+	10	60	24	85
50 mm concrete on polyethylene dpm laid on sand blinding	820470011	A+	A+	A+	A+	A+	A+	A+	A+	A+	A+	A+	A+	A+	A+	60+	9.9	1.1	0	85
50 mm fine aggregate on polyethylene dpm laid on sand blinding	820470012	A+	A+	A+	A+	A+	A+	A+	A+	A+	A+	A+	A+	A+	A+	60+	0	0.4	0	83

6.2 UPPER FLOORS

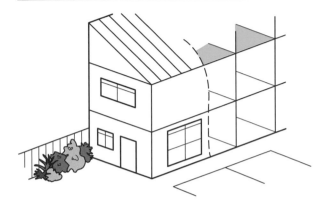

This section applies to all floor constructions that are not in contact with the ground, with the exception of separating floors between dwellings where ratings are provided in *section 6.3, Domestic*. Upper floors include floors to be constructed at ground level, but above a basement or cellar. For domestic construction, the upper floors include a plasterboard ceiling and paint finish, but for non-domestic upper floors, the ceiling finish is excluded.

Note: where descriptions refer to, say 20% recycled coarse aggregate, this refers to 20% of the coarse aggregate in the concrete being replaced with Recycled Concrete Aggregate (RCA).

Functional unit for upper floors for commercial buildings:

1 m² of upper floor construction, to satisfy Building Regulations in England & Wales, capable of supporting a live floor load of 2.5 kN/m², including any additional beams to span a 7.5 m column grid and surface-ready for the addition of a sub-structural floor system. Beams directly between columns are excluded between loadbearing walls. To include any repair, refurbishment or replacement over the 60-year study period.

Variation for housing:
As for commercial buildings but based on a 4 m span and area of 40 m², a live loading of 1.5 kN/m² and surface-ready for the addition of a sheet carpet and underlay. All domestic upper floors also include a painted plasterboard ceiling.

Variation for education:
As for commercial buildings but based on a floor between classrooms with a 8 m span and a live loading of 3 kN/m², and surface-ready for the addition of a sheet flooring.

Variation for health:
As for commercial buildings but based on a 6 m span, a live loading of 2 kN/m² and surface-ready for the addition of a sheet flooring.

Variation for retail:
As for commercial buildings but based on a 6 m span, a live loading of 4 kN/m² and surface-ready for the addition of a sub-structural floor system.

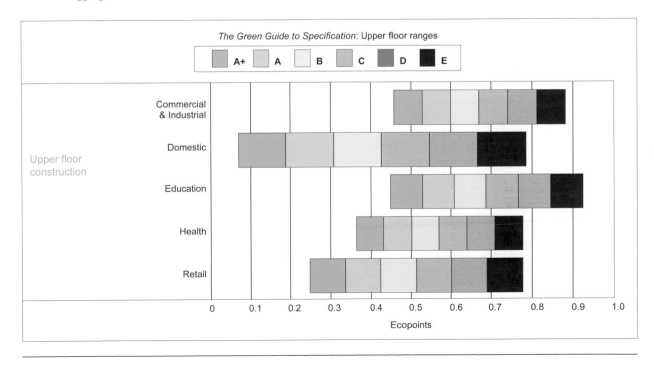

The Green Guide to Specification: Upper floor ranges

Concrete block solid densities are as follows:
- Dense block/blockwork ($\approx$ 1950 kg/m^3),
- Medium density block/blockwork ($\approx$ 1450 kg/m^3),
- Lightweight blockwork ($\approx$ 1100 kg/m^3),
- Superlightweight block/blockwork ($\approx$ 850 kg/m^3).

Upper floors
Commercial & Industrial

	Element number	Summary Rating	Climate change	Water extraction	Mineral resource extraction	Stratospheric ozone depletion	Human toxicity	Ecotoxicity to freshwater	Nuclear waste (higher level)	Ecotoxicity to land	Waste disposal	Fossil fuel depletion	Eutrophication	Photochemical ozone creation	Acidification	Typical replacement interval	Embodied CO₂ (kg CO₂ eq.)	Recycled content (kg)	Recycled content (%)	Recycled currently at EOL (%)
Lattice girder precast concrete floor with:																				
in situ concrete topping	807280012	B	B	B	B	A	B	C	B	A	B	A	B	A	B	60+	99	25	5	90
expanded polystyrene void formers and in situ concrete topping	807280013	A+	A+	A	A+	A	A+	A+	A+	A+	A+	A+	A+	A	A+	60+	68	18	4	90
Post-tensioned slabs with screed	807280010	C	C	D	D	B	C	D	C	B	D	C	C	B	C	60+	120	25	4	90
Power floated:																				
20% recycled coarse aggregate in situ reinforced concrete floor slab	807280060	C	D	D	C	A	C	D	C	B	D	B	B	B	C	60+	120	95.4	14	90
50% GGBS, 20% Recycled coarse aggregate in situ reinforced concrete floor slab	807280059	A	A	D	B	A	A+	A+	A	A	D	A+	A+	A+	A+	60+	79	137	21	90
in situ 50% GGBS reinforced concrete floor slab	807280057	B	A	D	C	A	A+	A+	A	A	D	A+	A+	A+	A+	60+	79	74	11	90
in situ reinforced 30% PFA, 20% recycled coarse aggregate concrete floor slab	807280058	B	B	D	B	A	B	B	A	B	D	A	B	A	B	60+	100	125	19	90
in situ reinforced concrete floor slab	807280054	C	D	D	D	A	C	D	C	B	D	B	B	B	C	60+	120	33	5	90
in situ reinforced concrete floor slab with 30% PFA	807280056	C	B	D	C	A	B	B	A	B	D	A	B	A	B	60+	100	62	9	90
in situ reinforced concrete ribbed/ trough slab	807280008	A+	A+	A	A	A+	A+	A	A+	A+	A+	A+	A+	A+	A+	60+	74	15	4	90
in situ reinforced concrete waffle slab	807280011	C	C	D	C	A	B	C	C	B	C	B	B	A	B	60+	110	31	5	90
post tensioned in situ reinforced concrete floor slab	807280055	A	B	B	B	A+	A	B	A	A	B	A	A	A+	A	60+	93	24	4	90
in situ reinforced concrete slab on 'deep' profiled metal decking	807280015	A+	A	C	A+	A+	A+	A+	C	A+	A	A	A+	A+	A+	60+	84	12	4	90
in situ reinforced concrete slab on 'shallow' profiled metal decking	807280074	A+	A+	A	A+	A+	A+	A+	A	A+	A+	A+	A+	A+	A+	60+	63	12	5	90

Upper floors
Commercial & Industrial

	Element number	Summary Rating	Climate change	Water extraction	Mineral resource extraction	Stratospheric ozone depletion	Human toxicity	Ecotoxicity to freshwater	Nuclear waste (higher level)	Ecotoxicity to land	Waste disposal	Fossil fuel depletion	Eutrophication	Photochemical ozone creation	Acidification	Typical replacement interval	Embodied CO2 (kg CO2 eq.)	Recycled content (kg)	Recycled content (%)	Recycled currently at EOL (%)
Screeded:																				
beam and aircrete block flooring	807280031	A+	B	A	A+	C	C	B	C	A+	A+	B	B	C	A	60+	94	5	1	90
beam and medium dense solid block flooring	807280016	A+	A	A	A+	D	C	B	A	A+	A+	B	B	B	B	60+	85	4.2	1	90
hollow precast prestressed concrete planks	807280045	A+	A	A+	A+	C	C	B	A	A+	A+	A	B	B	A	60+	81	4	1	90
hollow precast reinforced slab	807280006	D	E	C	B	E	E	D	E	E	C	E	E	E	E	60+	140	59	11	90
in situ concrete slab	807280017	E	E	E	E	C	E	E	E	C	E	D	E	D	E	60+	140	33	4	90
in situ reinforced concrete ribbed slab	807280062	B	B	B	B	B	B	C	B	A+	B	A	B	B	B	60+	97	16	3	90
in situ reinforced concrete waffle slab	807280061	E	E	E	E	C	E	E	E	C	E	D	D	C	D	60+	140	31	4	90
Structural topping on:																				
beam and aircrete block flooring	807280003	A+	A	A	A+	B	B	B	C	A+	A+	A	A	A	A	60+	89	6.9	2	90
grouted beam and dense solid block flooring	807280038	A+	A+	A+	A	B	A	A	A+	A+	A+	A+	A+	A	A+	60+	65	5.8	1	90
grouted beam and medium dense solid block flooring	807280037	A+	A	A	A+	B	B	B	A	A+	A+	A	A	A	A	60+	80	6.1	1	90
hollow precast prestressed concrete slabs	807280053	A+	A+	A+	A+	B	B	B	A	A+	A+	A+	A	A	A+	60+	76	5.9	2	90
hollow precast reinforced slab	807280007	C	E	C	B	D	E	D	E	E	C	E	E	D	E	60+	140	61	11	90

Upper floors

Domestic

	Element number	Summary Rating	Climate change	Water extraction	Mineral resource extraction	Stratospheric ozone depletion	Human toxicity	Ecotoxicity to freshwater	Nuclear waste (higher level)	Ecotoxicity to land	Waste disposal	Fossil fuel depletion	Eutrophication	Photochemical ozone creation	Acidification	Typical replacement interval	Embodied CO_2 (kg CO_2 eq.)	Recycled content (kg)	Recycled content (%)	Recycled currently at EOL (%)
Chipboard decking on:																				
galvanised steel joists	807280080	A	A	B	A+	A+	A+	B	A	A	A	A	A	A+	A	60+	27	10.9	36	27
metal web joists	807280005	A+	A+	A	A+	A	A	B	A	A+	A	A	A+	A	A+	60+	3.8	10.9	32	17
timber battens on grouted beam and dense solid block flooring	807280033	B	B	A	B	B	B	C	B	A	C	B	B	B	A	60+	34	12	5	82
timber battens, grouted beam and aircrete block flooring	807280002	A	B	B	A+	A	B	C	B	A	B	B	B	A	A	60+	41	12	8	76
timber battens, grouted beam and medium dense solid block flooring	807280043	B	B	B	A	B	B	C	A	A	B	C	B	B	B	60+	41	12	6	80
timber battens, grouted hollow precast prestressed concrete planks	807280048	C	B	B	B	B	C	C	B	B	C	C	C	B	B	60+	57	13	5	82
timber battens, grouted hollow precast reinforced slab flooring	807280047	E	E	D	C	D	E	D	D	D	E	E	E	E	E	60+	110	45	11	86
timber I joists	807280024	A+	A+	A	A+	A+	A	B	A	A+	A	A	A+	A+		60+	6.3	12	44	5
timber joists	807280081	A+	A+	A+	A+	A	A+	B	A	A+	A	A	A+	A+	A+	60+	-0.7	10.9	35	11
OSB-2 decking on:																				
galvanised steel joists	807280040	A+	A	B	A+	A+	A	B	A	A+	A	A	A+	A+	A+	60+	20	8.9	33	29
timber battens, grouted beam and aircrete block flooring	807280032	A	B	B	A	A	B	C	A	A+	A	B	A	A	A	60+	34	10	7	78
timber battens, grouted beam and dense solid block flooring	807280034	B	A	B	B	B	B	C	A	A+	B	A	A	A	A	60+	28	10	4	83
timber battens, grouted beam and medium dense solid block flooring	807280001	A	B	B	A	B	B	C	A	A+	B	B	B	A	B	60+	34	10	5	82
timber battens, grouted hollow precast prestressed concrete planks	807280050	B	B	B	B	B	C	C	B	A	C	B	B	B	B	60+	50	11	5	83
timber battens, grouted hollow precast reinforced slab flooring	807280049	D	D	E	C	D	E	D	C	C	E	E	E	D	E	60+	100	43	10	86
timber I joists	807280044	A+	A+	A	A+	A+	A	B	A+	A+	A+	A+	A+	A+	A+	60+	-1	10	41	5
timber joists	807280041	A+	A+	A+	A+	A+	A	B	A+	A+	A+	A+	A+	A+	A+	60+	-8	8.9	32	12
Panelised steel floor cassette with:																				
chipboard decking	807280066	A	A	B	A+	A+	A+	A+	A	A	A	A	A+	A	A	60+	26	12.8	36	27
OSB-2 decking	807280027	A+	A	B	A+	A+	A	A+	A	A+	A	A	A+	A+	A	60+	18	10.7	33	29
plywood (softwood, 636-1) decking	807280068	A	A	B	A+	A	A	A	C	B	A	A	A+	A	A	60+	23	3.9	12	29

Upper floors
Domestic

	Element number	Summary Rating	Climate change	Water extraction	Mineral resource extraction	Stratospheric ozone depletion	Human toxicity	Ecotoxicity to freshwater	Nuclear waste (higher level)	Ecotoxicity to land	Waste disposal	Fossil fuel depletion	Eutrophication	Photochemical ozone creation	Acidification	Typical replacement interval	Embodied CO2 (kg CO2 eq.)	Recycled content (kg)	Recycled content (%)	Recycled currently at EOL (%)
Plywood (softwood, 636-1) decking on:																				
galvanised steel joists	807280020	A	A	B	A+	A	A	C	C	B	A	A	A	A	A	60+	23	3.3	11	27
grouted beam and aircrete block flooring	807280030	B	B	B	A	B	B	D	C	C	A	B	B	B	B	60+	38	4.4	3	76
grouted beam and dense solid block flooring	807280035	B	A	B	B	C	C	D	C	C	C	B	B	B	B	60+	31	4.7	2	82
grouted beam and medium dense solid block flooring	807280014	B	B	B	A	C	C	D	C	C	B	B	B	C	B	60+	37	4.7	2	81
timber battens on grouted hollow precast prestressed concrete planks	807280052	C	B	B	B	C	C	E	D	C	C	C	C	C	C	60+	54	5.6	2	82
timber battens on grouted hollow precast reinforced slab	807280051	E	D	E	C	E	E	E	E	E	E	E	E	E	E	60+	110	37	9	86
timber I joists	807280025	A+	A+	A	A+	A	B	C	B	B	A	A	A	A	A	60+	2.8	4.4	16	5
timber joists	807280022	A+	A+	A	A+	B	A	C	B	B	A	A	A	A	A+	60+	-4	3.3	11	11
Post-tensioned slabs with screed	807280010	D	D	D	E	B	C	D	B	A	D	C	C	C	C	60+	96	12	2	89
Power floated:																				
20% recycled coarse aggregate in situ reinforced concrete floor slab	807280060	D	D	D	D	A	B	C	B	A	D	C	C	B	C	60+	89	61	12	88
50% GGBS, 20% recycled coarse aggregate in situ reinforced concrete floor slab	807280059	C	B	D	C	A	A	B	A	A+	D	A	A	A	A	60+	56	92	17	88
in situ 50% GGBS reinforced concrete floor slab	807280057	C	B	D	D	A	A	B	A	A+	D	A	A	A	A	60+	56	14	3	88
in situ reinforced 30% PFA, 20% recycled coarse aggregate concrete floor slab	807280058	D	C	D	D	A	B	C	A	A	D	B	B	A	B	60+	72	83	16	88
in situ reinforced concrete floor slab	807280054	D	D	D	D	A	B	C	B	A	D	C	C	B	C	60+	89	14	3	88
in situ reinforced concrete floor slab with 30% PFA	807280056	D	C	D	D	A	B	C	A	A	D	B	B	A	B	60+	72	14	3	88
post tensioned in situ reinforced concrete floor slab	807280055	C	C	C	C	A	B	C	A	A	C	B	B	A	B	60+	73	11	3	88
Reclaimed timber flooring on:																				
timber I joists	807280046	A+	A+	A+	A+	A+	A+	B	A+	A+	A+	A+	A+	A+	A+	50	-11	12	54	18
timber joists	807280042	A+	A+	A+	A+	A+	A+	A	A+	A+	A+	A+	A+	A+	A+	50	-18	11	42	23

Upper floors

Domestic

	Element number	Summary Rating	Climate change	Water extraction	Mineral resource extraction	Stratospheric ozone depletion	Human toxicity	Ecotoxicity to freshwater	Nuclear waste (higher level)	Ecotoxicity to land	Waste disposal	Fossil fuel depletion	Eutrophication	Photochemical ozone creation	Acidification	Typical replacement interval	Embodied CO2 (kg CO2 eq.)	Recycled content (kg)	Recycled content (%)	Recycled currently at EOL (%)
Screeded:																				
beam and aircrete block flooring	807280031	B	C	B	B	B	B	C	A	A	A	B	B	B	B	60+	66	5	2	87
beam and dense solid block flooring	807280039	C	C	B	C	C	B	C	A	A+	B	B	B	B	B	60+	59	5.3	1	88
beam and medium dense solid block flooring	807280016	B	C	B	B	C	C	C	A	A	B	C	C	B	C	60+	65	5.3	2	87
hollow precast prestressed concrete planks	807280045	C	C	B	C	C	C	C	B	A	C	C	C	C	C	60+	82	6.2	2	88
hollow precast reinforced slab	807280006	E	E	E	D	E	E	D	C	C	E	E	E	E	E	60+	140	38	7	89
in situ 30% PFA concrete (20% RCA) slab	807280063	E	D	E	E	C	C	D	B	A	E	C	C	C	C	60+	95	83	13	89
in situ 30% PFA concrete slab	807280072	E	D	E	E	C	C	D	B	A	E	C	C	C	C	60+	95	15	2	89
in situ 50% GGBS concrete (20% RCA) slab	807280064	D	C	E	E	C	C	C	B	A	E	C	C	C	C	60+	79	92	14	89
in situ 50% GGBS concrete slab	807280073	E	C	E	E	C	C	C	B	A	E	C	B	C	60+	79	15	2	89
in situ concrete (20% RCA) slab	807280065	E	E	E	E	C	D	D	B	B	E	D	D	C	D	60+	110	62	9	89
in situ concrete slab	807280017	E	E	E	E	C	D	D	B	B	E	D	D	C	D	60+	110	15	2	89
Structural topping on:																				
beam and aircrete block flooring	807280003	B	C	B	B	A	B	C	A	A+	A	B	A	A	B	60+	61	7	3	87
grouted beam and dense solid block flooring	807280038	C	B	B	C	B	B	C	A	A+	B	B	B	A	B	60+	54	7.2	2	88
grouted beam and medium dense solid block flooring	807280037	B	C	B	B	B	B	C	A	A	B	B	B	A	B	60+	60	7.2	2	87
hollow precast prestressed concrete slabs	807280053	C	C	B	C	B	C	C	B	A	C	B	C	B	C	60+	77	8.1	2	88
hollow precast reinforced slab	807280007	E	E	E	D	D	E	D	C	C	E	E	E	D	E	60+	130	40	8	89
t&g floorboards on:																				
timber I joists	807280026	A+	A+	A+	A+	A+	A+	B	A+	A+	A+	A+	A+	A+	A+	60+	-1	4.4	19	18
timber joists	807280023	A+	A+	A+	A+	A	A+	B	A+	A+	A+	A+	A+	A+	A+	60+	-8	3.3	12	23

Upper floors Education	Element number	Summary Rating	Climate change	Water extraction	Mineral resource extraction	Stratospheric ozone depletion	Human toxicity	Ecotoxicity to freshwater	Nuclear waste (higher level)	Ecotoxicity to land	Waste disposal	Fossil fuel depletion	Eutrophication	Photochemical ozone creation	Acidification	Typical replacement interval	Embodied CO2 (kg CO2 eq.)	Recycled content (kg)	Recycled content (%)	Recycled currently at EOL (%)
Lattice girder precast concrete floor with:																				
in situ concrete topping	807280012	B	B	B	B	A	B	B	B	B	B	B	B	A	B	60+	100	36	7	90
polystyrene void formers and in situ concrete topping	807280013	A+	A+	A+	A+	A	A+	A+	A+	A+	A+	A+	A+	A	A+	60+	66	16	4	90
Post-tensioned slabs with screed	807280010	D	D	D	D	C	D	D	C	B	D	C	D	C	C	60+	120	26	4	90
Power floated:																				
20% recycled coarse aggregate in situ reinforced concrete floor slab	807280060	C	D	D	C	A	C	D	C	B	D	B	C	B	C	60+	120	100	14	90
50% GGBS, 20% Recycled coarse aggregate in situ reinforced concrete floor slab	807280059	B	A	C	B	A	A	A+	A	A	D	A+	A	A+	A+	60+	83	145	21	90
in situ 50% GGBS reinforced concrete floor slab	807280057	B	A	D	C	A	A	A+	A	A	D	A+	A+	A+	A+	60+	83	78	11	90
in situ reinforced 30% PFA, 20% recycled coarse aggregate concrete floor slab	807280058	C	C	C	B	A	B	B	A	B	D	B	B	A	B	60+	110	132	19	90
in situ reinforced concrete floor slab	807280054	D	D	D	D	A	C	D	C	B	D	B	C	B	C	60+	120	34	5	90
in situ reinforced concrete floor slab with 30% PFA	807280056	C	C	D	C	A	B	B	B	B	D	B	B	A	B	60+	110	65	9	90
in situ reinforced concrete ribbed/trough slab	807280008	A+	A+	A	A	A+	A	A	A+	A+	A+	A+	A+	A+	A+	60+	79	16	3	90
in situ reinforced concrete waffle slab	807280011	C	C	D	D	A	C	C	C	B	C	B	C	A	C	60+	120	31	5	90
post-tensioned in situ reinforced concrete floor slab	807280055	B	B	B	B	A+	B	B	A	A	B	A	A	A+	A	60+	99	25	4	90
in situ reinforced concrete slab on 'deep' profiled metal decking	807280015	A+	A	B	A+	A+	A+	A+	C	A+	A+	A+	A+	A+	A+	60+	84	12	4	90
in situ reinforced concrete slab on 'shallow' profiled metal decking	807280074	A+	A+	A+	A+	A+	A+	A+	A+	A+	A+	A+	A+	A+	A+	60+	64	12	5	90

Upper floors
Education

	Element number	Summary Rating	Climate change	Water extraction	Mineral resource extraction	Stratospheric ozone depletion	Human toxicity	Ecotoxicity to freshwater	Nuclear waste (higher level)	Ecotoxicity to land	Waste disposal	Fossil fuel depletion	Eutrophication	Photochemical ozone creation	Acidification	Typical replacement interval	Embodied CO₂ (kg CO₂ eq.)	Recycled content (kg)	Recycled content (%)	Recycled currently at EOL (%)
Screeded:																				
beam and aircrete block flooring	807280031	A	B	A	A+	D	D	C	D	A+	A+	C	C	C	B	60+	100	5.3	1	90
hollow precast prestressed concrete planks	807280045	A	B	A+	A	D	D	C	B	A+	A	B	C	B	B	60+	93	4.4	1	90
hollow precast reinforced slab	807280006	C	E	C	B	E	E	D	E	E	C	E	E	E	E	60+	140	59	11	90
in situ concrete slab	807280017	E	E	E	E	C	E	E	E	C	E	D	E	D	E	60+	150	34	4	90
in situ reinforced concrete ribbed slab	807280062	B	B	B	C	B	C	C	B	A+	B	B	B	B	B	60+	100	17	3	90
in situ reinforced concrete waffle slab	807280061	E	E	E	E	C	E	E	E	C	E	D	E	D	E	60+	140	31	4	90
Structural topping on:																				
beam and aircrete block flooring	807280003	A	B	A	A+	B	C	B	C	A+	A+	B	B	B	A	60+	99	7.2	2	90
hollow precast prestressed concrete slabs	807280053	A	A	A+	A	B	C	B	B	A+	A+	A	B	A	A	60+	88	6.3	1	90
hollow precast reinforced slab	807280007	C	E	C	B	D	E	C	E	E	C	E	E	D	E	60+	140	61	11	90

Upper floors

Health

	Element number	Summary Rating	Climate change	Water extraction	Mineral resource extraction	Stratospheric ozone depletion	Human toxicity	Ecotoxicity to freshwater	Nuclear waste (higher level)	Ecotoxicity to land	Waste disposal	Fossil fuel depletion	Eutrophication	Photochemical ozone creation	Acidification	Typical replacement interval	Embodied CO2 (kg CO2 eq.)	Recycled content (kg)	Recycled content (%)	Recycled currently at EOL (%)
Lattice girder precast concrete floor with:																				
in situ concrete topping	807280012	C	B	C	C	A	B	C	B	A	C	A	B	A	B	60+	96	19	3	90
polystyrene void formers and in situ concrete topping	807280013	A	A+	B	A	A	A+	A	A+	A+	B	A+	A+	A	A+	60+	66	14	3	90
Post-tensioned slabs with screed	807280010	C	B	C	D	B	C	D	B	A	D	B	B	B	B	60+	100	19	3	90
Power floated:																				
20% recycled coarse aggregate in situ reinforced concrete floor slab	807280060	C	B	D	C	A	B	C	B	A	D	A	A	A	B	60+	100	79.5	14	90
50% GGBS, 20% Recycled coarse aggregate in situ reinforced concrete floor slab	807280059	B	A+	C	B	A+	A+	A+	A+	A+	D	A+	A+	A+	A+	60+	66	116	20	90
in situ 50% GGBS reinforced concrete floor slab	807280057	B	A+	C	C	A+	A+	A+	A+	A+	D	A+	A+	A+	A+	60+	66	61	11	90
in situ reinforced 30% PFA, 20% recycled coarse aggregate concrete floor slab	807280058	B	A	C	B	A+	A	B	A+	A	D	A	A	A+	A	60+	86	106	18	90
in situ reinforced concrete floor slab	807280054	C	B	D	D	A+	B	C	B	A	D	A	A	A	B	60+	99	25	4	90
in situ reinforced concrete floor slab with 30% PFA	807280056	C	A	C	C	A+	A	B	A+	A	D	A	A	A+	A	60+	86	50	9	90
in situ reinforced concrete ribbed/ trough slab	807280008	A	A+	A	A	A+	A+	A	A+	A+	A	A+	A+	A+	A+	60+	71	15	4	90
post-tensioned in situ reinforced concrete floor slab	807280055	A	A	B	B	A+	A+	A	A+	A+	B	A+	A+	A+	A+	60+	76	18	4	90
in situ reinforced concrete slab on 'deep' profiled metal decking	807280015	A	A	D	A+	A+	A+	A+	C	A+	B	A	A+	A+	A+	60+	84	12	4	90
in situ reinforced concrete slab on 'shallow' profiled metal decking	807280074	A+	A+	A	A+	A+	A+	A+	A	A+	A+	A+	A+	A+	A+	60+	61	7.8	3	90
Screeded:																				
beam and aircrete block flooring	807280031	A+	A+	A+	A+	B	A	A	A+	A+	A+	A+	A+	A	A+	60+	69	3.4	1	90
beam and medium dense solid block flooring	807280016	A	A+	A	A	C	C	B	A	A+	A	A	B	B	A	60+	76	3.5	1	90
hollow precast prestressed concrete planks	807280045	A	A	A+	A	C	B	B	A	A+	A	A	A	B	A	60+	76	2.9	1	90
hollow precast reinforced slab	807280006	E	E	E	C	E	E	E	E	E	E	E	E	E	E	60+	140	59	11	90
in situ concrete slab	807280017	E	D	E	E	C	D	E	D	B	E	C	D	C	C	60+	120	26	4	90
in situ reinforced concrete ribbed slab	807280062	C	B	C	C	B	B	C	A	A	C	A	B	B	B	60+	94	16	3	90

Upper floors

Health

Structural topping on:	Element number	Summary Rating	Climate change	Water extraction	Mineral resource extraction	Stratospheric ozone depletion	Human toxicity	Ecotoxicity to freshwater	Nuclear waste (higher level)	Ecotoxicity to land	Waste disposal	Fossil fuel depletion	Eutrophication	Photochemical ozone creation	Acidification	Typical replacement interval	Embodied CO_2 (kg CO_2 eq.)	Recycled content (kg)	Recycled content (%)	Recycled currently at EOL (%)
beam and aircrete block flooring	807280003	A+	A+	A+	A+	A	A+	A	A+	A+	A+	A+	A+	A+	A+	60+	64	5.3	2	90
grouted beam and dense solid block flooring	807280038	A	A+	A+	A	A	A	A	A+	A+	A	A+	A+	A+	A+	60+	63	6.1	2	90
grouted beam and medium dense solid block flooring	807280037	A	A+	A	A	B	B	B	A+	A+	A	A	A	A	A	60+	71	5.4	1	90
hollow precast prestressed concrete slabs	807280053	A	A+	A+	A	A	A	B	A	A+	A	A+	A	A+	A+	60+	72	4.9	1	90
hollow precast reinforced slab	807280007	E	E	E	C	D	E	D	E	E	D	E	E	D	E	60+	140	61	11	90

Upper floors
Retail

	Element number	Summary Rating	Climate change	Water extraction	Mineral resource extraction	Stratospheric ozone depletion	Human toxicity	Ecotoxicity to freshwater	Nuclear waste (higher level)	Ecotoxicity to land	Waste disposal	Fossil fuel depletion	Eutrophication	Photochemical ozone creation	Acidification	Typical replacement interval	Embodied CO2 (kg CO2 eq.)	Recycled content (kg)	Recycled content (%)	Recycled currently at EOL (%)
Chipboard decking on:																				
galvanised steel joists	807280080	A+	A+	D	A+	A+	A	A	C	A	B	A	A+	A	A+	60+	56	7.7	20	64
timber joists	807280081	A+	A+	A+	A+	A+	A+	A	A+	A+	A+	A+	A+	A+	A+	60+	-0.4	7.7	62	0
OSB/2 decking on galvanised steel joists	807280040	A+	A+	D	A+	A+	A	A+	B	A+	A	A+	A+	A+	A+	60+	49	5.6	16	69
Lattice girder precast concrete floor with:																				
in situ concrete topping	807280012	D	B	C	D	B	C	D	A	B	C	B	C	A	B	60+	97	21	4	90
polystyrene void formers and in situ concrete topping	807280013	B	A+	B	C	B	B	C	A+	A	B	A+	B	A	A	60+	67	16	4	90
Plywood (softwood, 636-1) decking on galvanised steel joists	807280020	A+	A+	D	A+	A	A	C	E	C	B	A	A	A	A	60+	52	0	0	65
Post-tensioned slabs with screed	807280010	D	C	C	D	C	C	D	A	A	D	B	C	B	C	60+	100	19	3	90
Power floated:																				
20% recycled coarse aggregate in situ reinforced concrete floor slab	807280060	D	C	D	D	A	C	D	A	B	D	A	C	A	B	60+	100	79.5	14	90
50% GGBS, 20% Recycled coarse aggregate in situ reinforced concrete floor slab	807280059	B	A+	C	C	A	B	B	A+	A	D	A+	A	A+	A	60+	66	116	20	90
in situ 50% GGBS reinforced concrete floor slab	807280057	C	A+	C	D	A	A	B	A+	A	D	A+	A	A+	A	60+	66	61	11	90
in situ reinforced 30% PFA, 20% recycled coarse aggregate concrete floor slab	807280058	C	B	C	C	A	B	C	A+	A	D	A	B	A	B	60+	86	106	18	90
in situ reinforced concrete floor slab	807280054	D	C	D	D	A	C	D	A	B	D	A	C	A	B	60+	99	25	4	90
in situ reinforced concrete floor slab with 30% PFA	807280056	C	B	C	D	A	B	C	A+	A	D	A	B	A	B	60+	86	50	9	90
in situ reinforced concrete ribbed/trough slab	807280008	B	A	A	C	A	B	C	A+	A	A	A+	A	A+	A	60+	71	15	4	90
post-tensioned in situ reinforced concrete floor slab	807280055	B	A	B	C	A	B	C	A+	A	B	A+	B	A+	A	60+	76	18	4	90
in situ reinforced concrete slab on 'deep' profiled metal decking	807280015	B	B	D	B	A+	A	B	B	A	B	A	A	A	A	60+	84	12	4	90
in situ reinforced concrete slab on 'shallow' profiled metal decking	807280074	A	A+	A	A	A+	A	A	A+	A+	A+	A+	A+	A+	A+	60+	61	7.8	3	90

Upper floors
Retail

	Element number	Summary Rating	Climate change	Water extraction	Mineral resource extraction	Stratospheric ozone depletion	Human toxicity	Ecotoxicity to freshwater	Nuclear waste (higher level)	Ecotoxicity to land	Waste disposal	Fossil fuel depletion	Eutrophication	Photochemical ozone creation	Acidification	Typical replacement interval	Embodied CO$_2$ (kg CO$_2$ eq.)	Recycled content (kg)	Recycled content (%)	Recycled currently at EOL (%)
Screeded:																				
beam and aircrete block flooring	807280031	B	A	A+	B	C	C	D	A	A	A+	A	C	B	B	60+	82	4.5	1	90
beam and medium dense solid block flooring	807280016	B	A	A	C	D	D	D	A+	A	A	B	C	C	C	60+	82	3.9	1	90
hollow precast prestressed concrete planks	807280045	B	A	A+	B	C	C	D	A	A	A	A	C	B	B	60+	77	4.3	1	90
hollow precast reinforced slab	807280006	E	E	E	D	E	E	E	C	E	E	E	E	E	E	60+	140	59	11	90
in situ concrete slab	807280017	E	D	E	E	C	D	E	B	B	E	C	D	C	D	60+	120	26	4	90
in situ reinforced concrete ribbed slab	807280062	D	B	C	D	B	C	D	A	A	C	A	C	B	B	60+	94	16	3	90
Structural topping on:																				
beam and aircrete block flooring	807280003	B	A	A	B	B	C	C	A	A	A+	A	B	A	A	60+	78	6.4	2	90
grouted beam and dense solid block flooring	807280038	B	A+	A+	C	B	B	C	A+	A+	A	A+	B	A	A	60+	61	5.4	1	90
grouted beam and medium dense solid block flooring	807280037	B	A	A	B	C	C	C	A+	A	A	A	B	A	B	60+	77	5.8	1	90
hollow precast prestressed concrete slabs	807280053	B	A	A+	B	B	C	C	A+	A	A	A+	B	A	A	60+	72	6.2	2	90
hollow precast reinforced slab	807280007	E	E	E	D	D	E	E	C	E	D	E	E	D	E	60+	140	61	11	90

6.3 SEPARATING FLOORS

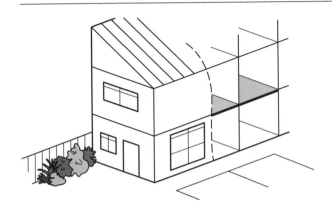

Functional unit for separating floors (party floors) for domestic buildings:

1 m² of separating floor to satisfy England & Wales Building Regulations, in particular a minimum airborne sound insulation $D_{nT,w} + C_x$ of 45 dB and Impact sound insulation Lntw of 62 dB (Source: Approved Document E 2003 incorporating 2004 amendments[41]). Floor to be based on a 5 m span and a live loading of 1.5 kN/m². To include any repair, refurbishment or replacement over the 60-year study period.

These ratings apply only to separating floors between dwellings. Where specifications state 'proprietary' products, please refer to *Robust Details* as only products designated by them can be used.

For full details of *Robust Details*, please refer to the *Robust Details Handbook*[44].

The following abbreviations used in the rating tables will assist in understanding the element descriptions and are based on *Robust Details*.

Floating Floor Treatments:
- **FFT1**: Proprietary resilient composite deep batten systems
- **FFT2**: Proprietary resilient cradle and batten systems
- **FFT3**: Proprietary resilient composite standard batten systems
- **FFT4**: Proprietary resilient overlay platform floor systems
- **FFT5**: Proprietary resilient overlay shallow platform floor systems
- **FFT6**: Proprietary composite platform type floating floor systems

Ceiling Treatments:
- **CT0/1/3**: Metal ceiling system with 150/100/75 mm minimum void and 8/8/10 kg/m² gypsum based board. Painted
- **CT2**: Timber battens and counterbattens with proprietary hangers and 1 layer 8 kg/m² gypsum based board. Painted
- **CT4**: Timber battens and resilient metal bars and 1 layer 10 kg/m² gypsum based board with 65 mm minimum void. Painted
- **A**: 2 layers plasterboard (20 kg/m² minimum) on independent timber joists (100 mm min clearance between top of joists and underside of base floor) with 100 mm minimum mineral wool (minimum density

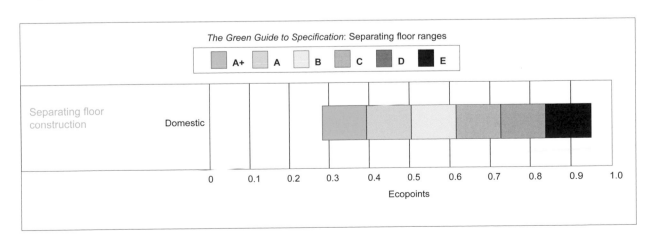

The Green Guide to Specification: Separating floor ranges

| A+ | A | B | C | D | E |

Separating floor construction — Domestic

Ecopoints
0   0.1   0.2   0.3   0.4   0.5   0.6   0.7   0.8   0.9   1.0

10 kg/m³) laid in the cavity formed by the ceiling. Painted
- **B**: 100 mm (minimum) mineral wool quilt insulation (10–36 kg/m³) between joists and with 2 layers gypsum based board with metal resilient ceiling bars (CT1, CT2 or CT3). Painted
- **C**: Resilient metal ceiling bars and 2 layers gypsum based board (25 kg/m² minimum). Painted

Metal Ceiling Systems:
- **A**: Metal ceiling system (CT0/1) with 50 mm minimum mineral wool quilt and 10 kg/m² gypsum based board (minimum 300 mm from top of beam to ceiling board). Painted
- **B**: Metal ceiling system (CT1/3) with 25 mm minimum mineral wool quilt and 10 kg/m² gypsum based board (minimum 300 mm from top of beam to ceiling board). Painted

Structure Options:
- **A**: 250 mm (minimum) timber I-Joists
- **B**: 18 mm OSB on 253 mm proprietary timber and metal web joists
- **C**: beam and dense block flooring with minimum 50 mm C30 concrete topping (minimum overall mass 300 kg/m²)

Proprietary Resilient Layers:
- **A**:   8 mm recycled rubber crumb resilient layer
- **B**:   6 mm resilient layer (recycled rubber)
- **C**: 10 mm high density polyethylene resilient layer

Division of separating floors into subsections
Separating floor specifications have been arranged into subsections for ease of use by designers. However, ratings have been arrived at through comparison of all separating floors shown across all subsections. The subsections are:
- In situ concrete,
- Precast concrete,
- Composite,
- Timber.

Note: where descriptions refer to, say, 100% RCA this refers to 100% of the coarse aggregate in the concrete being replaced with Recycled Concrete Aggregate (RCA).

Concrete block solid densities are as follows unless otherwise stated:
- Dense block/blockwork ($\approx$ 1950 kg/m³),
- Medium density block/blockwork ($\approx$ 1450 kg/m³),
- Lightweight blockwork ($\approx$ 1100 kg/m³),
- Superlightweight block/blockwork ($\approx$ 850 kg/m³).

Separating floors: in situ concrete construction

Domestic

	Element number	Summary Rating	Climate change	Water extraction	Mineral resource extraction	Stratospheric ozone	Human toxicity	Ecotoxicity to freshwater	Nuclear waste (higher level)	Ecotoxicity to land	Waste disposal	Fossil fuel depletion	Eutrophication	Photochemical ozone	Acidification	Typical replacement interval	Embodied CO2 (kg CO2 eq.)	Recycled content (kg)	Recycled content (%)	Recycled currently at EOL
Robust Detail E-FC-2: Floating Floor Treatment (FFT1/2/3 with OSB/3) on:																				
200 mm (min.) in situ slab with screed (80 kg/m²) with metal ceiling system with 75 mm void and one layer 10 kg/m² gypsum based board or 150 mm void and 8 kg/m² gypsum based board	829540151	D	D	C	E	C	B	A	A	A	B	C	D	B	A	60+	100	21	3	87
200 mm (min.) in situ slab with screed (80 kg/m²) with timber battens and metal resilient bars with 75 mm void and 8 kg/m² gypsum based board	829540153	D	D	C	E	C	C	A	A	A	B	C	D	C	A	60+	97	22	3	86
200 mm (min.) in situ slab with screed (80 kg/m²) with timber battens+counterbattens and 100 mm void and 8 kg/m² gypsum based board	829540152	D	D	C	E	C	B	A	A	A	B	C	D	C	A+	60+	94	21	3	87
250 mm (min.) in situ slab without screed with Ceiling Treatment (CT1/3)	829540148	D	D	C	E	A	B	A	A	A	B	C	C	A	A	60+	100	34	5	87
250 mm (min.) in situ slab without screed with Ceiling Treatment (CT2)	829540149	D	D	C	E	B	B	A	A+	A	B	B	C	C	A+	60+	92	33	5	87
250 mm (min.) in situ slab without screed with Ceiling Treatment (CT4)	829540150	D	D	C	E	B	B	A	A+	A	B	B	C	C	A	60+	95	34	5	86
Robust Detail E-FC-2: Floating Floor Treatment (FFT1/2/3 with plywood) on:																				
200 mm (min.) in situ slab with screed (80 kg/m²) with metal ceiling system with 75 mm min. void and one layer 10 kg/m² gypsum based board or 150 mm void and 8 kg/m² gypsum based board	829540157	E	E	C	E	D	B	B	C	D	B	D	E	B	A	60+	110	15	2	87
200 mm (min.) in situ slab with screed (80 kg/m²) with timber battens and metal resilient bars, 75 mm min. void and 10 kg/m² gypsum based board	829540159	E	D	C	E	D	B	B	C	C	B	D	E	D	A	60+	100	15	2	86
200 mm (min.) in situ slab with screed (80 kg/m²) with timber battens + counterbattens with 100 mm min. void and 8 kg/m² gypsum based board	829540158	E	D	C	E	D	B	B	C	C	B	D	D	D	A	60+	100	14	2	87
250 mm (min.) in situ slab without screed with Ceiling Treatment (CT1/3)	829540154	E	E	C	E	C	B	B	C	D	B	D	D	A	A	60+	110	27	4	87
250 mm (min.) in situ slab without screed with Ceiling Treatment (CT2)	829540155	D	D	C	E	C	B	B	C	D	B	C	D	C	A	60+	100	27	4	87
250 mm (min.) in situ slab without screed with Ceiling Treatment (CT4)	829540156	D	D	C	E	C	B	B	C	D	B	C	D	C	A	60+	100	27	4	86

Separating floors: in situ concrete construction Domestic	Element number	Summary Rating	Climate change	Water extraction	Mineral resource extraction	Stratospheric ozone depletion	Human toxicity	Ecotoxicity to freshwater	Nuclear waste (higher level)	Ecotoxicity to land	Waste disposal	Fossil fuel depletion	Eutrophication	Photochemical ozone creation	Acidification	Typical replacement interval	Embodied CO2 (kg CO2 eq.)	Recycled content (kg)	Recycled content (%)	Recycled currently at EOL (%)
Robust Detail E-FC-2: Floating Floor Treatment (FFT1/2/3/5 with chipboard) on:																				
200 mm (min.) in situ slab with screed (80 kg/m²) with metal ceiling system with 75 mm void and one layer 10 kg/m² gypsum based board or 150 mm void and 8 kg/m² gypsum based board	829540145	E	E	C	E	B	B	A	A	B	B	D	D	A	A	60+	110	24	4	87
200 mm (min.) in situ slab with screed (80 kg/m²) with timber battens + counterbattens with 100 mm void and 8 kg/m² gypsum based board	829540146	D	D	B	E	C	B	A	A	B	B	D	D	C	A	60+	100	23	3	86
200 mm (min.) in situ slab with screed (80 kg/m²) with timber battens and metal resilient bars with 75 mm void and 10 kg/m² gypsum based board	829540147	D	D	B	E	C	B	A	A	B	C	D	D	C	A	60+	100	24	4	86
250 mm (min.) in situ slab without screed with metal ceiling system with 75 mm void and one layer 10 kg/m² gypsum based board or 150 mm void and 8 kg/m² gypsum based board	829540142	D	E	C	E	A	A	A	A	B	B	C	C	A	A	60+	110	36	6	87
250 mm (min.) in situ slab without screed with timber battens and metal resilient bars with 75 mm void and 10 kg/m² gypsum based board	829540144	D	D	B	E	A	A	A	B	B	B	C	C	B	A	60+	100	36	6	86
250 mm (min.) in situ slab without screed with timber battens + counterbattens with 75 mm void and one layer 10 kg/m² gypsum based board or 150 mm void and 8 kg/m² gypsum based board	829540143	D	D	B	E	A	A	A	A	B	B	C	C	B	A+	60+	100	36	5	86

Separating floors: in situ concrete construction

Domestic

	Element number	Summary Rating	Climate change	Water extraction	Mineral resource extraction	Stratospheric ozone depletion	Human toxicity	Ecotoxicity to freshwater	Nuclear waste (higher level)	Ecotoxicity to land	Waste disposal	Fossil fuel depletion	Eutrophication	Photochemical ozone creation	Acidification	Typical replacement interval	Embodied CO2 (kg CO2 eq.)	Recycled content (kg)	Recycled content (%)	Recycled currently at EOL (%)
Robust Detail E-FC-2: Floating Floor Treatment (FFT2) any decking with 10 mm virgin foam density > 100 kg/m³) on:																				
200 mm min. in situ slab with screed (80 kg/m²) with metal ceiling w75 mm void + 10 kg/m² gypsum based board or 150 mm void + 8 kg/m² gypsum based board	829540163	E	E	E	E	C	B	B	C	B	C	E	E	A	A	60+	120	23.5	3	87
200 mm min. in situ slab with screed (80 kg/m²) with timber battens and metal resilient bars, 75 mm void and 10 kg/m² gypsum based board	829540165	E	E	E	E	D	B	B	C	B	C	E	E	C	A	60+	120	24	4	86
200 mm min. in situ slab with screed (80 kg/m²) with timber battens+counterbattens with 100 mm void and 8 kg/m² gypsum based board	829540164	E	E	E	E	D	B	B	C	B	C	E	E	C	A	60+	110	23	3	86
250 mm (min.) in situ slab without screed with Ceiling Treatment (CT1/3)	829540160	E	E	E	E	B	B	A	C	C	B	E	D	A	A	60+	120	36	6	86
250 mm (min.) in situ slab without screed with Ceiling Treatment (CT2)	829540161	E	E	E	E	B	A	B	B	C	B	D	D	C	A	60+	110	36	5	86
250 mm (min.) in situ slab without screed with Ceiling Treatment (CT4)	829540162	E	E	E	E	B	B	B	C	C	C	E	D	C	A	60+	110	36	6	86
Robust Detail E-FC-2: Floating Floor Treatment (FFT4a proprietary system with chipboard with mineral wool resilient layer) on:																				
200 mm (min.) in situ slab with screed (80 kg/m²) with Ceiling Treatment (CT1/3)	829540169	E	E	C	E	C	C	B	B	B	C	E	E	A	A	60+	130	28.6	4	86
200 mm (min.) in situ slab with screed (80 kg/m²) with Ceiling Treatment (CT2)	829540170	E	E	C	E	C	C	B	B	B	C	E	E	C	A	60+	120	28.3	4	86
200 mm (min.) in situ slab with screed (80 kg/m²) with Ceiling Treatment (CT4)	829540171	E	E	C	E	C	C	B	B	B	C	E	E	B	B	60+	120	29	4	85
250 mm (min.) in situ slab without screed with Ceiling Treatment (CT1/3)	829540166	E	E	C	E	A	B	A	B	B	C	E	D	A+	A	60+	130	41	6	86
250 mm (min.) in situ slab without screed with Ceiling Treatment (CT2)	829540167	E	E	C	E	B	B	B	A	B	C	D	D	B	A	60+	120	40.6	6	85
250 mm (min.) in situ slab without screed with Ceiling Treatment (CT4)	829540168	E	E	C	E	B	B	B	B	B	C	E	D	B	A	60+	120	41.4	6	85

Separating floors: in situ concrete construction

Domestic

	Element number	Summary Rating	Climate change	Water extraction	Mineral resource extraction	Stratospheric ozone depletion	Human toxicity	Ecotoxicity to freshwater	Nuclear waste (higher level)	Ecotoxicity to land	Waste disposal	Fossil fuel depletion	Eutrophication	Photochemical ozone creation	Acidification	Typical replacement interval	Embodied CO$_2$ (kg CO$_2$ eq.)	Recycled content (kg)	Recycled content (%)	Recycled currently at EOL (%)
Robust Detail E-FC-2: Floating Floor Treatment (FFT4b proprietary system with gypsum screed on virgin foam) on:																				
200 mm (min.) in situ slab with screed (80 kg/m²) with Ceiling Treatment (CT1/3)	829540175	E	E	B	E	B	A	A	A+	A	E	C	C	A+	A	35	120	15	2	86
200 mm (min.) in situ slab with screed (80 kg/m²) with Ceiling Treatment (CT2)	829540176	E	E	B	E	C	A	A	A+	A	E	B	C	B	A+	35	110	15	2	85
200 mm (min.) in situ slab with screed (80 kg/m²) with Ceiling Treatment (CT4)	829540178	E	E	B	E	C	A	A	A+	A	E	C	C	B	A	35	110	15	2	85
250 mm (min.) in situ slab without screed with Ceiling Treatment (CT1/3)	829540172	E	E	B	E	A	A	A+	A+	A	E	B	C	A+	A+	35	120	27	4	86
250 mm (min.) in situ slab without screed with Ceiling Treatment (CT2)	829540173	E	E	B	E	A	A	A	A+	A	E	B	C	B	A+	35	110	27	4	85
250 mm (min.) in situ slab without screed with Ceiling Treatment (CT4)	829540174	E	E	B	E	A	A	A	A+	A	E	B	C	A	A	35	110	28	4	85
Robust Detail E-FC-2: Floating Floor Treatment (FFT4c proprietary system with chipboard on virgin foam and rubber resilient layers) on:																				
200 mm (min.) in situ slab with screed (80 kg/m²) with Ceiling Treatment (CT1/3)	829540182	E	E	C	E	C	B	A	B	B	B	E	D	A	A	60+	120	23.4	3	87
200 mm (min.) in situ slab with screed (80 kg/m²) with Ceiling Treatment (CT2)	829540183	E	E	C	E	D	B	B	B	B	B	E	D	C	A	60+	110	23	3	86
200 mm (min.) in situ slab with screed (80 kg/m²) with Ceiling Treatment (CT4)	829540184	E	E	C	E	D	B	B	B	B	C	E	D	B	A	60+	110	24	4	86
250 mm (min.) in situ slab without screed with Ceiling Treatment (CT1/3)	829540179	E	E	C	E	B	B	A	B	B	B	E	D	A+	A	60+	120	36	6	87
250 mm (min.) in situ slab without screed with Ceiling Treatment (CT2)	829540180	D	D	C	E	B	B	A	B	B	D	D	B	A	A	60+	110	35	5	86
250 mm (min.) in situ slab without screed with Ceiling Treatment (CT4)	829540181	D	E	C	E	B	B	A	B	B	D	D	B	A	A	60+	110	36	6	86

Separating floors: precast concrete construction Domestic	Element number	Summary Rating	Climate change	Water extraction	Mineral resource extraction	Stratospheric ozone depletion	Human toxicity	Ecotoxicity to freshwater	Nuclear waste (higher level)	Ecotoxicity to land	Waste disposal	Fossil fuel depletion	Eutrophication	Photochemical ozone creation	Acidification	Typical replacement interval	Embodied CO2 (kg CO2 eq.)	Recycled content (kg)	Recycled content (%)	Recycled currently at EOL (%)
Robust Detail E-FC-1: Floating Floor Treatment (FFT1/2/3 with 18 mm min. OSB/3) on 40 mm min. screed (80 kg/m² min.) on:																				
150 mm (min.) precast prestressed hollow planks (300 kg/m² min.) with Ceiling Treatment (CT1/3)	829550106	B	C	A	C	C	B	A	A	A	A+	B	C	B	A+	60+	82	14	3	85
150 mm (min.) precast prestressed hollow planks (300 kg/m² min.) with Ceiling Treatment (CT2)	829550107	B	C	A+	C	D	B	A	A+	A	A+	B	C	C	A+	60+	71	13	3	84
150 mm (min.) precast prestressed hollow planks (300 kg/m² min.) with Ceiling Treatment (CT4)	829550108	B	C	A	C	D	B	A	A+	A	A+	B	C	C	A+	60+	74	14	3	84
150 mm (min.) precast reinforced hollow planks (300 kg/m² min.) with Ceiling Treatment (CT1/3)	829550109	B	C	A	C	C	B	A	A	A	A+	B	C	B	A+	60+	82	14	3	85
150 mm (min.) precast reinforced hollow planks (300 kg/m² min.) with Ceiling Treatment (CT2)	829550110	B	C	A+	C	D	B	A	A+	A	A+	B	C	C	A+	60+	71	13	3	84
150 mm (min.) precast reinforced hollow planks (300 kg/m² min.) with Ceiling Treatment (CT4)	829550111	B	C	A	C	D	B	A	A+	A	A+	B	C	C	A+	60+	74	14	3	84
Robust Detail E-FC-1: Floating Floor Treatment (FFT1/2/3 with 18 mm min. plywood) on 40 mm min. screed (80 kg/m² min.) on:																				
150 mm (min.) precast prestressed hollow planks (300 kg/m² min.) with Ceiling Treatment (CT1/3)	829550112	C	D	A	C	E	B	B	C	C	A+	C	D	B	A	60+	89	6.7	2	85
150 mm (min.) precast prestressed hollow planks (300 kg/m² min.) with Ceiling Treatment (CT2)	829550113	C	C	A+	C	E	B	B	C	C	A+	C	D	D	A+	60+	78	6.4	2	84
150 mm (min.) precast prestressed hollow planks (300 kg/m² min.) with Ceiling Treatment (CT4)	829550114	C	C	A	C	E	B	B	C	C	A+	C	D	C	A	60+	81	7.1	2	84
150 mm (min.) precast reinforced hollow planks (300 kg/m² min.) with Ceiling Treatment (CT1/3)	829550115	C	D	A	C	E	B	B	C	C	A+	C	D	B	A	60+	89	6.7	2	85
150 mm (min.) precast reinforced hollow planks (300 kg/m² min.) with Ceiling Treatment (CT2)	829550116	C	C	A+	C	E	B	B	C	C	A+	C	D	D	A+	60+	78	6.4	2	84
150 mm (min.) precast reinforced hollow planks (300 kg/m² min.) with Ceiling Treatment (CT4)	829550117	C	C	A	C	E	B	B	C	C	A+	C	D	C	A	60+	81	7.1	2	84

Separating floors: precast concrete construction

Domestic

	Element number	Summary Rating	Climate change	Water extraction	Mineral resource extraction	Stratospheric ozone depletion	Human toxicity	Ecotoxicity to freshwater	Nuclear waste (higher level)	Ecotoxicity to land	Waste disposal	Fossil fuel depletion	Eutrophication	Photochemical ozone creation	Acidification	Typical replacement interval	Embodied CO2 (kg CO2 eq.)	Recycled content (kg)	Recycled content (%)	Recycled currently at EOL (%)
Robust Detail E-FC-1: Floating Floor Treatment (FFT1/2/3/5 with 18 mm min. chipboard) on 40 mm min. screed (80 kg/m² min.) on:																				
150 mm (min.) precast prestressed hollow planks (300 kg/m² min.) with Ceiling Treatment (CT1/3)	829550100	C	D	A+	C	C	B	A	A	B	A+	C	C	A	A+	60+	91	16	4	85
150 mm (min.) precast prestressed hollow planks (300 kg/m² min.) with Ceiling Treatment (CT2)	829550101	B	C	A+	C	D	B	A	A	A	A+	C	C	C	A+	60+	80	15	4	84
150 mm (min.) precast prestressed hollow planks (300 kg/m² min.) with Ceiling Treatment (CT4)	829550102	B	C	A+	C	D	B	A	A	B	A+	C	C	C	A	60+	82	16	4	84
150 mm (min.) precast reinforced hollow planks (300 kg/m² min.) with Ceiling Treatment (CT1/3)	829550103	C	D	A+	C	C	B	A	A	B	A+	C	C	A	A+	60+	91	16	4	85
150 mm (min.) precast reinforced hollow planks (300 kg/m² min.) with Ceiling Treatment (CT2)	829550104	B	C	A+	C	D	B	A	A	A	A+	C	C	C	A+	60+	80	15	4	84
150 mm (min.) precast reinforced hollow planks (300 kg/m² min.) with Ceiling Treatment (CT4)	829550105	B	C	A+	C	D	B	A	A	B	A+	C	C	C	A	60+	82	16	4	84
Robust Detail E-FC-1: Floating Floor Treatment (FFT2 any decking (18 mm min.) with 10 mm virgin resilient foam with density > 100 kg/m³ on screed (80 kg/m² min.) on:																				
150 mm (min.) precast prestressed hollow planks (300 kg/m² min.) with Ceiling Treatment (CT1/3)	829550118	C	D	C	C	D	B	A	C	B	A+	E	E	A	A	60+	100	16	4	84
150 mm (min.) precast prestressed hollow planks (300 kg/m² min.) with Ceiling Treatment (CT2)	829550119	C	D	C	C	E	B	A	B	B	A+	D	E	C	A	60+	91	15	4	84
150 mm (min.) precast prestressed hollow planks (300 kg/m² min.) with Ceiling Treatment (CT4)	829550120	C	D	C	C	E	B	A	C	B	A	D	E	C	A	60+	93	16	4	83
150 mm (min.) precast reinforced hollow planks (300 kg/m² min.) with Ceiling Treatment (CT1/3)	829550121	C	D	C	C	D	B	A	C	B	A+	E	E	A	A	60+	100	16	4	84
150 mm (min.) precast reinforced hollow planks (300 kg/m² min.) with Ceiling Treatment (CT2)	829550122	C	D	C	C	E	B	A	B	B	A+	D	E	C	A	60+	91	15	4	84
150 mm (min.) precast reinforced hollow planks (300 kg/m² min.) with Ceiling Treatment (CT4)	829550123	C	D	C	C	E	B	A	C	B	A	D	E	C	A	60+	93	16	4	83

Separating floors: precast concrete construction

Domestic

	Element number	Summary Rating	Climate change	Water extraction	Mineral resource extraction	Stratospheric ozone depletion	Human toxicity	Ecotoxicity to freshwater	Nuclear waste (higher level)	Ecotoxicity to land	Waste disposal	Fossil fuel depletion	Eutrophication	Photochemical ozone creation	Acidification	Typical replacement interval	Embodied CO₂ (kg CO₂ eq.)	Recycled content (kg)	Recycled content (%)	Recycled currently at EOL (%)
Robust Detail E-FC-1: Floating Floor Treatment (FFT4a proprietary system chipboard on mineral wool resilient layer total 16 kg/m²) on screed (80 kg/m² min.) on:																				
150 mm (min.) precast prestressed hollow planks (300 kg/m² min.) with Ceiling Treatment (CT2)	829550125	C	D	A	C	D	C	A	A	B	A	D	D	B	A	60+	95	20.4	5	83
150 mm (min.) precast prestressed hollow planks (300 kg/m² min.) with Ceiling Treatment (CT1/3)	829550124	C	D	A	C	C	C	A	B	B	A	D	D	A	A	60+	110	20.7	5	83
150 mm (min.) precast prestressed hollow planks (300 kg/m² min.) with Ceiling Treatment (CT4)	829550126	C	D	A	C	D	C	A	B	B	A	D	D	B	A	60+	97	21.1	5	82
150 mm (min.) precast reinforced hollow planks (300 kg/m² min.) with Ceiling Treatment (CT1/3)	829550127	C	D	A	C	C	C	A	B	B	A	D	D	A	A	60+	110	20.7	5	83
150 mm (min.) precast reinforced hollow planks (300 kg/m² min.) with Ceiling Treatment (CT2)	829550128	C	D	A	C	D	C	A	A	B	A	D	D	B	A	60+	95	20.4	5	83
150 mm (min.) precast reinforced hollow planks (300 kg/m² min.) with Ceiling Treatment (CT4)	829550129	C	D	A	C	D	C	A	B	B	A	D	D	B	A	60+	97	21.1	5	82
Robust Detail E-FC-1: Floating Floor Treatment (FFT4b proprietary system with gypsum screed on virgin foam overall 16 kg/m²) on screed (80 kg/m² min.) on:																				
150 mm (min.) precast prestressed hollow planks (300 kg/m² min.) with Ceiling Treatment (CT1/3)	829550136	D	D	A+	C	C	A	A+	A+	A	C	B	C	A+	A+	35	100	7	2	83
150 mm (min.) precast prestressed hollow planks (300 kg/m² min.) with Ceiling Treatment (CT2)	829550137	C	D	A+	C	C	A	A+	A+	A	C	B	C	B	A+	35	89	6.6	2	82
150 mm (min.) precast prestressed hollow planks (300 kg/m² min.) with Ceiling Treatment (CT4)	829550138	C	D	A+	C	C	A	A+	A+	A	C	B	C	B	A+	35	92	7.3	2	82
150 mm (min.) precast reinforced hollow planks (300 kg/m² min.) with Ceiling Treatment (CT1/3)	829550139	D	D	A+	C	C	A	A+	A+	A	C	B	C	A+	A+	35	100	7	2	83
150 mm (min.) precast reinforced hollow planks (300 kg/m² min.) with Ceiling Treatment (CT2)	829550140	C	D	A+	C	C	A	A+	A+	A	C	B	C	B	A+	35	89	6.6	2	82
150 mm (min.) precast reinforced hollow planks (300 kg/m² min.) with Ceiling Treatment (CT4)	829550141	C	D	A+	C	C	A	A+	A+	A	C	B	C	B	A+	35	92	7.3	2	82

Separating floors: precast concrete construction Domestic	Element number	Summary Rating	Climate change	Water extraction	Mineral resource extraction	Stratospheric ozone depletion	Human toxicity	Ecotoxicity to freshwater	Nuclear waste (higher level)	Ecotoxicity to land	Waste disposal	Fossil fuel depletion	Eutrophication	Photochemical ozone creation	Acidification	Typical replacement interval	Embodied CO2 (kg CO2 eq.)	Recycled content (kg)	Recycled content (%)	Recycled currently at EOL (%)
Robust Detail E-FC-1: Floating Floor Treatment (FFT4c proprietary system chipboard on virgin foam and rubber resilient layers 16 kg/m²) on screed (80 kg/m² min.) on:																				
150 mm (min.) precast prestressed hollow planks (300 kg/m² min.) with Ceiling Treatment (CT1/3)	829550130	C	D	A	C	D	B	A	B	B	A+	D	D	A	A	60+	98	16	4	85
150 mm (min.) precast prestressed hollow planks (300 kg/m² min.) with Ceiling Treatment (CT2)	829550131	C	D	A	C	D	B	A	B	B	A+	D	D	B	A+	60+	87	15	4	84
150 mm (min.) precast prestressed hollow planks (300 kg/m² min.) with Ceiling Treatment (CT4)	829550132	C	D	A	C	D	B	A	B	B	A+	D	D	B	A	60+	90	16	4	84
150 mm (min.) precast reinforced hollow planks (300 kg/m² min.) with Ceiling Treatment (CT1/3)	829550133	C	D	A	C	D	B	A	B	B	A+	D	D	A	A	60+	98	16	4	85
150 mm (min.) precast reinforced hollow planks (300 kg/m² min.) with Ceiling Treatment (CT2)	829550134	C	D	A	C	D	B	A	B	B	A+	D	D	B	A+	60+	87	15	4	84
150 mm (min.) precast reinforced hollow planks (300 kg/m² min.) with Ceiling Treatment (CT4)	829550135	C	D	A	C	D	B	A	B	B	A+	D	D	B	A	60+	90	16	4	84
Robust Detail E-FC-4: 40 mm min. Proprietary Screed (80 kg/m²) on polythene sheet on Proprietary Resilient Layer B on:																				
precast prestressed hollow planks (150 mm min., 300 kg/m² min) with CT2 (timber battens and counterbattens, proprietary hangers)	829550190	C	D	A	C	E	B	A	B	A	A+	C	C	E	A+	50	110	10	3	86
precast prestressed hollow planks (150 mm min., 300 kg/m² min.) with Ceiling Treatment (CT0/1 Metal Ceiling System)	829550189	C	E	A	C	D	B	A	C	A	A+	C	C	C	A	50	120	11	3	87
precast reinforced hollow planks (150 mm min., 300 kg/m² min) with CT2 (timber battens and counterbattens, proprietary hangers)	829550192	C	D	A	C	E	B	A	B	A	A+	C	C	E	A+	50	110	10	3	86
precast reinforced hollow planks (150 mm min., 300 kg/m² min.) with Ceiling Treatment (CT0/1 Metal Ceiling System)	829550191	C	E	A	C	D	B	A	C	A	A+	C	C	C	A	50	120	11	3	87

Separating floors: precast concrete construction

Domestic

	Element number	Summary Rating	Climate change	Water extraction	Mineral resource extraction	Stratospheric ozone depletion	Human toxicity	Ecotoxicity to freshwater	Nuclear waste (higher level)	Ecotoxicity to land	Waste disposal	Fossil fuel depletion	Eutrophication	Photochemical ozone creation	Acidification	Typical replacement interval	Embodied CO2 (kg CO2 eq.)	Recycled content (kg)	Recycled content (%)	Recycled currently at EOL (%)
Robust Detail E-FC-4: 65 mm min. sand:cement screed (80 kg/m²) onto Proprietary Resilient Layer B on:																				
precast prestressed hollow planks (150 mm min, 300 kg/m² min) with Ceiling Treatment (CT0/1 metal ceiling system)	829550185	D	E	A	D	E	B	A	B	A	A+	D	D	D	A	50	130	11	2	87
precast prestressed hollow planks (150 mm min., 300 kg/m² min) with Ceiling Treatment (CT2 timber battens and counterbattens with proprietary hangers)	829550186	D	E	A	D	E	B	A	B	A	A+	D	D	E	A	50	120	10	2	87
precast reinforced hollow planks (150 mm min., 300 kg/m² min.) with Ceiling Treatment (CT0/1 metal ceiling system)	829550187	D	E	A	D	E	B	A	B	A	A+	D	D	D	A	50	130	11	2	87
precast reinforced hollow planks (150 mm min., 300 kg/m² min.) with Ceiling Treatment (CT2 timber battens and counterbattens with proprietary hangers)	829550188	D	E	A	D	E	B	A	B	A	A+	D	D	E	A	50	120	10	2	87
Robust Detail E-FC-5: 65 mm (min.) cement:sand screed on Proprietary Resilient Layer C on:																				
precast prestressed hollow planks (150 mm min, 300 kg/m² min.) with metal ceiling system (CT0/1)	829550193	C	E	A	D	E	B	A	A	A	A+	D	D	A	A	50	120	6.9	2	88
precast reinforced hollow planks (150 mm min, 300 kg/m² min.) with metal ceiling system (CT0/1)	829550194	C	E	A	D	E	B	A	A	A	A+	D	D	A	A	50	120	6.9	2	88
Robust Detail E-FC-6: 40 mm min. Proprietary Screed (80 kg/m²) with polythene sheet on DPM on Proprietary Layer A on Structure Option C with Metal Ceiling System Option A	829550196	C	D	A	D	D	A	A	B	A	A+	C	C	C	A+	50	97	10.1	2	87
Robust Detail E-FC-6: 65 mm min. sand:cement screed (80 kg/m²) on DPM on Proprietary Layer A on Structure Option C with Metal Ceiling System Option A	829550195	D	D	A	D	E	B	A	B	A	A	C	D	C	A	50	110	10.3	2	87

Separating floors: precast concrete construction

Domestic

	Element number	Summary Rating	Climate change	Water extraction	Mineral resource extraction	Stratospheric ozone depletion	Human toxicity	Ecotoxicity to freshwater	Nuclear waste (higher level)	Ecotoxicity to land	Waste disposal	Fossil fuel depletion	Eutrophication	Photochemical ozone creation	Acidification	Typical replacement interval	Embodied CO2 (kg CO2 eq.)	Recycled content (kg)	Recycled content (%)	Recycled currently at EOL (%)
Robust Detail E-FC-7: Floating Floor Treatment (FFT1/3 with 18 mm min. t&g chipboard) on 20 mm levelling screed on Structure Option C with Metal Ceiling System Option B	829550197	B	C	A+	C	C	A	A+	A+	A	A+	B	B	A	A+	50	66	14	4	83
Robust Detail E-FC-7: Floating Floor Treatment (FFT1/3 with 18 mm min. t&g OSB/3) on 20 mm levelling screed on Structure Option C with Metal Ceiling System Option B	829550198	B	B	A	C	C	B	A+	A+	A+	A+	A	B	A	A+	50	58	12.9	3	85
Robust Detail E-FC-7: Floating Floor Treatment (FFT1/3 with 18 mm min. t&g plywood) on 20 mm levelling screed on Structure Option C with Metal Ceiling System Option B	829550199	B	C	A	C	D	A	A	B	C	A+	B	C	A	A+	50	65	6.2	1	85
Robust Detail E-FC-7: Floating Floor Treatment (FFT2 with any t&g decking 18 mm min. with 10 mm virgin foam with density > 100 kg/m³ with 25 mm mineral wool quilt) on Structure Option C with Metal Ceiling System Option B	829550200	B	C	C	C	B	A	A	B	A	A+	B	C	A+	A+	60+	66	15.1	4	84
Robust Detail E-FC-7: Floating Floor Treatment (FFT2 with 18 mm min. t&g chipboard with 25 mm mineral wool quilt) on Structure Option C with Metal Ceiling System Option B	829550201	B	B	A+	B	A	A	A+	A+	A	A+	A	A	A+	A+	60+	55	15.2	4	84
Robust Detail E-FC-7: Floating Floor Treatment (FFT2 with 18 mm min. t&g OSB/3 with 25 mm mineral wool quilt) on Structure Option C with Metal Ceiling System Option B	829550202	A	B	A+	C	B	A	A+	A+	A+	A+	A+	A	A	A+	60+	47	13.1	3	84
Robust Detail E-FC-7: Floating Floor Treatment (FFT2 with: 18 mm min. t&g plywood with 25 mm mineral wool quilt) on Structure Option C with Metal Ceiling System Option B	829550203	B	B	A+	C	C	A	A	B	B	A+	A	B	A	A+	60+	54	6.3	2	84

Separating floors: steel and composite construction

Domestic

	Element number	Summary Rating	Climate change	Water extraction	Mineral resource extraction	Stratospheric ozone depletion	Human toxicity	Ecotoxicity to freshwater	Nuclear waste (higher level)	Ecotoxicity to land	Waste disposal	Fossil fuel depletion	Eutrophication	Photochemical ozone creation	Acidification	Typical replacement interval	Embodied CO$_2$ (kg CO$_2$ eq.)	Recycled content (kg)	Recycled content (%)	Recycled currently at EOL (%)
Panelised steel floor cassette, insulation with OSB/3 floor decking above and plasterboard and OSB/3 floating floor on timber battens. Plasterboard (2 layers with staggered joints) ceiling fixed to joists using resilient bars with paint	829560015	A	A	B	A+	A+	E	A+	A	A+	B	B	A+	C	E	35	28	25.6	35	18
Volumetric galvanised steel floor structure (units above and below) with chipboard and plasterboard floor decking, OSB/3 sheathing and 2 layer plasterboard ceiling with paint	829560055	B	C	B	A+	A+	D	B	B	A	B	D	A	B	E	60	70	29.5	35	20
Robust Detail E-FS-1: Floating Floor Treatment (FFT1/2/3 with 18 mm min. t&g OSB/3) on:																				
in situ concrete slab (2200 kg/m³ min.) supported by 'deep' profiled metal decking and Ceiling Treatment (CT1/3)	829560216	B	C	C	B	A+	A	A+	A	A	A+	B	A	A	A+	60+	85	22	6	84
in situ concrete slab (2200 kg/m³ min.) supported by 'deep' profiled metal decking and Ceiling Treatment (CT2)	829560217	B	C	B	B	A+	A	A+	A	A	A+	B	A	C	A+	60+	75	21	6	84
in situ concrete slab (2200 kg/m³ min.) supported by 'deep' profiled metal decking and Ceiling Treatment (CT4)	829560218	B	C	C	B	A+	A	A+	A	A	A	B	A	C	A+	60+	77	22	6	83
in situ concrete slab (2200 kg/m³ min.) supported by 'shallow' profiled metal decking and Ceiling Treatment (CT1/3)	829560237	A	C	A	B	A+	A+	A+	A+	A+	A+	A	A+	A+	A+	60+	65	22	8	83
in situ concrete slab (2200 kg/m³ min.) supported by 'shallow' profiled metal decking and Ceiling Treatment (CT2)	829560238	A	B	A	B	A+	A+	A+	A+	A+	A+	A+	A+	B	A+	60+	54	22	8	82
in situ concrete slab (2200 kg/m³ min.) supported by 'shallow' profiled metal decking and Ceiling Treatment (CT4)	829560239	A	B	A	B	A+	A+	A+	A+	A+	A+	A	A+	B	A+	60+	57	22	8	81

Separating floors: steel and composite construction Domestic	Element number	Summary Rating	Climate change	Water extraction	Mineral resource extraction	Stratospheric ozone depletion	Human toxicity	Ecotoxicity to freshwater	Nuclear waste (higher level)	Ecotoxicity to land	Waste disposal	Fossil fuel depletion	Eutrophication	Photochemical ozone creation	Acidification	Typical replacement interval	Embodied CO2 (kg CO2 eq.)	Recycled content (kg)	Recycled content (%)	Recycled currently at EOL (%)
Robust Detail E-FS-1: Floating Floor Treatment (FFT1/2/3 with 18 mm min. t&g plywood) on:																				
in situ concrete slab (2200 kg/m³ min.) supported by 'deep' profiled metal decking and Ceiling Treatment (CT1/3)	829560219	C	D	C	C	A	A	A	C	C	A+	C	B	A	A+	60+	93	15	4	84
in situ concrete slab (2200 kg/m³ min.) supported by 'deep' profiled metal decking and Ceiling Treatment (CT2)	829560220	C	C	B	B	B	A	A	C	C	A+	C	B	C	A+	60+	82	15	4	84
in situ concrete slab (2200 kg/m³ min.) supported by 'deep' profiled metal decking and Ceiling Treatment (CT4)	829560221	C	C	C	B	B	A	A	C	C	A	C	B	C	A+	60+	84	15	4	83
in situ concrete slab (2200 kg/m³ min.) supported by 'shallow' profiled metal decking and Ceiling Treatment (CT1/3)	829560240	B	C	A	B	A	A+	A	B	C	A+	B	A	A	A+	60+	72	15	6	83
in situ concrete slab (2200 kg/m³ min.) supported by 'shallow' profiled metal decking and Ceiling Treatment (CT2)	829560241	A	B	A	B	B	A+	A	B	C	A+	A	A	B	A+	60+	61	15	5	82
in situ concrete slab (2200 kg/m³ min.) supported by 'shallow' profiled metal decking and Ceiling Treatment (CT4)	829560242	B	C	A	B	A	A+	A	B	C	A+	A	A	B	A+	60+	64	15	6	81

Separating floors: steel and composite construction Domestic	Element number	Summary Rating	Climate change	Water extraction	Mineral resource extraction	Stratospheric ozone depletion	Human toxicity	Ecotoxicity to freshwater	Nuclear waste (higher level)	Ecotoxicity to land	Waste disposal	Fossil fuel depletion	Eutrophication	Photochemical ozone creation	Acidification	Typical replacement interval	Embodied CO₂ (kg CO₂ eq.)	Recycled content (kg)	Recycled content (%)	Recycled currently at EOL (%)
Robust Detail E-FS-1: Floating Floor Treatment (FFT1/2/3/5 with 18 mm min. t&g chipboard) on:																				
in situ concrete slab (2200 kg/m³ min.) supported by 'deep' profiled metal decking and Ceiling Treatment (CT1/3)	829560213	C	D	B	B	A+	A+	A+	A	A	A	C	B	A+	A+	60+	94	24	7	84
in situ concrete slab (2200 kg/m³ min.) supported by 'deep' profiled metal decking and Ceiling Treatment (CT2)	829560214	B	C	B	B	A+	A+	A+	A	A	A	B	B	B	A+	60+	83	23	7	83
in situ concrete slab (2200 kg/m³ min.) supported by 'deep' profiled metal decking and Ceiling Treatment (CT4)	829560215	B	C	B	B	A+	A+	A+	A	A	A	C	B	B	A+	60+	85	24	7	83
in situ concrete slab (2200 kg/m³ min.) supported by 'shallow' profiled metal decking and Ceiling Treatment (CT1/3)	829560234	A	C	A	B	A+	A+	A+	A+	A	A+	B	A	A+	A+	60+	74	24	9	82
in situ concrete slab (2200 kg/m³ min.) supported by 'shallow' profiled metal decking and Ceiling Treatment (CT2)	829560235	A	C	A	B	A+	A+	A+	A+	A	A+	A	A	B	A+	60+	63	24	9	81
in situ concrete slab (2200 kg/m³ min.) supported by 'shallow' profiled metal decking and Ceiling Treatment (CT4)	829560236	A	C	A	B	A+	A+	A+	A+	A	A+	A	A	A	A+	60+	65	24	9	81

Separating floors: steel and composite construction

Domestic

	Element number	Summary Rating	Climate change	Water extraction	Mineral resource extraction	Stratospheric ozone depletion	Human toxicity	Ecotoxicity to freshwater	Nuclear waste (higher level)	Ecotoxicity to land	Waste disposal	Fossil fuel depletion	Eutrophication	Photochemical ozone creation	Acidification	Typical replacement interval	Embodied CO_2 (kg CO_2 eq.)	Recycled content (kg)	Recycled content (%)	Recycled currently at EOL (%)
Robust Detail E-FS-1: Floating Floor Treatment (FFT2 any t&g decking (18 mm min) with 10 mm virgin foam density >100 kg/m³ with 25 mm mineral wool quilt) on:																				
in situ concrete slab (2200 kg/m³ min.) with 'shallow' profiled metal decking + Ceiling Treatment (CT2)	829560244	B	C	C	B	A	A+	A+	B	A	A+	B	B	B	A+	60+	74	24	9	81
in situ concrete slab (2200 kg/m³ min.) with 'shallow' profiled metal decking + Ceiling Treatment (CT4)	829560245	B	C	D	B	A	A+	A+	B	A	A+	C	B	B	A+	60+	76	24	9	80
in situ concrete slab (2200 kg/m³ min.) with 'deep' profiled metal decking and Ceiling Treatment (CT2)	829560223	C	D	E	B	A	A+	A	C	B	A	D	C	B	A+	60+	94	23	7	83
in situ concrete slab (2200 kg/m³ min.) with 'deep' profiled metal decking and Ceiling Treatment (CT4)	829560224	C	D	E	B	A	A	A	C	B	A	D	C	B	A	60+	96	24	7	83
in situ concrete slab (2200 kg/m³ min.) with 'shallow' profiled metal decking & Ceiling Treatment (CT1/3)	829560243	B	C	D	B	A+	A+	A+	B	A	A+	C	B	A+	A+	60+	85	24	9	82
in situ concrete slab (2200 kg/m³ min.) with 'deep' profiled metal decking and Ceiling Treatment (CT1/3)	829560222	C	D	E	B	A	A+	A+	C	B	A	D	C	A	A+	60+	100	24	7	84
Robust Detail E-FS-1: Floating Floor Treatment (FFT4a proprietary system with chipboard with mineral wool resilient layer (16 kg/m² min.)) on:																				
in situ concrete slab (2200 kg/m³ min.) with "deep" profiled metal decking and Ceiling Treatment (CT1/3)	829560225	C	D	C	C	A+	A	A+	B	B	A	D	B	A+	A	60+	110	28.8	8	82
in situ concrete slab (2200 kg/m³ min.) with "deep" profiled metal decking and Ceiling Treatment (CT2)	829560226	C	D	C	C	A	A	A	B	B	A	D	B	B	A+	60+	98	28.5	8	82
in situ concrete slab (2200 kg/m³ min.) with "deep" profiled metal decking and Ceiling Treatment (CT4)	829560227	C	D	C	C	A	A	A	B	B	B	D	B	B	A	60+	100	29.2	8	81
in situ concrete slab (2200 kg/m³ min.) with "shallow" profiled metal decking and Ceiling Treatment (CT1/3)	829560246	C	D	C	C	A+	A	A+	B	B	A	D	B	A+	A	60+	110	28.8	8	82
in situ concrete slab (2200 kg/m³ min.) with "shallow" profiled metal decking and Ceiling Treatment (CT2)	829560247	A	C	A+	B	A+	A+	A+	A+	A+	A+	A+	A+	C	A	60+	67	18	7	82
in situ concrete slab (2200 kg/m³ min.) with "shallow" profiled metal decking and Ceiling Treatment (CT4)	829560248	B	C	A	B	A+	A	A+	A	A	A+	C	A	A	A+	60+	80	29.4	11	79

Separating floors: steel and composite construction / Domestic	Element number	Summary Rating	Climate change	Water extraction	Mineral resource extraction	Stratospheric ozone depletion	Human toxicity	Ecotoxicity to freshwater	Nuclear waste (higher level)	Ecotoxicity to land	Waste disposal	Fossil fuel depletion	Eutrophication	Photochemical ozone creation	Acidification	Typical replacement interval	Embodied CO$_2$ (kg CO$_2$ eq.)	Recycled content (kg)	Recycled content (%)	Recycled currently at EOL (%)
Robust Detail E-FS-1: Floating Floor Treatment (FFT4b proprietary system with gypsum screed on virgin foam (16 kg/m² min.)) on:																				
in situ concrete slab (2200 kg/m³ min.) with 'deep' profiled metal decking and Ceiling Treatment (CT1/3)	829560228	C	D	B	C	A+	A+	A+	A	A	D	B	A	A+	A+	35	100	15	4	82
in situ concrete slab (2200 kg/m³ min.) with 'deep' profiled metal decking and Ceiling Treatment (CT2)	829560229	C	D	A	C	A+	A+	A+	A+	A+	D	A	A	A	A+	35	93	15	4	81
in situ concrete slab (2200 kg/m³ min.) with 'deep' profiled metal decking and Ceiling Treatment (CT4)	829560230	C	D	B	C	A+	A+	A+	A+	A+	D	A	A	A	A+	35	95	16	4	81
in situ concrete slab (2200 kg/m³ min.) with 'shallow' profiled metal decking and Ceiling Treatment (CT1/3)	829560249	B	C	A	B	A+	A+	A+	A+	A+	C	A+	A+	A+	A+	35	83	15.3	5	80
in situ concrete slab (2200 kg/m³ min.) with 'shallow' profiled metal decking and Ceiling Treatment (CT2)	829560250	B	C	A+	B	A+	A+	A+	A+	A+	C	A+	A+	A	A+	35	72	15	5	79
in situ concrete slab (2200 kg/m³ min.) with 'shallow' profiled metal decking and Ceiling Treatment (CT4)	829560251	B	C	A+	B	A+	A+	A+	A+	A+	C	A+	A+	A	A+	35	75	16	6	78
Robust Detail E-FS-1: Floating Floor Treatment (FFT4c proprietary system with chipboard on virgin foam and rubber resilient layers (16 kg/m² min.)) on:																				
in situ concrete slab (2200 kg/m³ min.) with 'deep' profiled metal decking and Ceiling Treatment (CT1/3)	829560231	C	D	C	B	A	A+	A+	B	B	A	D	B	A+	A+	60+	100	24	7	84
in situ concrete slab (2200 kg/m³ min.) with 'deep' profiled metal decking and Ceiling Treatment (CT2)	829560232	C	D	C	B	A	A+	A+	B	B	A	D	B	B	A+	60+	91	23	7	83
in situ concrete slab (2200 kg/m³ min.) with 'deep' profiled metal decking and Ceiling Treatment (CT4)	829560233	C	D	C	B	A	A	A+	B	B	A	D	B	B	A+	60+	93	24	7	83
in situ concrete slab (2200 kg/m³ min.) with 'shallow' profiled metal decking & Ceiling Treatment (CT1/3)	829560252	B	C	B	B	A+	A+	A+	A	A	A+	C	A	A+	A+	60+	81	24	9	82
in situ concrete slab (2200 kg/m³ min.) with 'shallow' profiled metal decking and Ceiling Treatment (CT2)	829560253	A	C	A	B	A	A+	A+	A	A	A+	B	A	A	A+	60+	70	24	9	81
in situ concrete slab (2200 kg/m³ min.) with 'shallow' profiled metal decking and Ceiling Treatment (CT4)	829560254	B	C	A	B	A	A+	A+	A	A	A+	C	A	A	A+	60+	73	24	9	81

Separating floors: timber construction

Domestic

	Element number	Summary Rating	Climate change	Water extraction	Mineral resource extraction	Stratospheric ozone depletion	Human toxicity	Ecotoxicity to freshwater	Nuclear waste (higher level)	Ecotoxicity to land	Waste disposal	Fossil fuel depletion	Eutrophication	Photochemical ozone creation	Acidification	Typical replacement interval	Embodied CO2 (kg CO2 eq.)	Recycled content (kg)	Recycled content (%)	Recycled currently at EOL (%)
Approved Document E: Floor type 3.1A: Platform floor:																				
18 mm OSB/3 on plasterboard (total min. 25 kg/m²) on 25 mm min. mineral wool (80 kg/m³) on OSB/3 deck (20 kg/m² min.) on timber frame floor structure with Ceiling Treatment A	829910234	A+	A+	A	A+	B	E	C	A	A+	B	A	A	B	D	60+	-8	33.4	37	8
18 mm plywood on plasterboard (total min. 25 kg/m²) on 25 mm min. mineral wool (80 kg/m³) on plywood (softwood) deck (20 kg/m² min.) on timber frame floor structure with Ceiling Treatment A	829910236	A	A+	A	A+	E	E	E	E	E	B	B	C	C	E	60+	4	14.6	16	8
19 mm chipboard on plasterboard (total min. 25 kg/m²) on 25 mm min. mineral wool (80 kg/m³) on chipboard deck (20 kg/m² min.) on timber frame floor structure with Ceiling Treatment A	829910235	A+	A+	A	A+	B	D	C	B	A	B	C	B	B	E	60+	12	34.7	38	8
2 × 12.5 mm cement-bonded particle board (25 kg/m² min.) on 25 mm min. mineral wool (80 kg/m³) on cement-bonded particle board deck (20 kg/m² min.) on timber frame floor base with Ceiling Treatment A	829910237	B	D	A+	A+	C	C	D	A	A+	B	B	B	A	B	60+	96	15.1	15	8
Robust Detail E-FT-1: Floating Floor Treatment (FFT1 with chipboard and gypsum based board with mineral wool quilt between battens) on 15 mm chipboard decking on Structure Option A with Ceiling Treatment B	829910204	A+	A	A+	A+	A+	D	A	A+	A	A	B	A	B	E	60+	22	31.6	41	7
Robust Detail E-FT-1: Floating Floor Treatment (FFT1 with OSB/3 and gypsum based board with mineral wool quilt between battens) on 15 mm OSB/3 decking on Structure Option A and Ceiling Treatment B	829910205	A+	A+	A+	A+	A+	E	A+	A+	A+	A+	A+	A+	B	E	60+	7.7	27.4	38	8
Robust Detail E-FT-1: Floating Floor Treatment (FFT1 with plywood and gypsum based board with mineral wool quilt between battens) on 15 mm plywood decking on Structure Option A and Ceiling Treatment B	829910206	A+	A	A	A+	C	E	B	C	D	A	B	B	C	E	60+	18	15	20	7

Separating floors: timber construction

Domestic

	Element number	Summary Rating	Climate change	Water extraction	Mineral resource extraction	Stratospheric ozone depletion	Human toxicity	Ecotoxicity to freshwater	Nuclear waste (higher level)	Ecotoxicity to land	Waste disposal	Fossil fuel depletion	Eutrophication	Photochemical ozone creation	Acidification	Typical replacement interval	Embodied CO2 (kg CO2 eq.)	Recycled content (kg)	Recycled content (%)	Recycled currently at EOL (%)
Robust Detail E-FT-2: Floating Floor Treatment (FFT1 with chipboard and gypsum based board with 60 mm (min.) mineral wool quilt between battens) on 11 mm (min.) OSB/3 decking on solid timber joists (220 mm min.) at 400 mm centres (max.) with Ceiling Treatment B	829910207	A+	A+	A+	A+	A	C	A+	A+	A+	A	A+	A+	B	E	60+	8.8	27.7	36	10
Robust Detail E-FT-2: Floating Floor Treatment (FFT1 with OSB/3 and gypsum based board with 60 mm (min.) mineral wool quilt between battens) on 11 mm (min.) OSB/3 decking on solid timber joists (220 mm min.) at 400 mm centres (max.) with Ceiling Treatment B	829910208	A+	A+	A+	A+	A	D	A+	A+	A+	A+	A+	A+	B	D	60+	0.4	25.6	34	10
Robust Detail E-FT-2: Floating Floor Treatment (FFT1 with plywood and gypsum based board with 60 mm (min.) mineral wool quilt between battens) on 11 mm (min.) OSB/3 decking on solid timber joists (220 mm min.) at 400 mm centres (max.) with Ceiling Treatment B	829910209	A+	A+	A+	A+	B	D	A	B	B	A+	A+	A+	C	E	60+	7.5	18.8	25	10
Robust Detail E-FT-3: Floating Floor Treatment (FFT1 with: chipboard and gypsum based board (13.5 kg/m²) with mineral wool quilt between battens) on Structure Option B and Ceiling Treatment C	829910210	A+	A+	A+	A+	A	D	A+	A+	A+	A	A	A+	B	E	60+	14	28.8	36	12
Robust Detail E-FT-3: Floating Floor Treatment (FFT1 with: OSB/3 and gypsum based board (13.5 kg/m²) with mineral wool quilt between battens) on Structure Option B and Ceiling Treatment C	829910211	A+	A+	A	A+	A	D	A+	A+	A+	A	A+	A+	B	D	60+	5.7	26.7	34	12
Robust Detail E-FT-3: Floating Floor Treatment (FFT1 with: plywood and gypsum based board (13.5 kg/m²) with mineral wool quilt between battens) on Structure Option B and Ceiling Treatment C	829910212	A+	A+	A	A+	B	D	A	B	B	A	A	A+	C	E	60+	13	19.9	26	12
Proprietary Floor Construction: Floating Floor Treatment (FFT6 with chipboard, polyethylene sheet, MDF, polyester felt, 36 mm pre-bonded composite board) on Structure Option B and Ceiling Treatment B (BRE Global has received evidence that this specification meets the requirements of the functional unit.)	029911071	A+	A+	A+	A+	A	B	A+	A+	A	A+	A	A+	A+	A	60+	11	26.9	38	13

6.4 ROOFS

Based on the different functional units, separate roofing ratings are provided for the following building types:

* Commercial, Education & Industrial,
* Domestic,
* Health & Retail.

A roof has greater impact for say, low-rise buildings in comparison with high-rise buildings. This is because the roof area is equivalent to 33% of the floor area for a three-storey building and only 5% of the floor area for a 20-storey building.

Walls and roofs, as the primary building elements, are inextricably linked structurally and aesthetically and are the principal components of the weather-proofing building envelope. Hence, wall and roof systems must

Functional unit for roofs for commercial/industrial buildings:

1 m² of roof area (measured horizontally) to satisfy Building Regulations in England & Wales and a U-value of 0.16 W/m²K (pitched roof) or 0.25 W/m²K (flat roof). Based on an overall span of 15 m with support at 7.5 m. To include any repair, refurbishment or replacement over the 60-year study period.

Variation for education:

As for commercial buildings and based on a span of 15 m with supports at a central corridor.

Variation for retail/health:

As for commercial buildings with a span of 8 m.

Functional unit for roofs for domestic buildings:

1 m² of roof area (measured horizontally), to satisfy England & Wales Building Regulations, particularly a U-value of 0.16 W/m²K (pitched roof) or 0.25 W/m²K (flat roof). Span of 8 m to include a plasterboard ceiling and emulsion paint finish. To include any repair, refurbishment or replacement over the 60-year study period.

be compatible in both functional and visual terms and designers should take care not to compromise these essential requirements by mixing incompatible wall and roofing solutions, purely on the grounds of perceived environmental preference.

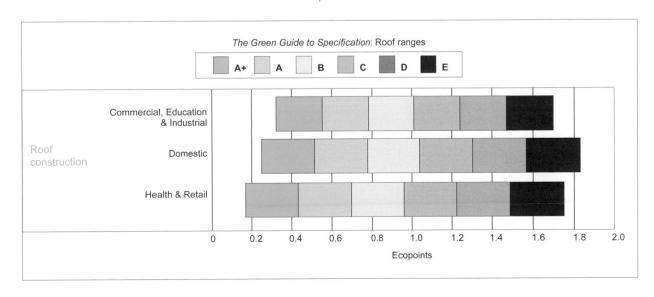

Division of roofing into subsections

Roofing specifications have been arranged into subsections for ease of use by designers. However, ratings have been arrived at through comparison of all roofing types shown across all subsections. The subsections are:

- **Flat roofs**, further subdivided into three systems, the position of the insulation being the primary difference between them:
  - cold deck,
  - inverted deck, and
  - warm deck.
- **Low pitched roofs** (eg pitched profiled roof decking, composite cladding panels, etc. up to a 15° pitch).
- **Pitched roofs** (eg roofs with a pitch of 16–45°, including tiled roofs on a timber roof structure and profiled sheet roofing).

Flat roofs: inverted deck

Commercial, Education & Industrial

	Element number	Summary Rating	Climate change	Water extraction	Mineral resource extraction	Stratospheric ozone depletion	Human toxicity	Ecotoxicity to freshwater	Nuclear waste (higher level)	Ecotoxicity to land	Waste disposal	Fossil fuel depletion	Eutrophication	Photochemical ozone creation	Acidification	Typical replacement interval	Embodied CO₂ (kg CO₂ eq.)	Recycled content (kg)	Recycled content (%)	Recycled currently at EOL (%)
Beam and dense block deck:																				
EPDM single ply roofing membrane, insulation, paving slabs	812530009	D	D	D	D	E	A	B	D	C	B	D	E	E	D	35	230	11	2	90
EPDM single ply roofing membrane, insulation, rounded pebbles	812530028	C	C	C	C	D	A	A	C	B	B	C	D	D	C	35	180	5.8	1	88
felt isolating layer, mastic asphalt roofing, insulation, paving slabs	812530033	D	D	C	D	E	A	C	C	C	E	E	E	E	D	50	210	11	1	84
felt isolating layer, mastic asphalt roofing, insulation, rounded pebbles	812530034	D	C	C	D	D	A	B	B	B	D	D	D	D	C	50	180	5.7	1	83
oxidised polyester reinforced bitumen roofing membranes, insulation, paving slabs	812530014	D	D	D	D	E	B	B	D	D	C	E	E	E	E	35	230	11	2	90
oxidised polyester reinforced bitumen roofing membranes, insulation, rounded pebbles	812530012	C	C	D	C	D	A	B	C	C	B	D	D	D	C	35	190	5.8	1	87
polymer modified polyester reinforced bitumen roofing membranes, insulation, paving slabs	812530011	C	C	C	D	D	A	B	C	C	B	D	D	D	D	50	200	11.4	2	88
polymer modified polyester reinforced bitumen roofing membranes, insulation, rounded pebbles	812530010	C	B	C	C	D	A	A	B	B	B	C	C	D	C	50	170	5.7	1	88
PVC single ply roofing membrane, insulation, paving slabs	812530029	D	D	D	D	E	A	B	D	D	C	D	E	E	D	35	230	11	2	90
PVC single ply roofing membrane, insulation, rounded pebbles	812530030	C	C	D	C	E	A	B	C	C	B	C	D	D	C	35	180	5.8	1	88
TPO single ply roofing membrane, insulation, paving slabs	812530031	D	D	D	D	E	A	B	D	D	B	D	E	E	E	35	230	11	2	90
TPO single ply roofing membrane, insulation, rounded pebbles	812530032	C	C	C	C	D	A	A	C	C	B	C	D	D	C	35	180	5.8	1	88
In situ reinforced concrete with 50% GGBS and 20% recycled coarse aggregate:																				
EPDM single ply roofing membrane, insulation, paving slabs	812530045	D	D	E	E	D	A	B	D	D	C	D	D	E	D	35	230	146	15	89
EPDM single ply roofing membrane, insulation, rounded pebbles	812530046	C	C	E	D	C	A	A	C	C	C	C	C	C	C	35	190	139	16	89
felt isolating layer, mastic asphalt roofing, insulation, paving slabs	812530055	E	D	D	E	D	A	C	C	D	E	E	D	D	D	50	220	145	14	85
felt isolating layer, mastic asphalt roofing, insulation, rounded pebbles	812530056	D	C	D	D	C	A	B	B	C	E	D	C	C	C	50	190	139	15	85

Cont'd . . . .

Flat roofs: inverted deck

Commercial, Education & Industrial

	Element number	Summary Rating	Climate change	Water extraction	Mineral resource extraction	Stratospheric ozone depletion	Human toxicity	Ecotoxicity to freshwater	Nuclear waste (higher level)	Ecotoxicity to land	Waste disposal	Fossil fuel depletion	Eutrophication	Photochemical ozone creation	Acidification	Typical replacement interval	Embodied CO$_2$ (kg CO$_2$ eq.)	Recycled content (kg)	Recycled content (%)	Recycled currently at EOL (%)
In situ reinforced concrete with 50% GGBS and 20% recycled coarse aggregate (cont'd):																				
oxidised polyester reinforced bitumen roofing membranes, insulation, paving slabs	812530047	E	D	E	E	D	A	B	D	E	D	E	E	E	E	35	240	146	15	88
oxidised polyester reinforced bitumen roofing membranes, insulation, rounded pebbles	812530048	D	C	E	D	C	A	B	C	D	C	D	D	D	C	35	200	139	15	88
polymer modified polyester reinforced bitumen roofing membranes, insulation, paving slabs	812530049	D	C	D	D	D	A	A	C	D	C	D	D	D	D	50	210	145	15	88
polymer modified polyester reinforced bitumen roofing membranes, insulation, rounded pebbles	812530050	C	C	D	D	C	A	A	B	C	C	C	C	C	C	50	180	139	15	88
PVC single ply roofing membrane, insulation, paving slabs	812530051	D	D	E	E	E	A	B	D	D	C	D	E	E	D	35	240	146	15	89
PVC single ply roofing membrane, insulation, rounded pebbles	812530052	C	C	E	D	D	A	A	C	C	C	C	C	D	C	35	190	139	15	89
TPO single ply roofing membrane, insulation, paving slabs	812530053	D	D	E	E	D	A	B	D	D	C	D	E	D	E	35	240	146	15	89
TPO single ply roofing membrane, insulation, rounded pebbles	812530054	C	C	E	D	C	A	A	C	D	C	C	C	C	C	35	190	139	16	89
In situ reinforced concrete:																				
EPDM single ply roofing membrane, insulation, paving slabs	812530035	E	E	E	E	D	A	B	E	E	C	E	E	E	E	35	270	40	4	90
EPDM single ply roofing membrane, insulation, rounded pebbles	812530036	D	D	E	D	C	A	B	C	D	C	D	D	D	D	35	230	33	4	90
felt isolating layer, mastic asphalt roofing, insulation, paving slabs	812530003	E	E	D	E	D	A	C	C	E	E	E	E	D	E	50	260	39	4	86
felt isolating layer, mastic asphalt roofing, insulation, rounded pebbles	812530027	E	D	D	E	C	A	C	B	D	E	E	D	D	D	50	230	33	4	86
oxidised polyester reinforced bitumen roofing membranes, insulation, paving slabs	812530037	E	E	E	E	D	B	B	E	E	D	E	E	E	E	35	280	40	4	90
oxidised polyester reinforced bitumen roofing membranes, insulation, rounded pebbles	812530038	D	D	E	E	C	A	B	C	E	C	E	D	D	D	35	230	33	4	90
polymer modified polyester reinforced bitumen roofing membranes, insulation, paving slabs	812530039	D	E	D	E	D	A	B	C	E	C	D	E	D	E	50	250	39	4	90

Cont'd . . . .

Flat roofs: inverted deck

Commercial, Education & Industrial

	Element number	Summary Rating	Climate change	Water extraction	Mineral resource extraction	Stratospheric ozone depletion	Human toxicity	Ecotoxicity to freshwater	Nuclear waste (higher level)	Ecotoxicity to land	Waste disposal	Fossil fuel depletion	Eutrophication	Photochemical ozone creation	Acidification	Typical replacement interval	Embodied CO2 (kg CO2 eq.)	Recycled content (kg)	Recycled content (%)	Recycled currently at EOL (%)
In situ reinforced concrete (cont'd):																				
polymer modified polyester reinforced bitumen roofing membranes, insulation, rounded pebbles	812530040	D	D	D	D	C	A	B	B	D	C	D	D	C	D	50	210	33	4	90
PVC single ply roofing membrane, insulation, paving slabs	812530041	E	E	E	E	E	A	B	D	E	C	E	E	E	E	35	280	40	4	90
PVC single ply roofing membrane, insulation, rounded pebbles	812530042	D	D	E	E	D	A	B	C	D	C	D	D	D	D	35	230	33	4	90
TPO single ply roofing membrane, insulation, paving slabs	812530043	E	E	E	E	D	A	B	D	E	C	E	E	E	E	35	280	40	4	90
TPO single ply roofing membrane, insulation, rounded pebbles	812530044	D	D	E	D	C	A	B	C	D	C	D	D	D	D	35	230	33	4	90
Precast prestressed concrete hollow slab, with screed:																				
EPDM single ply roofing membrane, insulation, paving slabs	812530068	D	D	D	D	E	A	B	E	D	C	D	E	E	E	35	240	12	2	90
EPDM single ply roofing membrane, insulation, rounded pebbles	812530069	C	C	D	C	D	A	A	C	C	B	C	D	D	D	35	190	6.1	1	88
mastic asphalt roofing, insulation, paving slabs	812530007	E	D	C	D	E	A	C	C	C	E	E	E	E	D	50	230	11.7	2	83
mastic asphalt roofing, insulation, rounded pebbles	812530070	D	C	C	D	D	A	C	B	C	E	D	D	D	C	50	200	6	1	83
oxidised polyester reinforced bitumen roofing membranes, insulation, paving slabs	812530071	D	E	D	D	E	B	B	D	D	C	E	E	E	E	35	250	12	2	90
oxidised polyester reinforced bitumen roofing membranes, insulation, rounded pebbles	812530072	C	C	D	C	D	A	B	C	C	C	D	D	D	D	35	200	6.1	1	87
polymer modified polyester reinforced bitumen roofing membranes, insulation, paving slabs	812530073	D	D	C	D	D	A	B	C	D	C	D	D	D	D	50	210	11	2	90
polymer modified polyester reinforced bitumen roofing membranes, insulation, rounded pebbles	812530074	C	C	C	C	D	A	A	B	C	B	D	D	D	C	50	180	6	1	87
PVC single ply roofing membrane, insulation, paving slabs	812530077	D	E	D	D	E	B	B	D	D	C	E	E	E	E	35	250	12	2	90
PVC single ply roofing membrane, insulation, rounded pebbles	812530070	C	C	D	C	E	A	B	C	C	B	D	D	D	D	35	200	6.1	1	88
TPO single ply roofing membrane, insulation, paving slabs	812530075	D	D	D	D	E	A	B	D	D	C	D	E	E	E	35	240	12	2	90
TPO single ply roofing membrane, insulation, rounded pebbles	812530076	C	C	D	C	D	A	B	C	C	B	C	D	D	D	35	200	6.1	1	88

Flat roofs: inverted deck

Commercial, Education & Industrial

	Element number	Summary Rating	Climate change	Water extraction	Mineral resource extraction	Stratospheric ozone depletion	Human toxicity	Ecotoxicity to freshwater	Nuclear waste (higher level)	Ecotoxicity to land	Waste disposal	Fossil fuel depletion	Eutrophication	Photochemical ozone creation	Acidification	Typical replacement interval	Embodied CO2 (kg CO2 eq.)	Recycled content (kg)	Recycled content (%)	Recycled currently at EOL (%)
Profiled metal 'deep' decking with in situ concrete:																				
EPDM single ply roofing membrane, insulation, paving slabs	812530058	D	E	E	D	D	A	A	E	D	C	D	D	E	D	35	250	25	4	90
EPDM single ply roofing membrane, insulation, rounded pebbles	812530059	C	C	D	C	C	A	A	D	C	B	C	C	D	C	35	200	18	3	90
felt isolating layer, mastic asphalt roofing, insulation, paving slabs	812530004	E	D	D	D	D	A	C	D	D	E	E	D	D	D	50	240	24	4	84
felt isolating layer, mastic asphalt roofing, insulation, rounded pebbles	812530057	D	C	D	C	C	A	B	C	C	E	D	C	D	C	50	200	18	3	83
oxidised polyester reinforced bitumen roofing membranes, insulation, paving slabs	812530060	D	E	E	D	D	A	B	E	D	C	E	E	E	E	35	260	25	4	90
oxidised polyester reinforced bitumen roofing membranes, insulation, rounded pebbles	812530061	C	D	E	C	C	A	A	D	D	C	D	C	D	C	35	210	18	3	90
polymer modified polyester reinforced bitumen roofing membranes, paving slabs	812530062	D	D	D	C	C	A	A	D	D	C	D	D	D	D	50	220	24	4	90
polymer modified polyester reinforced bitumen roofing membranes, rounded pebbles	812530063	C	C	D	C	C	A	A	C	C	B	D	C	C	C	50	190	18	3	90
PVC single ply roofing membrane, insulation, paving slabs	812530064	D	E	E	D	D	A	B	E	D	C	D	D	E	D	35	260	25	4	90
PVC single ply roofing membrane, insulation, rounded pebbles	812530065	C	C	E	C	C	A	A	D	C	B	D	C	D	C	35	210	18	3	90
TPO single ply roofing membrane, insulation, paving slabs	812530066	D	E	E	D	D	A	B	E	D	C	D	D	E	E	35	250	25	4	90
TPO single ply roofing membrane, insulation, rounded pebbles	812530067	C	C	D	C	C	A	A	D	C	B	C	C	D	C	35	210	18	3	90
Structural steel trusses, galvanised steel purlins and deck, plywood (temperate EN 636-2) decking:																				
EPDM single ply roofing membrane, insulation, paving slabs	812530079	B	C	E	B	C	A	B	E	D	B	D	C	D	C	35	180	13	7	79
EPDM single ply roofing membrane, insulation, rounded pebbles	812530080	A	A	D	A	B	A	A	D	C	A	C	B	C	B	35	130	6.4	7	70
felt isolating layer, mastic asphalt roofing, insulation, paving slabs	812530085	C	B	D	A	C	A	C	D	D	D	D	C	D	B	50	170	11	6	64
felt isolating layer, mastic asphalt roofing, insulation, rounded pebbles	812530086	B	A	C	A	B	A	B	C	C	D	C	B	C	B	50	140	6.3	4	49

Cont'd . . . .

Flat roofs: inverted deck

Commercial, Education & Industrial

	Element number	Summary Rating	Climate change	Water extraction	Mineral resource extraction	Stratospheric ozone depletion	Human toxicity	Ecotoxicity to freshwater	Nuclear waste (higher level)	Ecotoxicity to land	Waste disposal	Fossil fuel depletion	Eutrophication	Photochemical ozone creation	Acidification	Typical replacement interval	Embodied CO₂ (kg CO₂ eq.)	Recycled content (kg)	Recycled content (%)	Recycled currently at EOL (%)
Structural steel trusses, galvanised steel purlins and deck, plywood (temperate EN 636-2) decking (cont'd):																				
oxidised polyester reinforced bitumen roofing membrane, insulation, paving slabs	812530001	C	C	E	B	C	B	B	E	E	B	D	C	D	C	35	190	13	7	75
oxidised polyester reinforced bitumen roofing membranes, insulation, rounded pebbles	812530025	B	B	D	A	B	A	B	D	D	B	D	B	C	B	35	140	6.4	6	65
polymer modified polyester reinforced bitumen roofing membranes, insulation, paving slabs	812530002	B	B	D	A	B	A	A	D	D	B	C	B	C	B	50	150	12	7	74
polymer modified polyester reinforced bitumen roofing membranes, insulation, rounded pebbles	812530026	A	A	C	A+	B	A	A	C	C	B	C	A	B	A	50	120	6.3	6	65
PVC single ply roofing membrane, insulation, paving slabs	812530081	C	C	E	B	C	A	B	E	D	B	D	C	D	C	35	190	13	7	78
PVC single ply roofing membrane, insulation, rounded pebbles	812530082	B	B	D	A	C	A	A	D	D	A	C	B	C	B	35	140	6.4	7	69
TPO single ply roofing membrane, insulation, paving slabs	812530083	B	C	E	B	C	A	B	E	E	B	D	C	D	C	35	180	12	7	83
TPO single ply roofing membrane, insulation, rounded pebbles	812530084	A	A	D	A	B	A	A	D	D	A	C	B	C	B	35	140	6.4	7	69

Flat roofs: warm deck

Commercial, Education & Industrial

	Element number	Summary Rating	Climate change	Water extraction	Mineral resource extraction	Stratospheric ozone depletion	Human toxicity	Ecotoxicity to freshwater	Nuclear waste (higher level)	Ecotoxicity to land	Waste disposal	Fossil fuel depletion	Eutrophication	Photochemical ozone creation	Acidification	Typical replacement interval	Embodied CO2 (kg CO2 eq.)	Recycled content (kg)	Recycled content (%)	Recycled currently at EOL (%)
Beam and dense block deck:																				
vapour control layer, insulation, EPDM single ply roofing membrane	812540069	B	A	A	C	C	A	A	A	A	A	B	C	B	B	35	140	4.8	1	90
vapour control layer, insulation, felt isolating layer, mastic asphalt roofing	812540070	C	B	A	C	D	A	B	A	B	D	C	C	C	B	50	150	4.8	1	83
vapour control layer, insulation, oxidised polyester reinforced bitumen roofing membranes with mineral finish	812540049	B	B	A	C	C	A	A	A	B	B	C	C	C	B	35	140	4.8	1	90
vapour control layer, insulation, polymer modified polyester reinforced bitumen roofing membranes with mineral finish	812540071	B	B	A	C	C	A	A	A	B	B	B	C	C	B	50	140	4.8	1	90
vapour control layer, insulation, PVC single ply roofing membrane	812540072	B	B	A	C	D	A	A	A	B	A	B	C	C	B	35	140	4.8	1	90
vapour control layer, insulation, TPO single ply roofing membrane	812540073	B	B	A	C	C	A	A	A	B	A	B	C	B	B	35	140	4.8	1	90
In situ reinforced concrete slab with 50% GGBS and 20% recycled coarse aggregate:																				
vapour control layer, insulation, EPDM single ply roofing membrane	812540074	B	B	B	C	B	A+	A	A	B	B	B	B	B	B	35	150	139	17	90
vapour control layer, insulation, felt isolating layer, mastic asphalt roofing	812540075	C	B	B	C	C	A	B	A	C	E	C	C	B	B	50	160	139	16	85
vapour control layer, insulation, oxidised polyester reinforced bitumen roofing membranes with mineral finish	812540076	C	B	B	C	B	A	A	A	C	C	C	C	B	B	35	150	139	16	89
vapour control layer, insulation, polymer modified polyester reinforced bitumen roofing membranes with mineral finish	812540077	B	B	B	C	B	A	A	A	C	B	B	B	B	B	50	150	139	16	89
vapour control layer, insulation, PVC single ply roofing membrane	812540078	B	B	B	C	C	A	A	A	C	B	B	B	B	B	35	150	139	17	89
vapour control layer, insulation, TPO single ply roofing membrane	812540079	B	B	B	C	B	A+	A	A	C	B	B	B	B	B	35	150	139	17	89
In situ reinforced concrete slab:																				
vapour control layer, insulation, EPDM single ply roofing membrane	812540025	C	C	B	D	B	A	A	B	C	B	B	C	B	C	35	190	33	4	90
vapour control layer, insulation, felt isolating layer, mastic asphalt roofing	812540021	D	C	B	D	C	A	B	A	C	E	C	C	C	C	50	200	33	4	85

Cont'd . . . .

Flat roofs: warm deck

Commercial, Education & Industrial

	Element number	Summary Rating	Climate change	Water extraction	Mineral resource extraction	Stratospheric ozone depletion	Human toxicity	Ecotoxicity to freshwater	Nuclear waste (higher level)	Ecotoxicity to land	Waste disposal	Fossil fuel depletion	Eutrophication	Photochemical ozone creation	Acidification	Typical replacement interval	Embodied CO2 (kg CO2 eq.)	Recycled content (kg)	Recycled content (%)	Recycled currently at EOL (%)
In situ reinforced concrete slab (cont'd):																				
vapour control layer, insulation, oxidised polyester reinforced bitumen roofing membranes with mineral finish	812540022	C	C	C	D	B	A	A	B	D	C	C	C	C	C	35	190	33	4	90
vapour control layer, insulation, polymer modified polyester reinforced bitumen roofing membranes with mineral finish	812540023	C	C	B	D	B	A	A	A	C	B	C	C	B	C	50	190	33	4	90
vapour control layer, insulation, PVC single ply roofing membrane	812540026	C	C	C	D	C	A	A	A	C	B	B	C	C	C	35	190	33	4	90
vapour control layer, insulation, TPO single ply roofing membrane	812540027	C	C	B	D	B	A	A	A	C	B	B	C	B	C	35	190	33	4	90
Precast concrete formwork with lattice reinforcement and in situ concrete:																				
vapour control layer, insulation, EPDM single ply waterproofing membrane	812540024	B	B	B	C	B	A	A	A	C	B	B	C	B	C	35	170	22	3	90
vapour control layer, insulation, mastic asphalt roofing	812540011	D	C	B	D	C	A	B	A	C	D	C	C	C	C	50	180	22	3	85
vapour control layer, insulation, oxidised polyester reinforced bitumen roofing membranes with mineral finish	812540016	C	B	B	C	B	A	A	A	C	B	C	C	C	C	35	170	22	3	90
vapour control layer, insulation, polymer modified polyester reinforced bitumen roofing membranes with mineral finish	812540017	C	B	B	C	B	A	A	A	C	B	C	C	B	C	50	170	22	3	90
vapour control layer, insulation, PVC single ply waterproofing membrane	812540012	B	B	B	C	C	A	A	A	C	B	B	C	C	C	35	170	22	3	90
vapour control layer, insulation, TPO single ply waterproofing membrane	812540013	B	B	B	C	B	A	A	A	C	B	B	C	B	C	35	170	22	3	90
Precast prestressed concrete hollow slab, with screed:																				
vapour control layer, insulation, EPDM single ply waterproofing membrane	812540033	B	B	A	C	C	A	A	A	B	A	B	C	C	B	35	150	5.1	1	90
vapour control layer, insulation, felt isolating layer, mastic asphalt roofing	812540030	C	B	A	C	C	A	B	A	B	D	C	C	C	C	50	170	5.1	1	83
vapour control layer, insulation, oxidised polyester reinforced bitumen roofing membranes with mineral finish	812540031	B	B	A	C	C	A	A	A	C	B	C	C	C	C	35	160	5.1	1	90

Cont'd . . . .

Flat roofs: warm deck

Commercial, Education & Industrial

	Element number	Summary Rating	Climate change	Water extraction	Mineral resource extraction	Stratospheric ozone depletion	Human toxicity	Ecotoxicity to freshwater	Nuclear waste (higher level)	Ecotoxicity to land	Waste disposal	Fossil fuel depletion	Eutrophication	Photochemical ozone creation	Acidification	Typical replacement interval	Embodied CO_2 (kg CO_2 eq.)	Recycled content (kg)	Recycled content (%)	Recycled currently at EOL (%)
Precast prestressed concrete hollow slab, with screed (cont'd):																				
vapour control layer, insulation, polymer modified polyester reinforced bitumen roofing membranes with mineral finish	812540032	B	B	A	C	C	A	A	A	B	B	C	C	C	B	50	150	5.1	1	90
vapour control layer, insulation, PVC single ply waterproofing membrane	812540034	B	B	A	C	D	A	A	A	B	A	B	C	C	B	35	160	5.1	1	90
vapour control layer, insulation, TPO single ply waterproofing membrane	812540035	B	B	A	C	C	A	A	A	B	A	B	C	C	C	35	160	5.1	1	90
Profiled metal 'deep' decking with in situ concrete:																				
vapour control layer, insulation, EPDM single ply roofing membrane	812540080	B	B	B	B	B	A+	A	B	B	B	B	B	B	B	35	160	18	4	90
vapour control layer, insulation, felt isolating layer, mastic asphalt roofing	812540038	C	C	B	C	B	A	B	B	B	D	C	C	C	B	50	180	18	3	83
vapour control layer, insulation, oxidised polyester reinforced bitumen roofing membranes with mineral finish	812540081	B	B	B	B	B	A	A	B	C	B	C	B	B	B	35	170	18	4	90
vapour control layer, insulation, polymer modified polyester reinforced bitumen roofing membranes with mineral finish	812540039	B	B	B	B	B	A	A	B	B	B	C	B	B	B	50	160	18	4	90
vapour control layer, insulation, PVC single ply roofing membrane	812540082	B	B	B	B	B	A+	A	B	B	B	B	B	C	B	35	170	18	4	90
vapour control layer, insulation, TPO single ply roofing membrane	812540083	B	B	B	B	B	A+	A	B	B	B	B	B	B	B	35	170	18	4	90
Structural steel trusses, galvanised steel purlins and deck:																				
vapour control layer, insulation, EPDM single ply roofing membrane	812540001	A+	A+	A+	A+	A+	A+	A+	A+	A+	A+	A+	A+	A+	A+	35	72	4	20	70
vapour control layer, insulation, felt isolating layer, mastic asphalt roofing	812540002	A	A+	A+	A+	A	A+	A	A+	A+	C	A	A+	A	A+	50	89	4	6	24
vapour control layer, insulation, oxidised polyester reinforced bitumen roofing membranes with mineral finish	812540009	A+	A+	A	A+	A+	A+	A+	A+	A+	A	A	A+	A+	A+	35	80	4	15	51
vapour control layer, insulation, polymer modified polyester reinforced bitumen roofing membranes with mineral finish	812540010	A+	A+	A+	A+	A+	A+	A+	A+	A+	A+	A	A+	A+	A+	50	77	4	14	49
vapour control layer, insulation, PVC single ply waterproofing membrane	812540003	A+	A+	A	A+	A	A+	A+	A+	A+	A+	A+	A+	A	A+	35	78	4	20	68
vapour control layer, insulation, TPO single ply waterproofing membrane	812540004	A+	A+	A+	A+	A+	A+	A+	A+	A+	A+	A+	A+	A+	A+	35	75	4	20	69

Low pitched roofs — Commercial, Education & Industrial	Element number	Summary Rating	Climate change	Water extraction	Mineral resource extraction	Stratospheric ozone depletion	Human toxicity	Ecotoxicity to freshwater	Nuclear waste (higher level)	Ecotoxicity to land	Waste disposal	Fossil fuel depletion	Eutrophication	Photochemical ozone creation	Acidification	Typical replacement interval	Embodied CO_2 (kg CO_2 eq.)	Recycled content (kg)	Recycled content (%)	Recycled currently at EOL (%)
Galvanised steel rafters and joists:																				
composite profiled roof cladding (steel inner lining, pentane blown PUR/PIR insulation, coated aluminium outer skin)	812550014	A+	A+	C	A+	A	B	B	A	B	A+	A	A	B	A	35	98	4.6	27	73
composite profiled roof cladding (steel inner lining, pentane blown PUR/PIR insulation, coated steel outer skin)	812550001	A+	A+	D	A+	A+	A+	A+	A+	A	A+	A	A	B	A+	35	95	3.6	18	77
double skin built up profiled roof cladding (coated aluminium inner and outer skin, insulation)	812550013	A	A	A	A+	A	E	E	D	B	A+	A	A+	A	A	35	110	7.4	37	64
double skin built up profiled roof cladding (coated steel inner and outer skin, insulation)	812550016	A+	A+	B	A+	A+	A+	A+	B	A+	A+	A	A+	A	A+	35	100	4.6	18	70
double skin built up profiled roof cladding (mill finished aluminium inner and outer skin, insulation)	812550018	A+	A+	A+	A+	A+	B	D	B	A+	A+	A+	A+	A+	A+	50	83	7.4	37	64
double skin built up roof cladding (aluminium inner lining, insulation, mill finished aluminium standing seam outer skin)	812550002	A	A	A	A+	A	E	E	D	B	A+	A	A+	A	A	35	110	7.4	37	64
double skin built up roof cladding (steel inner lining, insulation, coated aluminium standing seam outer skin)	812550007	A	A	A	A+	A	D	D	C	B	A+	A	A+	A	A	35	110	6.3	29	66
double skin built up roof cladding (steel inner lining, insulation, copper standing seam outer skin)	812550019	A	A+	C	B	A	A+	A+	B	A+	A+	A+	A+	A+	A+	45	91	8.2	32	71
double skin built up roof cladding (steel inner lining, insulation, mill finished aluminium standing seam outer skin)	812550034	A+	A+	A	A+	A+	A	B	B	A+	A+	A+	A+	A+	A+	50	82	6.3	29	66

Flat roofs: cold deck
Domestic

	Element number	Summary Rating	Climate change	Water extraction	Mineral resource extraction	Stratospheric ozone depletion	Human toxicity	Ecotoxicity to freshwater	Nuclear waste (higher level)	Ecotoxicity to land	Waste disposal	Fossil fuel depletion	Eutrophication	Photochemical ozone creation	Acidification	Typical replacement interval	Embodied CO2 (kg CO2 eq.)	Recycled content (kg)	Recycled content (%)	Recycled currently at EOL (%)
Vapour control layer, insulation, timber joists, OSB/3:																				
EPDM single ply roofing membrane	812520030	A+	A+	A+	A+	A	A+	A+	A+	A+	A+	A+	A+	A+	A+	35	15	10.7	26	11
oxidised polyester reinforced bitumen roofing membranes with mineral finish	812520029	A+	A+	A+	A+	A	A+	A+	A+	A+	A	A	A+	A+	A+	35	22	10.7	22	9
PVC single ply roofing membrane	812520032	A+	A+	A+	A+	A	A+	A+	A+	A+	A+	A+	A+	A+	A+	35	20	10.7	26	11
TPO single ply roofing membrane	812520031	A+	A+	A+	A+	A	A+	A+	A+	A+	A+	A+	A+	A+	A+	35	17	10.7	26	11
Vapour control layer, insulation, timber joists, plywood (temperate EN 636-2) decking:																				
EPDM single ply roofing membrane	812520009	A+	A+	A+	A+	A	A	A	A	B	A+	A+	A+	A	A+	35	22	3.9	10	11
oxidised polyester reinforced bitumen roofing membranes with mineral finish	812520002	A+	A+	A	A+	A	A	A	A	B	A	A	A+	A	A	35	29	3.9	8	9
PVC single ply roofing membrane	812520006	A+	A+	A	A+	B	A	A	A	B	A+	A+	A+	A	A+	35	27	3.9	9	11
TPO single ply roofing membrane	812520007	A+	A+	A+	A+	A	A	A	A	B	A+	A+	A+	A	A+	35	24	3.9	10	11

Flat roofs: inverted deck

Domestic

	Element number	Summary Rating	Climate change	Water extraction	Mineral resource extraction	Stratospheric ozone depletion	Human toxicity	Ecotoxicity to freshwater	Nuclear waste (higher level)	Ecotoxicity to land	Waste disposal	Fossil fuel depletion	Eutrophication	Photochemical ozone creation	Acidification	Typical replacement interval	Embodied CO2 (kg CO2 eq.)	Recycled content (kg)	Recycled content (%)	Recycled currently at EOL (%)
Beam and dense block deck:																				
EPDM single ply roofing membrane, insulation, paving slabs	812530009	D	D	D	D	E	A	B	D	C	B	D	D	D	D	35	220	13	2	89
EPDM single ply roofing membrane, insulation, rounded pebbles	812530028	C	C	C	C	D	A	A	C	B	B	C	C	C	C	35	170	7.3	1	87
felt isolating layer, mastic asphalt roofing, insulation, paving slabs	812530033	D	D	C	D	E	A	C	C	B	D	D	D	C	D	50	200	12	2	83
felt isolating layer, mastic asphalt roofing, insulation, rounded pebbles	812530034	C	C	B	C	D	A	B	B	B	D	D	C	C	C	50	170	7.1	1	81
oxidised polyester reinforced bitumen roofing membranes, insulation, paving slabs	812530014	D	D	D	D	E	B	B	D	C	C	E	E	D	D	35	220	13	2	89
oxidised polyester reinforced bitumen roofing membranes, insulation, rounded pebbles	812530012	C	C	C	C	D	A	B	C	B	B	D	C	C	C	35	180	7.3	1	86
polymer modified polyester reinforced bitumen roofing membranes, insulation, paving slabs	812530011	C	C	C	C	D	A	B	C	C	B	D	D	C	C	50	190	12	2	89
polymer modified polyester reinforced bitumen roofing membranes, insulation, rounded pebbles	812530010	C	C	B	C	C	A	A	B	B	B	C	C	B	C	50	160	7.1	1	86
PVC single ply roofing membrane, insulation, paving slabs	812530029	D	D	D	D	E	A	B	D	C	B	D	D	D	D	35	220	13	2	89
PVC single ply roofing membrane, insulation, rounded pebbles	812530030	C	C	C	C	D	A	A	C	B	B	C	C	C	C	35	180	7.3	1	87
TPO single ply roofing membrane, insulation, paving slabs	812530031	D	D	D	D	D	A	B	D	C	B	D	D	D	D	35	220	13	2	89
TPO single ply roofing membrane, insulation, rounded pebbles	812530032	C	C	C	C	D	A	A	C	B	B	C	C	C	C	35	170	7.3	1	87
In situ reinforced concrete with 50% GGBS and 20% recycled coarse aggregate:																				
EPDM single ply roofing membrane, insulation, paving slabs	812530045	D	D	E	E	D	A	B	D	D	C	D	D	C	D	35	240	144	14	89
EPDM single ply roofing membrane, insulation, rounded pebbles	812530046	D	C	E	D	C	A	A	C	C	C	C	C	C	C	35	190	137	15	89
felt isolating layer, mastic asphalt roofing, insulation, paving slabs	812530055	E	D	D	E	D	A	C	C	D	E	E	D	C	D	50	230	143	14	85
felt isolating layer, mastic asphalt roofing, insulation, rounded pebbles	812530056	D	C	D	D	C	A	B	C	C	E	D	C	C	C	50	200	137	14	85

Cont'd . . . .

Flat roofs: inverted deck
Domestic

	Element number	Summary Rating	Climate change	Water extraction	Mineral resource extraction	Stratospheric ozone depletion	Human toxicity	Ecotoxicity to freshwater	Nuclear waste (higher level)	Ecotoxicity to land	Waste disposal	Fossil fuel depletion	Eutrophication	Photochemical ozone creation	Acidification	Typical replacement interval	Embodied CO2 (kg CO2 eq.)	Recycled content (kg)	Recycled content (%)	Recycled currently at EOL (%)
In situ reinforced concrete with 50% GGBS and 20% recycled coarse aggregate (cont'd):																				
oxidised polyester reinforced bitumen roofing membranes, insulation, paving slabs	812530047	E	D	E	E	D	A	B	D	E	D	E	E	D	E	35	250	144	14	89
oxidised polyester reinforced bitumen roofing membranes, insulation, rounded pebbles	812530048	D	D	E	D	C	A	B	C	D	C	D	C	C	C	35	200	138	14	87
polymer modified polyester reinforced bitumen roofing membranes, insulation, paving slabs	812530049	D	D	D	D	D	A	A	C	D	C	D	D	C	D	50	210	143	14	89
polymer modified polyester reinforced bitumen roofing membranes, insulation, rounded pebbles	812530050	C	C	D	D	C	A	A	B	C	C	C	C	B	C	50	180	138	14	88
PVC single ply roofing membrane, insulation, paving slabs	812530051	E	D	E	E	E	A	B	D	D	C	D	D	D	D	35	250	144	14	89
PVC single ply roofing membrane, insulation, rounded pebbles	812530052	D	D	E	D	D	A	A	C	C	C	C	C	C	C	35	200	137	15	89
TPO single ply roofing membrane, insulation, paving slabs	812530053	D	D	E	E	D	A	B	D	D	C	D	D	C	D	35	240	144	14	89
TPO single ply roofing membrane, insulation, rounded pebbles	812530054	D	C	E	D	C	A	A	C	C	C	C	C	C	C	35	200	137	15	89
In situ reinforced concrete slab:																				
EPDM single ply roofing membrane, insulation, paving slabs	812530035	E	E	E	E	D	A	B	E	E	C	E	E	D	E	35	280	43	4	89
EPDM single ply roofing membrane, insulation, rounded pebbles	812530036	D	D	E	E	C	A	B	D	D	C	D	D	C	D	35	240	36	4	89
felt isolating layer, mastic asphalt roofing, insulation, paving slabs	812530003	E	E	D	E	D	A	C	D	E	E	E	E	C	E	50	270	42	4	85
felt isolating layer, mastic asphalt roofing, insulation, rounded pebbles	812530027	E	D	D	E	D	A	C	C	D	E	D	D	C	D	50	240	36	4	85
oxidised polyester reinforced bitumen roofing membranes, insulation, paving slabs	812530037	E	E	E	E	D	B	B	E	E	D	E	E	D	E	35	290	43	4	89
oxidised polyester reinforced bitumen roofing membranes, insulation, rounded pebbles	812530038	D	D	E	E	C	A	B	D	E	C	E	D	C	D	35	250	36	4	89

Cont'd . . . .

Flat roofs: inverted deck

Domestic

	Element number	Summary Rating	Climate change	Water extraction	Mineral resource extraction	Stratospheric ozone depletion	Human toxicity	Ecotoxicity to freshwater	Nuclear waste (higher level)	Ecotoxicity to land	Waste disposal	Fossil fuel depletion	Eutrophication	Photochemical ozone creation	Acidification	Typical replacement interval	Embodied CO2 (kg CO2 eq.)	Recycled content (kg)	Recycled content (%)	Recycled currently at EOL (%)
In situ reinforced concrete slab (cont'd):																				
polymer modified polyester reinforced bitumen roofing membranes, insulation, paving slabs	812530039	E	E	D	E	D	A	B	D	E	C	D	E	C	E	50	260	42	4	89
polymer modified polyester reinforced bitumen roofing membranes, insulation, rounded pebbles	812530040	D	D	D	D	C	A	B	C	D	C	D	D	C	D	50	230	36	4	89
PVC single ply roofing membrane, insulation, paving slabs	812530041	E	E	E	E	E	B	B	E	E	C	E	E	D	E	35	290	43	4	89
PVC single ply roofing membrane, insulation, rounded pebbles	812530042	D	D	E	E	D	A	B	D	D	C	D	D	C	D	35	240	36	4	89
TPO single ply roofing membrane, insulation, paving slabs	812530043	E	E	E	E	D	A	B	E	E	C	E	E	D	E	35	290	43	4	89
TPO single ply roofing membrane, insulation, rounded pebbles	812530044	D	D	E	E	C	A	B	D	D	C	D	D	C	D	35	240	36	4	89
Precast prestressed concrete hollow slab, with screed:																				
EPDM single ply roofing membrane, insulation, paving slabs	812530068	D	E	D	D	E	A	B	E	D	C	D	E	D	E	35	250	15	2	89
EPDM single ply roofing membrane, insulation, rounded pebbles	812530069	C	D	D	C	D	A	A	D	C	B	C	D	C	D	35	210	9.4	1	87
mastic asphalt roofing, insulation, paving slabs	812530007	E	D	C	D	E	A	C	D	C	E	E	E	D	D	50	240	14	2	83
mastic asphalt roofing, insulation, rounded pebbles	812530070	D	D	C	D	D	A	C	C	C	D	D	D	C	D	50	210	9.3	1	82
oxidised polyester reinforced bitumen roofing membranes, insulation, paving slabs	812530071	D	E	D	D	E	B	B	E	D	C	E	E	D	E	35	260	15	2	89
oxidised polyester reinforced bitumen roofing membranes, insulation, rounded pebbles	812530072	C	D	D	C	D	A	B	D	C	C	D	D	C	D	35	210	9.4	1	86
polymer modified polyester reinforced bitumen roofing membranes, insulation, paving slabs	812530073	D	D	C	D	D	A	B	C	D	C	D	D	C	D	50	230	14	2	89
polymer modified polyester reinforced bitumen roofing membranes, insulation, rounded pebbles	812530074	C	C	C	C	D	A	B	C	C	B	D	D	C	C	50	190	9.3	1	86

Cont'd . . . .

Flat roofs: inverted deck
Domestic

	Element number	Summary Rating	Climate change	Water extraction	Mineral resource extraction	Stratospheric ozone depletion	Human toxicity	Ecotoxicity to freshwater	Nuclear waste (higher level)	Ecotoxicity to land	Waste disposal	Fossil fuel depletion	Eutrophication	Photochemical ozone creation	Acidification	Typical replacement interval	Embodied CO$_2$ (kg CO$_2$ eq.)	Recycled content (kg)	Recycled content (%)	Recycled currently at EOL (%)
Precast prestressed concrete hollow slab, with screed (cont'd):																				
PVC single ply roofing membrane, insulation, paving slabs	812530077	D	E	D	D	E	B	B	D	D	C	D	E	D	E	35	260	15	2	89
PVC single ply roofing membrane, insulation, rounded pebbles	812530078	C	D	D	C	E	A	B	C	C	B	D	D	C	D	35	210	9.4	1	87
TPO single ply roofing membrane, insulation, paving slabs	812530075	D	E	D	D	E	A	B	D	D	C	D	E	D	E	35	250	15	2	89
TPO single ply roofing membrane, insulation, rounded pebbles	812530076	C	D	D	C	D	A	B	C	C	B	D	D	C	D	35	210	9.4	1	87
Profiled metal 'deep' decking with in situ concrete:																				
EPDM single ply roofing membrane, insulation, paving slabs	812530058	D	E	E	D	D	A	B	E	D	C	D	D	D	D	35	260	28	4	89
EPDM single ply roofing membrane, insulation, rounded pebbles	812530059	C	D	D	C	C	A	A	D	C	B	C	C	C	C	35	220	21	4	89
felt isolating layer, mastic asphalt roofing, insulation, paving slabs	812530004	E	D	D	D	D	A	C	D	D	E	E	D	C	D	50	250	27	4	83
felt isolating layer, mastic asphalt roofing, insulation, rounded pebbles	812530057	D	D	C	C	C	A	B	C	C	E	D	C	C	C	50	220	21	3	82
oxidised polyester reinforced bitumen roofing membranes, insulation, paving slabs	812530060	D	E	E	D	D	A	B	E	D	C	E	E	D	E	35	270	28	4	89
oxidised polyester reinforced bitumen roofing membranes, insulation, rounded pebbles	812530061	D	D	E	C	C	A	B	D	D	C	D	C	C	D	35	220	21	4	89
polymer modified polyester reinforced bitumen roofing membranes, paving slabs	812530062	D	D	D	C	C	A	A	D	D	C	D	D	C	D	50	230	27	4	89
polymer modified polyester reinforced bitumen roofing membranes, rounded pebbles	812530063	C	D	D	C	C	A	A	C	C	B	D	C	B	C	50	200	21	4	89
PVC single ply roofing membrane, insulation, paving slabs	812530064	D	E	E	D	D	A	B	E	D	C	D	D	D	D	35	270	28	4	89
PVC single ply roofing membrane, insulation, rounded pebbles	812530065	C	D	E	C	C	A	A	D	C	B	D	C	C	C	35	220	21	4	89
TPO single ply roofing membrane, insulation, paving slabs	812530066	D	E	E	D	D	A	B	E	D	C	D	D	D	E	35	260	28	4	89
TPO single ply roofing membrane, insulation, rounded pebbles	812530067	C	D	D	C	C	A	A	D	C	B	D	C	C	C	35	220	21	4	89

Flat roofs: inverted deck

Domestic

	Element number	Summary Rating	Climate change	Water extraction	Mineral resource extraction	Stratospheric ozone depletion	Human toxicity	Ecotoxicity to freshwater	Nuclear waste (higher level)	Ecotoxicity to land	Waste disposal	Fossil fuel depletion	Eutrophication	Photochemical ozone creation	Acidification	Typical replacement interval	Embodied CO_2 (kg CO_2 eq.)	Recycled content (kg)	Recycled content (%)	Recycled currently at EOL (%)
Structural steel trusses, galvanised steel purlins and deck, plywood (temperate EN 636-2) decking:																				
EPDM single ply roofing membrane, insulation, paving slabs	812530079	C	C	E	B	C	A	B	E	D	B	D	C	C	C	35	190	16.3	9	75
EPDM single ply roofing membrane, insulation, rounded pebbles	812530080	B	B	D	A	B	A	A	E	C	A	C	B	B	B	35	140	9.7	9	64
felt isolating layer, mastic asphalt roofing, insulation, paving slabs	812530085	C	C	D	A	C	A	C	D	D	D	D	C	C	C	50	180	14	7	61
felt isolating layer, mastic asphalt roofing, insulation, rounded pebbles	812530086	C	B	C	A	B	A	B	D	C	D	C	B	B	B	50	140	9.6	6	46
oxidised polyester reinforced bitumen roofing membrane, insulation, paving slabs	812530001	C	C	E	B	C	B	B	E	E	B	D	C	C	C	35	200	16.3	8	72
oxidised polyester reinforced bitumen roofing membranes, insulation, rounded pebbles	812530025	B	C	D	A	B	A	B	D	D	B	C	B	B	B	35	150	9.7	8	59
polymer modified polyester reinforced bitumen roofing membranes, insulation, paving slabs	812530002	B	C	D	A	B	A	B	D	D	B	C	B	B	B	50	160	15.3	9	70
polymer modified polyester reinforced bitumen roofing membranes, insulation, rounded pebbles	812530026	B	B	C	A+	B	A	A	D	C	B	C	A	B	B	50	130	9.6	8	60
PVC single ply roofing membrane, insulation, paving slabs	812530081	C	C	E	B	C	A	B	E	D	B	D	C	C	C	35	200	16.3	9	75
PVC single ply roofing membrane, insulation, rounded pebbles	812530082	B	B	D	A	C	A	A	D	D	A	C	B	C	B	35	150	9.7	9	63
TPO single ply roofing membrane, insulation, paving slabs	812530083	C	C	E	B	C	A	B	E	D	B	D	C	C	C	35	190	16.3	9	75
TPO single ply roofing membrane, insulation, rounded pebbles	812530084	B	B	D	A	B	A	A	D	D	A	C	B	B	B	35	150	9.7	9	63
Timber joists, OSB/3 decking:																				
EPDM single ply roofing membrane, insulation, paving slabs	812530087	A	A	B	A	B	A	A	B	A	A	B	B	B	A	35	97	17	10	74
EPDM single ply roofing membrane, insulation, rounded pebbles	812530088	A+	A+	A	A+	A	A+	A+	A	A+	A	A+	A	A+	A+	35	50	10.8	11	55
oxidised polyester reinforced bitumen roofing membranes, waterproof rigid insulation, paving slabs	812530024	A	B	B	A	C	A	A	B	A	A	B	B	B	B	35	100	17.4	10	68

Cont'd . . . .

Flat roofs: inverted deck
Domestic

	Element number	Summary Rating	Climate change	Water extraction	Mineral resource extraction	Stratospheric ozone depletion	Human toxicity	Ecotoxicity to freshwater	Nuclear waste (higher level)	Ecotoxicity to land	Waste disposal	Fossil fuel depletion	Eutrophication	Photochemical ozone creation	Acidification	Typical replacement interval	Embodied CO$_2$ (kg CO$_2$ eq.)	Recycled content (kg)	Recycled content (%)	Recycled currently at EOL (%)
Timber joists, OSB/3 decking (cont'd):																				
oxidised polyester reinforced bitumen roofing membranes, waterproof rigid insulation, rounded pebbles	812530023	A	A	B	A+	B	A	A	A	A	A	B	A	A	A	35	58	10.8	10	51
polymer modified polyester reinforced bitumen roofing membranes, waterproof rigid insulation, paving stones	812530022	A	A	A	A	B	A	A	B	A	A	B	A	A	A	50	80	16.5	10	65
polymer modified polyester reinforced bitumen roofing membranes, waterproof rigid insulation, rounded pebbles	812530021	A+	A+	A	A+	A	A	A	A	A	A	A	A	A	A	45	43	10.8	10	51
PVC single ply roofing membrane, insulation, paving slabs	812530089	A	B	B	A	C	A	A	B	A	A	B	B	B	A	35	100	17	10	74
PVC single ply roofing membrane, insulation, rounded pebbles	812530090	A+	A	B	A+	B	A+	A	A	A+	A	A	A+	A	A+	35	56	10.8	11	55
TPO single ply roofing membrane, insulation, paving slabs	812530091	A	A	B	A	B	A	A	B	A	A	B	B	B	B	35	99	17	10	74
TPO single ply roofing membrane, insulation, rounded pebbles	812530092	A+	A	A	A+	A	A+	A	A	A+	A	A	A+	A	A	35	52	10.8	11	55
Timber joists, plywood (temperate EN 636-2) decking:																				
EPDM single ply roofing membrane, insulation, paving slabs	812530093	A	B	B	A	C	A	A	C	C	A	B	B	B	B	35	100	9.9	6	74
EPDM single ply roofing membrane, insulation, rounded pebbles	812530094	A	A	B	A+	B	A	A	B	B	A	A	A	A	A	35	56	4	4	55
oxidised polyester reinforced bitumen roofing membrane, insulation, paving slabs	812530013	B	B	C	A	C	A	B	C	C	A	C	B	B	B	35	110	10.6	6	68
oxidised polyester reinforced bitumen roofing membranes, insulation, rounded pebbles	812530016	A	A	B	A+	B	A	A	B	B	A	B	A	A	A	35	63	4	4	51
polymer modified polyester reinforced bitumen roofing membranes, insulation, paving stones	812530006	A	A	B	A	B	A	A	C	C	A	B	B	B	A	50	85	9.7	6	65
polymer modified polyester reinforced bitumen roofing membranes, insulation, rounded pebbles	812530005	A	A	B	A+	B	A	A	B	B	A	A	A	A	A	50	54	4	4	51

Cont'd . . . .

Flat roofs: inverted deck / Domestic	Element number	Summary Rating	Climate change	Water extraction	Mineral resource extraction	Stratospheric ozone depletion	Human toxicity	Ecotoxicity to freshwater	Nuclear waste (higher level)	Ecotoxicity to land	Waste disposal	Fossil fuel depletion	Eutrophication	Photochemical ozone creation	Acidification	Typical replacement interval	Embodied CO₂ (kg CO₂ eq.)	Recycled content (kg)	Recycled content (%)	Recycled currently at EOL (%)
Timber joists, plywood (temperate EN 636-2) decking (cont'd):																				
PVC single ply roofing membrane, insulation, paving slabs	812530095	B	B	C	A	C	A	B	C	C	A	B	B	B	B	35	110	9.9	6	74
PVC single ply roofing membrane, insulation, rounded pebbles	812530096	A	A	B	A+	B	A	A	B	B	A	A	A	B	A	35	61	4	4	55
TPO single ply roofing membrane, insulation, paving slabs	812530097	A	B	B	A	C	A	B	C	C	A	B	B	B	B	35	100	9.9	6	74
TPO single ply roofing membrane, insulation, rounded pebbles	812530098	A	A	B	A+	B	A	A	B	B	A	A	A	A	A	35	58	4	4	55

Embodied CO_2 (kg CO_2 eq.)

Flat roofs: warm deck

Domestic

	Element number	Summary Rating	Climate change	Water extraction	Mineral resource extraction	Stratospheric ozone depletion	Human toxicity	Ecotoxicity to freshwater	Nuclear waste (higher level)	Ecotoxicity to land	Waste disposal	Fossil fuel depletion	Eutrophication	Photochemical ozone creation	Acidification	Typical replacement interval	Embodied CO2 (kg CO2 eq.)	Recycled content (kg)	Recycled content (%)	Recycled currently at EOL (%)
Beam and dense block deck:																				
vapour control layer, insulation, EPDM single ply roofing membrane	812540069	B	B	A	B	C	A+	A	A	A	A	B	B	B	B	35	130	6.2	1	88
vapour control layer, insulation, felt isolating layer, mastic asphalt roofing	812540070	C	B	A	C	C	A	B	A	A	D	C	C	B	B	50	140	6.2	1	81
vapour control layer, insulation, oxidised polyester reinforced bitumen roofing membranes with mineral finish	812540049	B	B	A	B	C	A	A	A	B	B	B	B	B	B	35	140	6.2	1	88
vapour control layer, insulation, polymer modified polyester reinforced bitumen roofing membranes with mineral finish	812540071	B	B	A	B	C	A	A	A	A	A	B	B	B	B	50	130	6.2	1	88
vapour control layer, insulation, PVC single ply roofing membrane	812540072	B	B	A	B	C	A	A	A	A	A	B	B	B	B	35	130	6.2	1	88
vapour control layer, insulation, TPO single ply roofing membrane	812540073	B	B	A	B	C	A+	A	A	A	A	B	B	B	B	35	130	6.2	1	88
In situ reinforced concrete slab with 50% GGBS and 20% recycled coarse aggregate:																				
vapour control layer, insulation, EPDM single ply roofing membrane	812540074	C	C	B	C	B	A+	A	B	B	B	B	B	B	B	35	150	137	15	89
vapour control layer, insulation, felt isolating layer, mastic asphalt roofing	812540075	D	C	B	D	C	A	B	A	C	E	C	C	B	B	50	170	137	15	85
vapour control layer, insulation, oxidised polyester reinforced bitumen roofing membranes with mineral finish	812540076	C	C	B	C	B	A	A	B	C	C	C	B	B	B	35	160	137	15	89
vapour control layer, insulation, polymer modified polyester reinforced bitumen roofing membranes with mineral finish	812540077	C	C	B	C	B	A	A	A	C	C	B	B	B	B	50	150	137	15	89
vapour control layer, insulation, PVC single ply roofing membrane	812540078	C	C	B	C	C	A+	A	A	C	B	B	B	B	B	35	160	137	15	89
vapour control layer, insulation, TPO single ply roofing membrane	812540079	C	C	B	C	B	A+	A	A	C	B	B	B	B	B	35	160	137	15	89
In situ reinforced concrete slab:																				
vapour control layer, insulation, EPDM single ply roofing membrane	812540025	C	C	C	D	B	A	A	B	C	B	B	C	B	C	35	200	36	4	89
vapour control layer, insulation, felt isolating layer, mastic asphalt roofing	812540021	D	D	B	D	C	A	B	B	C	E	D	C	B	C	50	210	36	4	85

Cont'd . . . .

Flat roofs: warm deck

Domestic

	Element number	Summary Rating	Climate change	Water extraction	Mineral resource extraction	Stratospheric ozone depletion	Human toxicity	Ecotoxicity to freshwater	Nuclear waste (higher level)	Ecotoxicity to land	Waste disposal	Fossil fuel depletion	Eutrophication	Photochemical ozone creation	Acidification	Typical replacement interval	Embodied CO$_2$ (kg CO$_2$ eq.)	Recycled content (kg)	Recycled content (%)	Recycled currently at EOL (%)
In situ reinforced concrete slab (cont'd):																				
vapour control layer, insulation, oxidised polyester reinforced bitumen roofing membranes with mineral finish	812540022	C	D	C	D	B	A	A	B	D	C	C	C	B	C	35	200	36	4	89
vapour control layer, insulation, polymer modified polyester reinforced bitumen roofing membranes with mineral finish	812540023	C	C	B	D	B	A	A	B	C	C	C	C	B	C	50	200	36	4	89
vapour control layer, insulation, PVC single ply roofing membrane	812540026	C	D	C	D	C	A	A	B	C	B	B	C	B	C	35	200	36	4	89
vapour control layer, insulation, TPO single ply roofing membrane	812540027	C	D	C	D	B	A	A	B	C	B	B	C	B	C	35	200	36	4	89
Precast concrete formwork with lattice reinforcement and in situ concrete:																				
vapour control layer, insulation, EPDM single ply waterproofing membrane	812540024	C	C	B	C	B	A	A	B	C	B	B	C	B	C	35	180	25	3	89
vapour control layer, insulation, mastic asphalt roofing	812540011	D	C	B	D	C	A	B	B	C	D	C	C	B	C	50	190	25	3	84
vapour control layer, insulation, oxidised polyester reinforced bitumen roofing membranes with mineral finish	812540016	C	C	B	C	C	A	A	B	C	B	C	C	B	C	35	190	25	3	89
vapour control layer, insulation, polymer modified polyester reinforced bitumen roofing membranes with mineral finish	812540017	C	C	B	C	B	A	A	B	C	B	C	C	B	C	50	180	25	3	89
vapour control layer, insulation, PVC single ply waterproofing membrane	812540012	C	C	B	C	C	A	A	B	C	B	B	C	B	C	35	180	25	3	89
vapour control layer, insulation, TPO single ply waterproofing membrane	812540013	C	C	B	C	B	A	A	B	C	B	B	C	B	C	35	180	25	3	89
Precast prestressed concrete hollow slab, with screed:																				
vapour control layer, insulation, EPDM single ply waterproofing membrane	812540033	B	C	A	C	C	A	A	B	B	A	B	C	B	C	35	170	8.4	1	88
vapour control layer, insulation, felt isolating layer, mastic asphalt roofing	812540030	C	C	A	C	D	A	B	B	B	D	C	C	B	C	50	180	8.4	1	82

Cont'd . . . .

Flat roofs: warm deck

Domestic

	Element number	Summary Rating	Climate change	Water extraction	Mineral resource extraction	Stratospheric ozone depletion	Human toxicity	Ecotoxicity to freshwater	Nuclear waste (higher level)	Ecotoxicity to land	Waste disposal	Fossil fuel depletion	Eutrophication	Photochemical ozone creation	Acidification	Typical replacement interval	Embodied CO2 (kg CO2 eq.)	Recycled content (kg)	Recycled content (%)	Recycled currently at EOL (%)
Precast prestressed concrete hollow slab, with screed (cont'd):																				
vapour control layer, insulation, oxidised polyester reinforced bitumen roofing membranes with mineral finish	812540031	C	C	B	C	C	A	A	B	C	B	C	C	B	C	35	170	8.4	1	89
vapour control layer, insulation, polymer modified polyester reinforced bitumen roofing membranes with mineral finish	812540032	B	C	A	C	C	A	A	B	B	B	C	C	B	C	50	170	8.4	1	89
vapour control layer, insulation, PVC single ply waterproofing membrane	812540034	B	C	B	C	D	A	A	B	B	A	B	C	B	C	35	170	8.4	1	88
vapour control layer, insulation, TPO single ply waterproofing membrane	812540035	B	C	A	C	C	A	A	B	B	A	B	C	B	C	35	170	8.4	1	88
Profiled metal 'deep' decking with in situ concrete:																				
vapour control layer, insulation, EPDM single ply roofing membrane	812540080	B	C	B	B	B	A+	A	B	B	B	B	B	B	B	35	170	21	4	88
vapour control layer, insulation, felt isolating layer, mastic asphalt roofing	812540038	C	C	B	C	B	A	B	B	B	D	C	C	B	C	50	190	21	4	81
vapour control layer, insulation, oxidised polyester reinforced bitumen roofing membranes with mineral finish	812540081	C	C	B	B	B	A	A	B	C	B	C	B	B	C	35	180	21	4	89
vapour control layer, insulation, polymer modified polyester reinforced bitumen roofing membranes with mineral finish	812540039	B	C	B	B	B	A	A	B	B	B	C	B	B	B	50	180	21	4	89
vapour control layer, insulation, PVC single ply roofing membrane	812540082	B	C	B	B	B	A+	A	B	B	B	B	B	B	B	35	180	21	4	88
vapour control layer, insulation, TPO single ply roofing membrane	812540083	B	C	B	B	B	A+	A	B	B	B	B	B	B	B	35	180	21	4	88
Structural steel trusses, galvanised steel purlins and deck:																				
vapour control layer, insulation, EPDM single ply roofing membrane	812540001	A+	A	A+	A+	A+	A+	A+	A	A+	A+	A+	A+	A+	A+	35	81	7.2	25	47
vapour control layer, insulation, felt isolating layer, mastic asphalt roofing	812540002	A	A	A+	A+	A	A+	A	A	A+	C	B	A+	A+	A+	50	98	6.9	9	22
vapour control layer, insulation, oxidised polyester reinforced bitumen roofing membranes with mineral finish	812540009	A+	A	A	A+	A+	A+	A+	A	A	A	A	A+	A+	A+	35	89	7.2	20	38

Cont'd . . . .

Flat roofs: warm deck

Domestic

	Element number	Summary Rating	Climate change	Water extraction	Mineral resource extraction	Stratospheric ozone depletion	Human toxicity	Ecotoxicity to freshwater	Nuclear waste (higher level)	Ecotoxicity to land	Waste disposal	Fossil fuel depletion	Eutrophication	Photochemical ozone creation	Acidification	Typical replacement interval	Embodied CO2 (kg CO2 eq.)	Recycled content (kg)	Recycled content (%)	Recycled currently at EOL (%)
Structural steel trusses, galvanised steel purlins and deck (cont'd):																				
vapour control layer, insulation, polymer modified polyester reinforced bitumen roofing membranes with mineral finish	812540010	A+	A	A+	A+	A+	A+	A+	A	A+	A+	A	A+	A+	A+	50	86	7.2	20	37
vapour control layer, insulation, PVC single ply waterproofing membrane	812540003	A+	A	A	A+	A	A+	A+	A	A+	A+	A+	A+	A+	A+	35	87	7.2	25	47
vapour control layer, insulation, TPO single ply waterproofing membrane	812540004	A+	A	A+	A+	A+	A+	A+	A	A+	A+	A+	A+	A+	A+	35	84	7.2	25	47
Timber joists, OSB/3 decking:																				
vapour control layer, insulation, EPDM single ply waterproofing membrane	812540057	A+	A+	A+	A+	A	A+	A+	A	A+	A+	A+	A+	A+	A+	35	26	10.5	27	12
vapour control layer, insulation, felt isolating layer, mastic asphalt roofing	812540051	A	A+	A+	A+	A	A+	A	A+	A+	C	A	A+	A+	A+	50	42	10	12	8
vapour control layer, insulation, oxidised polyester reinforced bitumen roofing membranes with mineral finish	812540041	A+	A+	A+	A+	A	A+	A+	A	A+	A+	A	A+	A+	A+	35	33	10.5	23	10
vapour control layer, insulation, polymer modified polyester reinforced bitumen roofing membranes with mineral finish	812540052	A+	A+	A+	A+	A	A+	A+	A+	A+	A+	A	A+	A+	A+	50	29	10.5	22	10
vapour control layer, insulation, PVC single ply waterproofing membrane	812540058	A+	A+	A+	A+	A	A+	A+	A+	A+	A+	A+	A+	A+	A+	35	31	10.5	27	11
vapour control layer, insulation, TPO single ply waterproofing membrane	812540059	A+	A+	A+	A+	A	A+	A+	A+	A+	A+	A+	A+	A+	A+	35	28	10.5	27	12
Timber joists, plywood (temperate EN 636-2) decking:																				
vapour control layer, insulation, EPDM single ply waterproofing membrane	812540042	A+	A+	A+	A+	A	A+	A	A	A	A+	A+	A+	A+	A+	35	31	3.7	10	11
vapour control layer, insulation, felt isolating layer, mastic asphalt roofing	812540048	A	A+	A+	A+	B	A	B	A	B	C	A	A	A	A+	50	47	3.7	4	8
vapour control layer, insulation, oxidised polyester reinforced bitumen roofing membranes with mineral finish	812540047	A+	A+	A	A+	A	A	A	A	B	A+	A	A+	A	A+	35	39	3.7	8	10

Cont'd . . . .

Flat roofs: warm deck **Domestic**	Element number	**Summary Rating**	Climate change	Water extraction	Mineral resource extraction	Stratospheric ozone depletion	Human toxicity	Ecotoxicity to freshwater	Nuclear waste (higher level)	Ecotoxicity to land	Waste disposal	Fossil fuel depletion	Eutrophication	Photochemical ozone creation	Acidification	Typical replacement interval	Embodied CO$_2$ (kg CO$_2$ eq.)	Recycled content (kg)	Recycled content (%)	Recycled currently at EOL (%)
Timber joists, plywood (temperate EN 636-2) decking:																				
vapour control layer, insulation, polymer modified polyester reinforced bitumen roofing membranes with mineral finish	812540050	A+	A+	A+	A+	A	A	A	A	B	A+	A	A+	A	A+	50	35	3.7	8	9
vapour control layer, insulation, PVC single ply waterproofing membrane	812540043	A+	A+	A	A+	B	A	A	A	B	A+	A+	A+	A	A+	35	37	3.7	9	11
vapour control layer, insulation, TPO single ply roofing membrane	812540055	A+	A+	A+	A+	A	A	A	A	B	A+	A+	A+	A+	A+	35	33	3.7	10	11

Low pitched roofs Domestic	Element number	Summary Rating	Climate change	Water extraction	Mineral resource extraction	Stratospheric ozone depletion	Human toxicity	Ecotoxicity to freshwater	Nuclear waste (higher level)	Ecotoxicity to land	Waste disposal	Fossil fuel depletion	Eutrophication	Photochemical ozone creation	Acidification	Typical replacement interval	Embodied CO2 (kg CO2 eq.)	Recycled content (kg)	Recycled content (%)	Recycled currently at EOL (%)
Galvanised steel rafters and joists:																				
composite profiled roof cladding (steel inner lining, pentane blown PUR/PIR insulation, coated aluminium outer skin)	812550014	A	B	C	A+	A	B	B	A	B	A+	A	A	B	A	35	110	7.8	30	47
composite profiled roof cladding (steel inner lining, pentane blown PUR/PIR insulation, coated steel outer skin)	812550001	A+	B	D	A+	A+	A+	A+	A+	A	A+	A	A	B	A	35	100	6.9	24	52
double skin built up profiled roof cladding (coated aluminium inner and outer skin, insulation)	812550013	A	B	A	A+	A	E	E	D	B	A+	A	A+	A+	A	35	120	10.7	36	44
double skin built up profiled roof cladding (coated steel inner and outer skin, insulation)	812550016	A	B	B	A+	A+	A+	A+	B	A+	A+	A	A+	A	A	35	110	7.8	23	51
double skin built up profiled roof cladding (mill finished aluminium inner and outer skin, insulation)	812550018	A+	A	A+	A+	A+	B	D	C	A+	A+	A+	A+	A+	A	50	92	10.7	36	44
double skin built up roof cladding (aluminium inner lining, insulation, mill finished aluminium standing seam outer skin)	812550002	A	B	A	A+	A	E	E	D	B	A+	A	A+	A+	A	35	120	10.7	36	44
double skin built up roof cladding (steel inner lining, insulation, coated aluminium standing seam outer skin)	812550007	A	B	B	A+	A	D	D	D	B	A+	A	A+	A	A	35	120	9.6	31	46
double skin built up roof cladding (steel inner lining, insulation, copper standing seam outer skin)	812550019	A	A	C	B	A	A+	A+	C	A+	A+	A	A+	A+	A+	45	100	11.5	33	52
double skin built up roof cladding (steel inner lining, insulation, mill finished aluminium standing seam outer skin)	812550034	A+	A	A	A+	A+	A	B	B	A+	A+	A+	A+	A+	A+	50	91	9.6	31	46

Pitched roofs: steel construction

Domestic

	Element number	Summary Rating	Climate change	Water extraction	Mineral resource extraction	Stratospheric ozone depletion	Human toxicity	Ecotoxicity to freshwater	Nuclear waste (higher level)	Ecotoxicity to land	Waste disposal	Fossil fuel depletion	Eutrophication	Photochemical ozone creation	Acidification	Typical replacement interval	Embodied CO2 (kg CO2 eq.)	Recycled content (kg)	Recycled content (%)	Recycled currently at EOL (%)
Galvanised steel rafters and joists with insulation:																				
battens, breather membrane, plywood (temperate EN 636-2) decking, standing seam copper roof	812150015	A	A	D	A	B	B	B	E	E	A+	A	A	A	A	45	72	10.8	21	28
roofing underlay, counterbattens, battens and concrete interlocking tiles	812150004	A+	A	A+	A+	A+	A+	A+	A	A+	A+	A+	A+	A	A+	60+	72	6.5	7	68
roofing underlay, counterbattens, battens and concrete plain tiles	812150005	A+	A	A+	A+	A	A+	A+	A	A	A+	A+	A+	A+	A+	60+	87	6.5	5	75
roofing underlay, counterbattens, battens and photovoltaic roofing tiles	812150007	A+	A+	A+	A+	A	A+	A	A+	A+	B	A+	A+	D	A+	25	49	6.5	12	15
roofing underlay, counterbattens, battens and polymer modified cement slates	812150010	A	B	A	A+	B	A	C	D	A	A	A	B	B	A	40	110	19.1	32	13
roofing underlay, counterbattens, battens and reclaimed clay tiles	812150012	A+	A+	A+	A+	A	A+	A+	A+	A+	A+	A+	A+	B	A+	50	46	88.3	77	71
roofing underlay, counterbattens, battens and reclaimed slates	812150011	A+	A+	A+	A+	A+	A+	A+	A+	A+	A+	A+	A+	A	A+	50	48	49.7	68	63
roofing underlay, counterbattens, battens and resin bonded slates	812150009	A	B	B	A+	B	A	E	D	C	A	A	A	B	A	40	110	14.6	30	15
roofing underlay, counterbattens, battens and UK produced clay plain tiles	812150001	A	A	A+	A	A	A+	A+	B	A+	A+	A	A+	B	A+	60+	97	6.5	6	71
roofing underlay, counterbattens, battens and UK produced fibre cement slates	812150013	A	B	A	A+	A	A+	A	B	A	A+	A	A	B	A	40	110	6.5	12	13
roofing underlay, counterbattens, battens and UK produced slate	812150008	A	A	A+	C	A	A+	A	A	A+	A+	A+	A	A	A	60+	68	6.5	9	64

Pitched roofs: timber construction

Domestic

	Element number	Summary Rating	Climate change	Water extraction	Mineral resource extraction	Stratospheric ozone depletion	Human toxicity	Ecotoxicity to freshwater	Nuclear waste (higher level)	Ecotoxicity to land	Waste disposal	Fossil fuel depletion	Eutrophication	Photochemical ozone creation	Acidification	Typical replacement interval	Embodied CO$_2$ (kg CO$_2$ eq.)	Recycled content (kg)	Recycled content (%)	Recycled currently at EOL (%)
Structurally insulated timber panel system with OSB/3 each side:																				
roofing underlay, counterbattens, battens and concrete interlocking tiles	812410018	A+	A+	A	A+	A	A+	A+	A+	A	A	A+	A	B	A	60+	28	18	15	50
roofing underlay, counterbattens, battens and concrete plain tiles	812410064	A+	A+	B	A+	A	A+	A+	A+	A	A	A	A	B	A	60+	44	18	12	59
roofing underlay, counterbattens, battens and photovoltaic roofing tiles	812410068	A+	A+	A	A+	B	A+	A	A+	A	B	A+	A	E	A+	25	6	18	22	8
roofing underlay, counterbattens, battens and polymer modified cement slates	812410066	A	A	C	A+	B	A	B	D	B	B	B	B	C	B	35	68	30	34	7
roofing underlay, counterbattens, battens and reclaimed clay tiles	812410025	A+	A+	A	A+	A	A+	A+	A+	A+	A	A+	A+	C	A+	50	1.7	100	69	56
roofing underlay, counterbattens, battens and reclaimed slates	812410067	A+	A+	A	A+	A	A+	A+	A+	A+	A	A+	A+	B	A+	50	3.8	61	60	44
roofing underlay, counterbattens, battens and resin bonded slates	812410022	A	A	D	A+	B	B	D	C	C	B	B	B	C	B	35	69	26	33	8
roofing underlay, counterbattens, battens and UK produced clay plain tiles	812410069	A	A	B	A+	B	A+	A+	B	A	A	A	A	C	A	60+	53	18	12	56
roofing underlay, counterbattens, battens and UK produced fibre cement slates	812410065	A	A	C	A+	B	A+	A+	B	A	A	A	A	C	A	30	64	18	21	7
roofing underlay, counterbattens, battens and UK produced slate	812410021	A	A+	A	C	B	A+	A+	A+	A+	A	A+	A	B	B	60+	25	18	18	44
Structurally insulated timber panel system with plywood (temperate EN 636-2) decking each side:																				
roofing underlay, counterbattens, battens and concrete interlocking tiles	812410049	A+	A+	B	A+	B	A	A+	A	C	A+	A+	A	B	A	60+	40	4	4	54
roofing underlay, counterbattens, battens and concrete plain tiles	812410050	A+	A	B	A+	B	A	A+	A	C	A	A	A	B	A	60+	55	4	3	63
roofing underlay, counterbattens, battens and photovoltaic roofing tiles	812410052	A+	A+	B	A+	B	A	A	A	B	B	A+	A	E	A	25	18	4	6	9
roofing underlay, counterbattens, battens and polymer modified cement slates	812410053	A	A	C	A+	C	A	C	D	D	B	B	C	D	B	35	79	17	21	8

Cont'd . . . .

Pitched roofs: timber construction

Domestic

	Element number	Summary Rating	Climate change	Water extraction	Mineral resource extraction	Stratospheric ozone depletion	Human toxicity	Ecotoxicity to freshwater	Nuclear waste (higher level)	Ecotoxicity to land	Waste disposal	Fossil fuel depletion	Eutrophication	Photochemical ozone creation	Acidification	Typical replacement interval	Embodied CO₂ (kg CO₂ eq.)	Recycled content (kg)	Recycled content (%)	Recycled currently at EOL (%)
Structurally insulated timber panel system with plywood (temperate EN 636-2) decking each side (cont'd):																				
roofing underlay, counterbattens, battens and reclaimed clay tiles	812410054	A+	A+	B	A+	B	A	A+	A+	B	A	A+	A+	C	A+	50	14	86	64	60
roofing underlay, counterbattens, battens and reclaimed slates	812410055	A+	A+	A	A+	A	A	A+	A+	B	A+	A+	A+	B	A+	50	15	47	51	48
roofing underlay, counterbattens, battens and resin bonded slates	812410056	A	A	D	A+	C	B	E	D	E	A	B	B	D	B	35	81	12	17	9
roofing underlay, counterbattens, battens and UK produced clay plain tiles	812410058	A	A	B	A	B	A	A+	B	B	A	B	A	C	A	60+	65	4	3	60
roofing underlay, counterbattens, battens and UK produced fibre cement slates	812410051	A	A	C	A+	B	A	A	C	C	A	A	B	C	B	30	76	4	5	8
roofing underlay, counterbattens, battens and UK produced slate	812410057	A	A+	B	C	B	A	A	A	B	A+	A	B	B	B	60+	37	4	4	49
Timber trussed rafters and joists with insulation:																				
battens, breather membrane, plywood (temperate EN 636-2) decking, standing seam copper roof	812410020	A	A	D	A	B	B	B	E	D	A+	A	A	A	A	45	52	8.5	17	20
roofing underlay, counterbattens, battens and concrete interlocking tiles	812410007	A+	A	A+	A+	A	A+	A+	A+	A+	A+	A+	A+	A	A+	60+	52	4.2	5	63
roofing underlay, counterbattens, battens and concrete plain tiles	812410017	A+	A	A+	A+	A	A+	A+	A	A+	A+	A+	A+	A+	A+	60+	67	4.2	3	71
roofing underlay, counterbattens, battens and integrated photovoltaic roof tiles	812410014	A+	A+	A+	A+	A	A+	A	A+	A+	B	A+	A+	D	A+	25	29	4.2	8	7
roofing underlay, counterbattens, battens and polymer modified cement slates	812410011	A	A	A	A+	B	A	C	D	A	A	A	B	B	A	40	93	16.8	28	5
roofing underlay, counterbattens, battens and reclaimed clay tiles	812410013	A+	A+	A+	A+	A	A+	A+	A+	A+	A+	A+	A+	B	A+	50	26	85.9	75	67
roofing underlay, counterbattens, battens and reclaimed slates	812410012	A+	A+	A+	A+	A+	A+	A+	A+	A+	A+	A+	A+	A	A+	50	28	47.4	65	57
roofing underlay, counterbattens, battens and resin bonded slates	812410010	A	A	B	A+	B	A	E	C	C	A	A	A	B	A	40	94	12.2	25	6
roofing underlay, counterbattens, battens and UK produced clay plain tiles	812410006	A+	A	A+	A+	A	A+	A+	B	A+	A+	A	A+	A	A+	60+	77	4.2	4	67

Cont'd . . . .

Pitched roofs: timber construction **Domestic**	Element number	**Summary Rating**	Climate change	Water extraction	Mineral resource extraction	Stratospheric ozone depletion	Human toxicity	Ecotoxicity to freshwater	Nuclear waste (higher level)	Ecotoxicity to land	Waste disposal	Fossil fuel depletion	Eutrophication	Photochemical ozone creation	Acidification	Typical replacement interval	Embodied CO$_2$ (kg CO$_2$ eq.)	Recycled content (kg)	Recycled content (%)	Recycled currently at EOL (%)
Timber trussed rafters and joists with insulation (cont'd):																				
roofing underlay, counterbattens, battens and UK produced fibre cement slates	812410008	A+	A	A	A+	A	A+	A	B	A	A+	A	A	B	A	40	90	4.2	7	6
roofing underlay, counterbattens, battens and UK produced slates	812410026	A	A+	A+	C	A	A+	A	A	A+	A+	A+	A	A	A	60+	49	4.2	6	58

Flat roofs: inverted deck

Health & Retail

	Element number	Summary Rating	Climate change	Water extraction	Mineral resource extraction	Stratospheric ozone depletion	Human toxicity	Ecotoxicity to freshwater	Nuclear waste (higher level)	Ecotoxicity to land	Waste disposal	Fossil fuel depletion	Eutrophication	Photochemical ozone creation	Acidification	Typical replacement interval	Embodied CO₂ (kg CO₂ eq.)	Recycled content (kg)	Recycled content (%)	Recycled currently at EOL (%)
Beam and dense block deck:																				
EPDM single ply roofing membrane, insulation, paving slabs	812530009	D	D	D	D	E	A	B	D	C	B	D	E	D	D	35	220	12	2	90
EPDM single ply roofing membrane, insulation, rounded pebbles	812530028	C	C	C	C	D	A	A	C	B	B	C	C	C	C	35	180	6.2	1	88
felt isolating layer, mastic asphalt roofing, insulation, paving slabs	812530033	D	D	C	D	E	A	C	C	C	E	D	D	C	D	50	210	11.7	2	83
felt isolating layer, mastic asphalt roofing, insulation, rounded pebbles	812530034	D	C	C	C	D	A	B	B	B	D	D	D	C	C	50	180	6	1	83
oxidised polyester reinforced bitumen roofing membranes, insulation, paving slabs	812530014	D	D	D	D	E	B	B	D	D	C	E	E	D	E	35	230	12	2	90
oxidised polyester reinforced bitumen roofing membranes, insulation, rounded pebbles	812530012	C	C	D	C	D	A	B	C	C	B	D	D	C	C	35	190	6.2	1	87
polymer modified polyester reinforced bitumen roofing membranes, insulation, paving slabs	812530011	C	D	C	D	D	A	B	C	C	B	D	D	C	D	50	200	11	2	90
polymer modified polyester reinforced bitumen roofing membranes, insulation, rounded pebbles	812530010	C	C	C	C	D	A	A	B	B	B	C	C	C	C	50	170	6	1	87
PVC single ply roofing membrane, insulation, paving slabs	812530029	D	D	D	D	E	A	B	D	D	B	D	E	D	D	35	230	12	2	90
PVC single ply roofing membrane, insulation, rounded pebbles	812530030	C	C	D	C	E	A	B	C	C	B	C	D	C	C	35	180	6.2	1	88
TPO single ply roofing membrane, insulation, paving slabs	812530031	D	D	D	D	E	A	B	D	C	B	D	E	D	D	35	230	12	2	90
TPO single ply roofing membrane, insulation, rounded pebbles	812530032	C	C	C	C	D	A	A	C	C	B	C	D	C	C	35	180	6.2	1	88
In situ reinforced concrete with 50% GGBS and 20% recycled coarse aggregate:																				
EPDM single ply roofing membrane, insulation, paving slabs	812530045	E	E	E	E	D	A	B	D	D	C	D	D	D	D	35	240	153	15	89
EPDM single ply roofing membrane, insulation, rounded pebbles	812530046	D	D	E	D	C	A	A	C	C	C	C	C	C	C	35	190	147	15	89
felt isolating layer, mastic asphalt roofing, insulation, paving slabs	812530055	E	D	D	E	D	A	C	C	D	E	E	D	C	D	50	230	152	14	85
felt isolating layer, mastic asphalt roofing, insulation, rounded pebbles	812530056	D	D	D	D	C	A	B	C	C	E	D	C	C	C	50	200	146	15	85

Cont'd . . . .

Flat roofs: inverted deck

Health & Retail

	Element number	Summary Rating	Climate change	Water extraction	Mineral resource extraction	Stratospheric ozone depletion	Human toxicity	Ecotoxicity to freshwater	Nuclear waste (higher level)	Ecotoxicity to land	Waste disposal	Fossil fuel depletion	Eutrophication	Photochemical ozone creation	Acidification	Typical replacement interval	Embodied CO2 (kg CO2 eq.)	Recycled content (kg)	Recycled content (%)	Recycled currently at EOL (%)
In situ reinforced concrete with 50% GGBS and 20% recycled coarse aggregate (cont'd):																				
oxidised polyester reinforced bitumen roofing membranes, insulation, paving slabs	812530047	E	E	E	E	D	B	B	D	E	D	E	E	D	E	35	250	153	15	88
oxidised polyester reinforced bitumen roofing membranes, insulation, rounded pebbles	812530048	D	D	E	D	C	A	B	C	D	C	D	D	C	D	35	200	147	15	88
polymer modified polyester reinforced bitumen roofing membranes, insulation, paving slabs	812530049	D	D	D	D	D	A	B	C	D	C	D	D	C	D	50	210	152	15	88
polymer modified polyester reinforced bitumen roofing membranes, insulation, rounded pebbles	812530050	C	C	D	D	C	A	A	C	C	C	C	C	B	C	50	180	146	15	88
PVC single ply roofing membrane, insulation, paving slabs	812530051	E	E	E	E	E	A	B	D	D	C	D	E	D	D	35	250	153	15	89
PVC single ply roofing membrane, insulation, rounded pebbles	812530052	D	D	E	D	D	A	A	C	D	C	C	C	C	C	35	200	147	15	89
TPO single ply roofing membrane, insulation, paving slabs	812530053	E	E	E	E	D	A	B	D	D	C	D	E	D	E	35	240	153	15	89
TPO single ply roofing membrane, insulation, rounded pebbles	812530054	D	D	E	D	C	A	A	C	D	C	C	C	C	D	35	200	147	15	89
In situ reinforced concrete:																				
EPDM single ply roofing membrane, insulation, paving slabs	812530035	E	E	E	E	D	A	B	E	E	C	E	E	D	E	35	280	41	4	90
EPDM single ply roofing membrane, insulation, rounded pebbles	812530036	D	D	E	E	C	A	B	D	D	C	D	D	C	D	35	230	35	4	90
felt isolating layer, mastic asphalt roofing, insulation, paving slabs	812530003	E	E	D	E	D	A	C	D	E	E	E	E	D	E	50	270	40	4	86
felt isolating layer, mastic asphalt roofing, insulation, rounded pebbles	812530027	E	D	D	E	D	A	C	C	D	E	E	D	C	D	50	240	35	4	86
oxidised polyester reinforced bitumen roofing membranes, insulation, paving slabs	812530037	E	E	E	E	D	B	B	E	E	D	E	E	D	E	35	290	41	4	90
oxidised polyester reinforced bitumen roofing membranes, insulation, rounded pebbles	812530038	D	E	E	E	C	A	B	D	E	C	E	D	C	D	35	240	35	4	90

Cont'd . . . .

Flat roofs: inverted deck
Health & Retail

	Element number	Summary Rating	Climate change	Water extraction	Mineral resource extraction	Stratospheric ozone depletion	Human toxicity	Ecotoxicity to freshwater	Nuclear waste (higher level)	Ecotoxicity to land	Waste disposal	Fossil fuel depletion	Eutrophication	Photochemical ozone creation	Acidification	Typical replacement interval	Embodied CO2 (kg CO2 eq.)	Recycled content (kg)	Recycled content (%)	Recycled currently at EOL (%)
In situ reinforced concrete (cont'd):																				
polymer modified polyester reinforced bitumen roofing membranes, insulation, paving slabs	812530039	E	E	D	E	D	A	B	D	E	C	D	E	C	E	50	250	40	4	90
polymer modified polyester reinforced bitumen roofing membranes, insulation, rounded pebbles	812530040	D	D	D	D	C	A	B	C	D	C	D	D	C	D	50	220	35	4	90
PVC single ply roofing membrane, insulation, paving slabs	812530041	E	E	E	E	E	B	B	E	E	C	E	E	D	E	35	290	41	4	90
PVC single ply roofing membrane, insulation, rounded pebbles	812530042	D	E	E	E	D	A	B	D	D	C	D	D	C	D	35	240	35	4	90
TPO single ply roofing membrane, insulation, paving slabs	812530043	E	E	E	E	D	A	B	E	E	C	E	E	D	E	35	280	41	4	90
TPO single ply roofing membrane, insulation, rounded pebbles	812530044	D	D	E	E	C	A	B	D	D	C	D	D	C	D	35	240	35	4	90
Precast prestressed concrete hollow slab, with screed:																				
EPDM single ply roofing membrane, insulation, paving slabs	812530068	D	E	D	D	E	A	B	E	D	C	D	E	D	E	35	240	12	2	90
EPDM single ply roofing membrane, insulation, rounded pebbles	812530069	C	D	D	C	D	A	A	D	C	B	C	D	C	D	35	200	6.2	1	88
mastic asphalt roofing, insulation, paving slabs	812530007	E	D	C	D	E	A	C	C	C	E	E	E	D	D	50	230	11.7	2	83
mastic asphalt roofing, insulation, rounded pebbles	812530070	D	D	C	D	D	A	C	C	C	D	D	D	C	D	50	200	6	1	83
oxidised polyester reinforced bitumen roofing membranes, insulation, paving slabs	812530071	D	E	D	D	E	B	B	E	D	C	E	E	D	E	35	250	12	2	90
oxidised polyester reinforced bitumen roofing membranes, insulation, rounded pebbles	812530072	C	D	D	C	D	A	B	D	C	C	D	D	C	D	35	200	6.2	1	87
polymer modified polyester reinforced bitumen roofing membranes, insulation, paving slabs	812530073	D	D	C	D	D	A	B	C	D	C	D	D	C	D	50	220	11	2	90
polymer modified polyester reinforced bitumen roofing membranes, insulation, rounded pebbles	812530074	C	C	C	C	D	A	A	C	C	B	D	D	C	C	50	180	6	1	88
PVC single ply roofing membrane, insulation, paving slabs	812530077	D	E	D	D	E	B	B	D	D	C	D	E	D	E	35	250	12	2	90

Cont'd . . . .

Flat roofs: inverted deck

Health & Retail

	Element number	Summary Rating	Climate change	Water extraction	Mineral resource extraction	Stratospheric ozone depletion	Human toxicity	Ecotoxicity to freshwater	Nuclear waste (higher level)	Ecotoxicity to land	Waste disposal	Fossil fuel depletion	Eutrophication	Photochemical ozone creation	Acidification	Typical replacement interval	Embodied CO2 (kg CO2 eq.)	Recycled content (kg)	Recycled content (%)	Recycled currently at EOL (%)
Precast prestressed concrete hollow slab, with screed (cont'd):																				
PVC single ply roofing membrane, insulation, rounded pebbles	812530078	C	D	D	C	E	A	B	C	C	B	D	D	C	D	35	200	6.2	1	88
TPO single ply roofing membrane, insulation, paving slabs	812530075	D	E	D	D	E	A	B	D	D	C	D	E	D	E	35	250	12	2	90
TPO single ply roofing membrane, insulation, rounded pebbles	812530076	C	D	D	C	D	A	B	C	C	B	D	D	C	D	35	200	6.2	1	88
Profiled metal 'deep' decking with in situ concrete:																				
EPDM single ply roofing membrane, insulation, paving slabs	812530058	D	E	E	D	D	A	B	E	D	C	D	D	D	D	35	250	25	4	90
EPDM single ply roofing membrane, insulation, rounded pebbles	812530059	C	D	D	C	C	A	A	D	C	B	C	C	C	C	35	210	18	3	90
felt isolating layer, mastic asphalt roofing, insulation, paving slabs	812530004	E	D	D	D	D	A	C	D	D	E	E	D	C	D	50	240	24.7	4	83
felt isolating layer, mastic asphalt roofing, insulation, rounded pebbles	812530057	D	D	C	C	C	A	B	C	C	E	D	C	C	C	50	210	18	3	83
oxidised polyester reinforced bitumen roofing membranes, insulation, paving slabs	812530060	D	E	E	D	D	A	B	E	D	C	E	E	D	E	35	260	25	4	90
oxidised polyester reinforced bitumen roofing membranes, insulation, rounded pebbles	812530061	D	D	E	C	C	A	A	D	D	C	D	C	C	D	35	210	18	3	90
polymer modified polyester reinforced bitumen roofing membranes, paving slabs	812530062	D	D	D	C	C	A	A	D	D	C	D	D	C	D	50	230	24	4	90
polymer modified polyester reinforced bitumen roofing membranes, rounded pebbles	812530063	C	D	D	C	C	A	A	C	C	B	D	C	B	C	50	190	18	3	90
PVC single ply roofing membrane, insulation, paving slabs	812530064	D	E	E	D	D	A	B	E	D	C	D	D	D	D	35	260	25	4	90
PVC single ply roofing membrane, insulation, rounded pebbles	812530065	C	D	E	C	C	A	A	D	C	B	D	C	C	C	35	210	18	3	90
TPO single ply roofing membrane, insulation, paving slabs	812530066	D	E	E	D	D	A	B	E	D	C	D	D	D	E	35	250	25	4	90
TPO single ply roofing membrane, insulation, rounded pebbles	812530067	C	D	D	C	C	A	A	D	C	B	D	C	C	C	35	210	18	3	90

Flat roofs: inverted deck

Health & Retail

	Element number	Summary Rating	Climate change	Water extraction	Mineral resource extraction	Stratospheric ozone depletion	Human toxicity	Ecotoxicity to freshwater	Nuclear waste (higher level)	Ecotoxicity to land	Waste disposal	Fossil fuel depletion	Eutrophication	Photochemical ozone creation	Acidification	Typical replacement interval	Embodied CO2 (kg CO2 eq.)	Recycled content (kg)	Recycled content (%)	Recycled currently at EOL (%)
Structural steel trusses, galvanised steel purlins and deck, plywood (temperate EN 636-2) decking:																				
EPDM single ply roofing membrane, insulation, paving slabs	812530079	C	C	E	B	C	A	B	E	D	B	D	C	C	C	35	180	13	7	79
EPDM single ply roofing membrane, insulation, rounded pebbles	812530080	B	B	D	A	B	A	A	D	C	A	C	B	B	B	35	130	6.4	7	70
felt isolating layer, mastic asphalt roofing, insulation, paving slabs	812530085	C	C	D	A	C	A	C	D	D	D	D	C	C	C	50	170	11	6	64
felt isolating layer, mastic asphalt roofing, insulation, rounded pebbles	812530086	C	B	C	A	B	A	B	D	C	D	C	B	B	B	50	140	6.3	4	49
oxidised polyester reinforced bitumen roofing membrane, insulation, paving slabs	812530001	C	C	E	B	C	B	B	E	E	B	D	C	C	C	35	190	13	7	75
oxidised polyester reinforced bitumen roofing membranes, insulation, rounded pebbles	812530025	B	B	D	A	B	A	B	D	D	B	C	B	B	B	35	140	6.4	6	65
polymer modified polyester reinforced bitumen roofing membranes, insulation, paving slabs	812530002	B	C	D	A	B	A	A	D	D	B	C	B	B	B	50	150	12	7	74
polymer modified polyester reinforced bitumen roofing membranes, insulation, rounded pebbles	812530026	B	B	C	A+	B	A	A	D	C	B	C	A	B	B	50	120	6.3	6	65
PVC single ply roofing membrane, insulation, paving slabs	812530081	C	C	E	B	C	A	B	E	D	B	D	C	C	C	35	190	13	7	78
PVC single ply roofing membrane, insulation, rounded pebbles	812530082	B	B	D	A	C	A	A	D	D	A	C	B	C	B	35	140	6.4	7	69
TPO single ply roofing membrane, insulation, paving slabs	812530083	C	C	E	B	C	A	B	E	D	B	D	C	C	C	35	180	12	7	83
TPO single ply roofing membrane, insulation, rounded pebbles	812530084	B	B	D	A	B	A	A	D	D	A	C	B	B	B	35	140	6.4	7	69

Flat roofs: warm deck
Health & Retail

	Element number	Summary Rating	Climate change	Water extraction	Mineral resource extraction	Stratospheric ozone depletion	Human toxicity	Ecotoxicity to freshwater	Nuclear waste (higher level)	Ecotoxicity to land	Waste disposal	Fossil fuel depletion	Eutrophication	Photochemical ozone creation	Acidification	Typical replacement interval	Embodied CO2 (kg CO2 eq.)	Recycled content (kg)	Recycled content (%)	Recycled currently at EOL (%)
In situ reinforced concrete slab with 50% GGBS and 20% recycled coarse aggregate:																				
vapour control layer, insulation, EPDM single ply roofing membrane	812540074	C	C	B	C	B	A+	A	B	C	B	B	B	B	B	35	150	146	16	90
vapour control layer, insulation, felt isolating layer, mastic asphalt roofing	812540075	D	C	B	D	C	A	B	A	C	E	C	C	B	C	50	170	146	16	85
vapour control layer, insulation, oxidised polyester reinforced bitumen roofing membranes with mineral finish	812540076	C	C	C	C	B	A	A	B	C	C	C	C	B	C	35	160	146	16	89
vapour control layer, insulation, polymer modified polyester reinforced bitumen roofing membranes with mineral finish	812540077	C	C	B	C	B	A	A	A	C	C	B	B	B	B	50	150	146	16	89
vapour control layer, insulation, PVC single ply roofing membrane	812540078	C	C	C	C	C	A	A	B	C	B	B	B	B	B	35	160	146	16	89
vapour control layer, insulation, TPO single ply roofing membrane	812540079	C	C	B	C	B	A+	A	A	C	B	B	B	B	C	35	160	146	16	90
In situ reinforced concrete slab:																				
vapour control layer, insulation, EPDM single ply roofing membrane	812540025	C	D	C	D	B	A	A	B	C	B	B	C	B	C	35	190	35	4	90
vapour control layer, insulation, felt isolating layer, mastic asphalt roofing	812540021	D	D	B	D	C	A	B	B	D	E	D	D	B	C	50	210	35	4	86
vapour control layer, insulation, oxidised polyester reinforced bitumen roofing membranes with mineral finish	812540022	D	D	C	D	B	A	A	B	D	C	C	C	B	C	35	200	35	4	90
vapour control layer, insulation, polymer modified polyester reinforced bitumen roofing membranes with mineral finish	812540023	C	D	B	D	B	A	A	B	D	C	C	C	B	C	50	200	35	4	90
vapour control layer, insulation, PVC single ply roofing membrane	812540026	C	D	C	D	C	A	A	B	D	B	C	C	B	C	35	200	35	4	90
vapour control layer, insulation, TPO single ply roofing membrane	812540027	C	D	C	D	B	A	A	B	D	B	B	C	B	C	35	200	35	4	90
Precast concrete formwork with lattice reinforcement and in situ concrete:																				
vapour control layer, insulation, EPDM single ply waterproofing membrane	812540024	C	C	B	C	B	A	A	B	C	B	B	C	B	C	35	170	22	3	90
vapour control layer, insulation, mastic asphalt roofing	812540011	D	C	B	D	C	A	B	B	C	D	C	C	B	C	50	180	22	3	85

Cont'd . . . .

Flat roofs: warm deck

Health & Retail

	Element number	Summary Rating	Climate change	Water extraction	Mineral resource extraction	Stratospheric ozone depletion	Human toxicity	Ecotoxicity to freshwater	Nuclear waste (higher level)	Ecotoxicity to land	Waste disposal	Fossil fuel depletion	Eutrophication	Photochemical ozone creation	Acidification	Typical replacement interval	Embodied CO2 (kg CO2 eq.)	Recycled content (kg)	Recycled content (%)	Recycled currently at EOL (%)
Precast concrete formwork with lattice reinforcement and in situ concrete (cont'd):																				
vapour control layer, insulation, oxidised polyester reinforced bitumen roofing membranes with mineral finish	812540016	C	C	B	C	C	A	A	B	C	B	C	C	B	C	35	180	22	3	90
vapour control layer, insulation, polymer modified polyester reinforced bitumen roofing membranes with mineral finish	812540017	C	C	B	C	B	A	A	B	C	B	C	C	B	C	50	170	22	3	90
vapour control layer, insulation, PVC single ply waterproofing membrane	812540012	C	C	B	C	C	A	A	B	C	B	B	C	B	C	35	170	22	3	90
vapour control layer, insulation, TPO single ply waterproofing membrane	812540013	C	C	B	C	B	A	A	B	C	B	B	C	B	C	35	170	22	3	90
Precast prestressed concrete hollow slab, with screed:																				
vapour control layer, insulation, EPDM single ply waterproofing membrane	812540033	B	C	A	C	C	A	A	B	B	A	B	C	B	C	35	160	5.1	1	90
vapour control layer, insulation, felt isolating layer, mastic asphalt roofing	812540030	C	C	A	C	D	A	B	B	B	D	C	C	B	C	50	170	5.1	1	83
vapour control layer, insulation, oxidised polyester reinforced bitumen roofing membranes with mineral finish	812540031	C	C	B	C	C	A	A	B	C	B	C	C	B	C	35	160	5.1	1	90
vapour control layer, insulation, polymer modified polyester reinforced bitumen roofing membranes with mineral finish	812540032	B	C	A	C	C	A	A	B	B	B	C	C	B	C	50	160	5.1	1	90
vapour control layer, insulation, PVC single ply waterproofing membrane	812540034	B	C	B	C	D	A	A	B	B	A	B	C	B	C	35	160	5.1	1	90
vapour control layer, insulation, TPO single ply waterproofing membrane	812540035	B	C	A	C	C	A	A	B	B	A	B	C	B	C	35	160	5.1	1	90
Profiled metal 'deep' decking with in situ concrete:																				
vapour control layer, insulation, EPDM single ply roofing membrane	812540080	B	C	B	B	B	A+	A	B	B	B	B	B	B	B	35	170	18	4	90
vapour control layer, insulation, felt isolating layer, mastic asphalt roofing	812540038	C	C	B	C	B	A	B	B	B	D	C	C	B	C	50	180	18	3	83
vapour control layer, insulation, oxidised polyester reinforced bitumen roofing membranes with mineral finish	812540081	C	C	B	B	B	A	A	B	C	B	C	B	B	C	35	170	18	4	90

Cont'd . . . .

Flat roofs: warm deck

Health & Retail

	Element number	Summary Rating	Climate change	Water extraction	Mineral resource extraction	Stratospheric ozone depletion	Human toxicity	Ecotoxicity to freshwater	Nuclear waste (higher level)	Ecotoxicity to land	Waste disposal	Fossil fuel depletion	Eutrophication	Photochemical ozone creation	Acidification	Typical replacement interval	Embodied CO₂ (kg CO₂ eq.)	Recycled content (kg)	Recycled content (%)	Recycled currently at EOL (%)
Profiled metal 'deep' decking with in situ concrete (cont'd):																				
vapour control layer, insulation, polymer modified polyester reinforced bitumen roofing membranes with mineral finish	812540039	B	C	B	B	B	A	A	B	B	B	C	B	B	B	50	170	18.5	3	88
vapour control layer, insulation, PVC single ply roofing membrane	812540082	B	C	B	B	B	A+	A	B	B	B	B	B	B	B	35	170	18.5	4	89
vapour control layer, insulation, TPO single ply roofing membrane	812540083	B	C	B	B	B	A+	A	B	B	B	B	B	B	B	35	170	18.5	4	89
Structural steel trusses, galvanised steel purlins and deck:																				
vapour control layer, insulation, EPDM single ply roofing membrane	812540001	A+	A	A+	A+	A+	A+	A+	A	A+	A+	A+	A+	A+	A+	35	72	4	20	70
vapour control layer, insulation, felt isolating layer, mastic asphalt roofing	812540002	A	A	A+	A+	A	A+	A	A	A+	C	B	A+	A+	A+	50	89	4	6	24
vapour control layer, insulation, oxidised polyester reinforced bitumen roofing membranes with mineral finish	812540009	A+	A	A	A+	A+	A+	A+	A	A	A	A	A+	A+	A+	35	80	4	15	51
vapour control layer, insulation, polymer modified polyester reinforced bitumen roofing membranes with mineral finish	812540010	A+	A	A+	A+	A+	A+	A+	A	A+	A+	A	A+	A+	A+	50	77	4	14	49
vapour control layer, insulation, PVC single ply waterproofing membrane	812540003	A+	A	A	A+	A	A+	A+	A	A+	A+	A+	A+	A+	A+	35	78	4	20	68
vapour control layer, insulation, TPO single ply waterproofing membrane	812540004	A+	A	A+	A+	A+	A+	A+	A	A+	A+	A+	A+	A+	A+	35	75	4	20	69

Low pitched roofs

Health & Retail

	Element number	Summary Rating	Climate change	Water extraction	Mineral resource extraction	Stratospheric ozone depletion	Human toxicity	Ecotoxicity to freshwater	Nuclear waste (higher level)	Ecotoxicity to land	Waste disposal	Fossil fuel depletion	Eutrophication	Photochemical ozone creation	Acidification	Typical replacement interval	Embodied CO_2 (kg CO_2 eq.)	Recycled content (kg)	Recycled content (%)	Recycled currently at EOL (%)
Galvanised steel rafters and joists:																				
composite profiled roof cladding (steel inner lining, pentane blown PUR/PIR insulation, coated aluminium outer skin)	812550014	A	B	C	A+	A	B	B	A	B	A+	A	A	B	A	35	98	4.6	27	73
composite profiled roof cladding (steel inner lining, pentane blown PUR/PIR insulation, coated steel outer skin)	812550001	A+	B	D	A+	A+	A+	A+	A+	A	A+	A	A	B	A	35	95	3.6	18	77
double skin built up profiled roof cladding (coated aluminium inner and outer skin, insulation)	812550013	A	B	A	A+	A	E	E	D	B	A+	A	A+	A+	A	35	110	7.4	37	64
double skin built up profiled roof cladding (coated steel inner and outer skin, insulation)	812550016	A	B	B	A+	A+	A+	A+	B	A+	A+	A	A+	A	A	35	100	4.6	18	70
double skin built up profiled roof cladding (mill finished aluminium inner and outer skin, insulation)	812550018	A+	A	A+	A+	A+	B	D	B	A+	A+	A+	A+	A+	A	50	83	7.4	37	64
double skin built up roof cladding (aluminium inner lining, insulation, mill finished aluminium standing seam outer skin)	812550002	A	B	A	A+	A	E	E	D	B	A+	A	A+	A+	A	35	110	7.4	37	64
double skin built up roof cladding (steel inner lining, insulation, coated aluminium standing seam outer skin)	812550007	A	B	B	A+	A	D	D	D	B	A+	A	A+	A	A	35	110	6.3	29	66
double skin built up roof cladding (steel inner lining, insulation, copper standing seam outer skin)	812550019	A	A	C	B	A	A+	A+	C	A+	A+	A	A+	A+	A+	45	91	8.2	32	71
double skin built up roof cladding (steel inner lining, insulation, mill finished aluminium standing seam outer skin)	812550034	A+	A	A	A+	A+	A	B	B	A+	A+	A+	A+	A+	A+	50	82	6.3	29	66

Pitched roofs: steel construction

Health & Retail

	Element number	Summary Rating	Climate change	Water extraction	Mineral resource extraction	Stratospheric ozone depletion	Human toxicity	Ecotoxicity to freshwater	Nuclear waste (higher level)	Ecotoxicity to land	Waste disposal	Fossil fuel depletion	Eutrophication	Photochemical ozone creation	Acidification	Typical replacement interval	Embodied CO2 (kg CO2 eq.)	Recycled content (kg)	Recycled content (%)	Recycled currently at EOL (%)
Galvanised steel rafters and joists with insulation:																				
battens, breather membrane, plywood (temperate EN 636-2) decking, standing seam copper roof	812150015	A	A	D	A	B	B	B	E	E	A+	A	A	A	A	45	62	7.6	18	34
roofing underlay, counterbattens, battens and concrete interlocking tiles	812150004	A+	A	A+	A+	A+	A+	A+	A+	A+	A+	A+	A+	A	A+	60+	62	3.3	4	76
roofing underlay, counterbattens, battens and concrete plain tiles	812150005	A+	A	A+	A+	A	A+	A+	A	A	A+	A+	A+	A+	A+	60+	78	3.3	3	81
roofing underlay, counterbattens, battens and photovoltaic roofing tiles	812150007	A+	A+	A+	A+	A	A+	A	A+	A+	B	A+	A+	D	A+	25	40	3.3	8	19
roofing underlay, counterbattens, battens and polymer modified cement slates	812150010	A	B	A	A+	B	A	C	D	A	A	A	B	B	A	40	100	15.9	31	15
roofing underlay, counterbattens, battens and reclaimed clay tiles	812150012	A+	A+	A+	A+	A	A+	A+	A+	A+	A+	A+	A+	B	A+	50	36	85.1	81	77
roofing underlay, counterbattens, battens and reclaimed slates	812150011	A+	A+	A+	A+	A+	A+	A+	A+	A+	A+	A+	A+	A	A+	50	39	46.5	72	72
roofing underlay, counterbattens, battens and resin bonded slates	812150009	A	B	B	A+	B	A	E	D	C	A	A	A	B	A	40	100	11.3	28	19
roofing underlay, counterbattens, battens and UK produced clay plain tiles	812150001	A	A	A+	A	A	A+	A+	B	A+	A+	A	A+	A	A+	60+	87	3.3	3	77
roofing underlay, counterbattens, battens and UK produced fibre cement slates	812150013	A	B	A	A+	A	A+	A	B	A	A+	A	A	B	A	40	100	3.3	7	16
roofing underlay, counterbattens, battens and UK produced slate	812150008	A	A	A+	C	A	A+	A	A	A+	A+	A+	A	A	A	60+	59	3.3	5	73

Pitched roofs: timber construction

Health & Retail

	Element number	Summary Rating	Climate change	Water extraction	Mineral resource extraction	Stratospheric ozone depletion	Human toxicity	Ecotoxicity to freshwater	Nuclear waste (higher level)	Ecotoxicity to land	Waste disposal	Fossil fuel depletion	Eutrophication	Photochemical ozone creation	Acidification	Typical replacement interval	Embodied CO2 (kg CO2 eq.)	Recycled content (kg)	Recycled content (%)	Recycled currently at EOL (%)
Structurally insulated timber panel system with OSB/3 each side:																				
roofing underlay, counterbattens, battens and concrete interlocking tiles	812410018	A+	A+	B	A+	A	A+	A+	A+	A	A	A+	A	B	A+	60+	23	14	13	55
roofing underlay, counterbattens, battens and concrete plain tiles	812410064	A+	A+	B	A+	A	A+	A	A+	A	A	A	A	B	A	60+	38	14	10	64
roofing underlay, counterbattens, battens and photovoltaic roofing tiles	812410068	A+	A+	B	A+	B	A+	A	A+	A	C	A+	A	F	A+	25	0.6	14	20	10
roofing underlay, counterbattens, battens and polymer modified cement slates	812410066	A	A	C	A+	B	A	C	D	B	B	B	B	C	B	35	62	26	34	8
roofing underlay, counterbattens, battens and reclaimed clay tiles	812410025	A+	A+	A	A+	A	A+	A+	A+	A+	A	A+	A+	C	A+	50	-4	96	72	61
roofing underlay, counterbattens, battens and reclaimed slates	812410067	A+	A+	A	A+	A	A+	A+	A+	A+	A	A+	A+	B	A+	50	-2	57	63	49
roofing underlay, counterbattens, battens and resin bonded slates	812410022	A	A	D	A+	C	B	E	C	D	B	B	B	C	B	35	64	22	33	9
roofing underlay, counterbattens, battens and UK produced clay plain tiles	812410069	A	A	B	A	B	A+	A+	B	A	A	B	A	C	A	60+	48	14	10	61
roofing underlay, counterbattens, battens and UK produced fibre cement slates	812410065	A	A	C	A+	B	A+	A	B	B	A	A	B	C	A	30	59	14	19	8
roofing underlay, counterbattens, battens and UK produced slate	812410021	A	A+	B	C	B	A+	A	A+	A	A	A	B	B	A	60+	20	14	15	50
Structurally insulated timber panel system with plywood (temperate EN 636-2) decking each side:																				
roofing underlay, counterbattens, battens and concrete interlocking tiles	812410049	A+	A+	B	A+	B	A	A	A	C	A+	A	A	B	A	60+	35	0	0	60
roofing underlay, counterbattens, battens and concrete plain tiles	812410050	A	A	B	A+	B	A	A	A	C	A	A	A	B	A	60+	50	0	0	68
roofing underlay, counterbattens, battens and photovoltaic roofing tiles	812410052	A	A+	B	A+	B	A	B	A	B	B	A	A	E	A+	25	12	0	0	11
roofing underlay, counterbattens, battens and polymer modified cement slates	812410053	B	A	C	A+	C	A	D	E	D	B	B	C	D	B	35	74	13	18	9
roofing underlay, counterbattens, battens and reclaimed clay tiles	812410054	A+	A+	B	A+	B	A	A	A+	B	A	A+	A	C	A+	50	8.8	82	66	65
roofing underlay, counterbattens, battens and reclaimed slates	812410055	A+	A+	B	A+	B	A	A	A+	B	A+	A+	A+	B	A+	50	10	43	52	55

Cont'd . . . .

Pitched roofs: timber construction

Health & Retail

	Element number	Summary Rating	Climate change	Water extraction	Mineral resource extraction	Stratospheric ozone depletion	Human toxicity	Ecotoxicity to freshwater	Nuclear waste (higher level)	Ecotoxicity to land	Waste disposal	Fossil fuel depletion	Eutrophication	Photochemical ozone creation	Acidification	Typical replacement interval	Embodied CO2 (kg CO2 eq.)	Recycled content (kg)	Recycled content (%)	Recycled currently at EOL (%)
Structurally insulated timber panel system with plywood (temperate EN 636-2) decking each side (cont'd):																				
roofing underlay, counterbattens, battens and resin bonded slates	812410056	B	A	D	A+	C	B	E	D	E	A	B	B	D	B	35	76	8	14	11
roofing underlay, counterbattens, battens and UK produced clay plain tiles	812410058	A	A	B	A	B	A	A	B	C	A	B	A	C	A	60+	60	0	0	65
roofing underlay, counterbattens, battens and UK produced fibre cement slates	812410051	A	A	C	A+	B	A	B	C	C	A	B	B	C	A	30	71	0	0	9
roofing underlay, counterbattens, battens and UK produced slate	812410057	A	A+	B	C	B	A	B	A	B	A+	A	B	B	B	60+	31	0	0	55
Timber trussed rafters and joists with insulation:																				
battens, breather membrane, plywood (temperate EN 636-2) decking, standing seam copper roof	812410020	A	A+	D	A	B	B	B	E	D	A+	A	A	A	A	45	43	5.2	12	24
roofing underlay, counterbattens, battens and concrete interlocking tiles	812410007	A+	A+	A+	A+	A	A+	A+	A+	A+	A+	A+	A+	A	A+	60+	43	0.9	1	71
roofing underlay, counterbattens, battens and concrete plain tiles	812410017	A+	A	A+	A+	A	A+	A+	A	A+	A+	A+	A+	A+	A+	60+	58	0.9	1	77
roofing underlay, counterbattens, battens and integrated photovoltaic roof tiles	812410014	A+	A+	A+	A+	A	A+	A	A+	A+	B	A+	A+	D	A+	25	20	0.9	2	9
roofing underlay, counterbattens, battens and polymer modified cement slates	812410011	A	A	A	A+	B	A	C	D	A	A	A	B	B	A	40	84	13.5	27	6
roofing underlay, counterbattens, battens and reclaimed clay tiles	812410013	A+	A+	A+	A+	A	A+	A+	A+	A+	A+	A+	A+	B	A+	50	17	82.7	79	73
roofing underlay, counterbattens, battens and reclaimed slates	812410012	A+	A+	A+	A+	A+	A+	A+	A+	A+	A+	A+	A+	A	A+	50	19	44.1	69	66
roofing underlay, counterbattens, battens and resin bonded slates	812410010	A	A	B	A+	B	A	E	C	C	A	A	A	B	A	40	85	8.9	23	8
roofing underlay, counterbattens, battens and UK produced clay plain tiles	812410006	A+	A	A+	A+	A	A+	A+	B	A+	A+	A	A+	A	A+	60+	68	0.9	1	73
roofing underlay, counterbattens, battens and UK produced fibre cement slates	812410008	A+	A	A	A+	A	A+	A	B	A	A+	A	A	B	A	40	81	0.9	2	7
roofing underlay, counterbattens, battens and UK produced slates	812410026	A	A+	A+	C	A	A+	A	A+	A+	A+	A+	A	A	A	60+	39	0.9	1	67

6.5 EXTERNAL WALLS

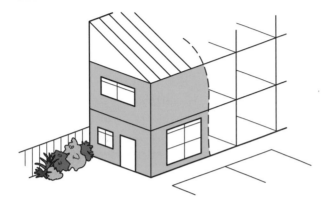

Functional unit for external walls:

1 m² of external wall construction, to satisfy current Building Regulations in England & Wales, and a U-value of 0.3 W/m²K. Where relevant, the specification will also include an internal wall finish. To include any repair, refurbishment or replacement over the 60-year study period.

External walls ratings are applicable to any building type.

Perhaps more than any other decision facing the designer, the choice of the external wall specification is subject to the widest range of practical, economic and visual considerations, some of which may be beyond the control of the design team. Client requirements or preferences and development control issues may largely determine the building form and the choice of external materials. Designers may therefore find themselves in a position where choice is limited and environmental compromise is inevitable.

The external envelope is also the key factor in portraying the character and design philosophy of the building and once established, compromise in the designer's original version of the building may be strongly resisted. For this reason, it is important that designers should not regard environmental considerations as 'bolt-on' extras to the building design. With careful thought at

the outset, building design can (and should) take a holistic and integrated approach, incorporating technical, cost and environmental considerations into the design strategy. The degree to which each of these aspects is prioritised or compromised should flow from a clearly established project philosophy agreed by the design team and client organisation at the outset and will vary project-to-project.

External walls can have a significant contribution to the impacts of the building. The external wall can also account for around 30% of building costs, so designers should consider the benefits of minimising the external wall area for a given plan area by avoiding excessively long and narrow or complex plan forms. Designs with a relatively low external wall area and maximum floor space will benefit the project in terms of capital cost, running cost (lower maintenance and heat loss) and environmental impact.

External wall specifications include a diverse range of construction types and materials; it is therefore no surprise that a wide range of environmental impacts is exhibited with this element.

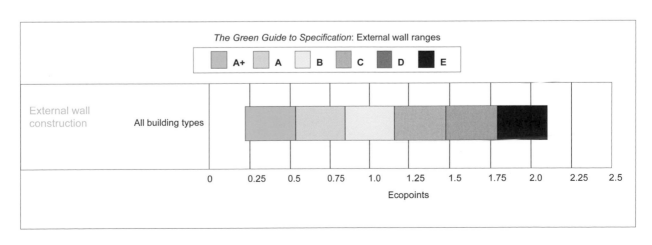

Superstructure

In a change to the previous editions of *The Green Guide to Specification*, an allowance for the structural frame has been included for non-loadbearing external wall constructions. This is based on typical column spacing around the perimeter of the building and is averaged to the amount per square metre of external wall.

Division of external walls into subsections

External wall specifications have been arranged into subsections for ease of use by designers. However, ratings have been arrived at through comparison of all external walls shown across all subsections. The subsections are listed in Box 6.1.

Note: where descriptions refer to, say 100% RCA this refers to 100% of the coarse aggregate in the concrete being replaced with Recycled Concrete Aggregate.

Concrete block solid densities are as follows unless otherwise stated:
- Dense block/blockwork ($\approx$ 1950 kg/m³),
- Medium density block/blockwork ($\approx$ 1450 kg/m³),
- Lightweight blockwork ($\approx$ 1100 kg/m³),
- Superlightweight block/blockwork ($\approx$ 850 kg/m³).

Box 6.1: External walls subsections

- Brick or stone and blockwork cavity walls
- Rendered or fairfaced blockwork cavity walls
- Brick and light steel-framed construction
- Brick and timber-framed construction
- Rendered or fairfaced blockwork and light steel-framed construction
- Rendered or fairfaced blockwork and timber-framed construction
- Cladding on light steel-framed construction
- Cladding on timber-framed construction
- Cladding on loadbearing masonry
- Insulated cladding on concrete frame with block infill
- Insulated cladding on concrete frame with metal stud infill
- Insulated cladding on steel frame with block infill
- Insulated cladding on steel frame with metal stud infill
- Insulated cladding on steel frame with no internal finish
- Rainscreen cladding on concrete frame with block infill
- Rainscreen cladding on concrete frame with metal stud infill
- Rainscreen cladding on concrete frame with timber stud infill
- Rainscreen cladding on steel frame with block infill
- Rainscreen cladding on steel frame with metal stud infill
- Rainscreen cladding on steel frame with timber stud infill
- Rainscreen cladding on loadbearing single-leaf blockwork walls with metal stud infill
- Rainscreen cladding on loadbearing single-leaf blockwork wall with timber stud infill
- Rainscreen cladding on loadbearing masonry cavity walls
- Insulated render systems on loadbearing single-leaf blockwork walls
- Aluminium curtain walling systems
- Timber curtain walling systems
- Loadbearing precast concrete systems

Brick or stone and blockwork cavity walls

All building types

	Element number	Summary Rating	Climate change	Water extraction	Mineral resource extraction	Stratospheric ozone depletion	Human toxicity	Ecotoxicity to freshwater	Nuclear waste (higher level)	Ecotoxicity to land	Waste disposal	Fossil fuel depletion	Eutrophication	Photochemical ozone creation	Acidification	Typical replacement interval	Embodied CO2 (kg CO2 eq.)	Recycled content (kg)	Recycled content (%)	Recycled currently at EOL (%)
Brickwork outer leaf, insulation, aircrete blockwork inner leaf:																				
cement mortar, plaster, paint	806170028	A+	A	A+	A+	A	A+	A+	A+	A+	A+	A+	A+	A+	A+	60+	73	0.6	0	83
cement mortar, plasterboard on battens, paint	806170615	A+	A	A+	A+	A	A+	A+	A+	A+	A+	A+	A+	A+	A	60+	74	3.5	2	86
cement:lime mortar, plaster, paint	806170061	A+	A	A+	A+	A	A+	A+	A+	A+	A+	A+	A+	A+	A+	60+	72	0.6	0	83
cement:lime mortar, plasterboard on battens, paint	806170065	A+	A	A+	A+	A	A+	A+	A+	A+	A+	A+	A+	A+	A	60+	74	3.5	2	86
Brickwork outer leaf, insulation, cellular dense blockwork inner leaf:																				
cement mortar, plaster, paint	806170091	A+	A	A+	A+	A	A+	A+	A+	A+	A+	A+	A+	A+	A+	60+	67	0.6	0	85
cement mortar, plasterboard on battens, paint	806170090	A+	A	A+	A+	A	A+	A+	A+	A+	A+	A+	A+	A+	A	60+	69	3.5	1	87
cement:lime mortar, plaster, paint	806170092	A+	A	A+	A+	A	A+	A+	A+	A+	A+	A+	A+	A+	A+	60+	67	0.6	0	85
cement:lime mortar, plasterboard on battens, paint	806170093	A+	A	A+	A+	A	A+	A+	A+	A+	A+	A+	A+	A+	A	60+	68	3.5	1	87
Brickwork outer leaf, insulation, dense solid blockwork inner leaf:																				
cement mortar, plaster, paint	806170027	A+	A	A+	A+	A	A+	A+	A+	A+	A	A+	A+	A+	A+	60+	70	0.6	0	86
cement mortar, plasterboard on battens, paint	806170033	A+	A	A+	A+	A	A+	A+	A+	A+	A+	A+	A+	A+	A	60+	72	3.5	1	88
cement:lime mortar, plaster, paint	806170060	A+	A	A+	A+	A	A+	A+	A+	A+	A	A+	A+	A+	A+	60+	70	0.6	0	86
cement:lime mortar, plasterboard on battens, paint	806170066	A+	A	A+	A+	A	A+	A+	A+	A+	A+	A+	A+	A+	A	60+	71	3.5	1	88
Brickwork outer leaf, insulation, lightweight solid blockwork inner leaf: cement mortar, plasterboard on battens, paint	806170616	A+	A	A+	A+	A	A+	A+	A+	A+	A+	A+	A+	A+	A	60+	81	3.5	1	87

Brick or stone and blockwork cavity walls

All building types

	Element number	Summary Rating	Climate change	Water extraction	Mineral resource extraction	Stratospheric ozone depletion	Human toxicity	Ecotoxicity to freshwater	Nuclear waste (higher level)	Ecotoxicity to land	Waste disposal	Fossil fuel depletion	Eutrophication	Photochemical ozone creation	Acidification	Typical replacement interval	Embodied CO$_2$ (kg CO$_2$ eq.)	Recycled content (kg)	Recycled content (%)	Recycled currently at EOL (%)
Brickwork outer leaf, insulation, medium density solid blockwork inner leaf:																				
cement mortar, plaster, paint	806170046	A+	A	A+	A+	A	A+	A+	A+	A+	A+	A+	A+	A+	A+	60+	78	0.6	0	85
cement mortar, plasterboard on battens, paint	806170047	A+	A	A+	A+	A	A+	A+	A+	A+	A+	A+	A+	A+	A	60+	79	3.5	1	87
cement:lime mortar, plaster, paint	806170084	A+	A	A+	A+	A	A+	A+	A+	A+	A+	A+	A+	A+	A+	60+	77	0.6	0	85
cement:lime mortar, plasterboard on battens, paint	806170087	A+	A	A+	A+	A	A+	A+	A+	A+	A+	A+	A+	A+	A	60+	79	3.5	1	87
Brickwork outer leaf, insulation, superlightweight solid blockwork inner leaf:																				
cement mortar, plaster, paint	806170030	A+	A	A+	A+	A	A+	A+	A+	A+	A+	A+	A+	A+	A+	60+	79	0.6	0	84
cement mortar, plasterboard on battens, paint	806170063	A+	A	A+	A+	A	A+	A+	A+	A+	A+	A+	A+	A+	A	60+	81	3.5	1	87
cement:lime mortar, plaster, paint	806170020	A+	A	A+	A+	A	A+	A+	A+	A+	A+	A+	A+	A+	A+	60+	79	0.6	0	84
cement:lime mortar, plasterboard on battens, paint	806170023	A+	A	A+	A+	A	A+	A+	A+	A+	A+	A+	A+	A+	A	60+	80	3.5	1	87
Limestone split faced outer leaf, insulation, dense solid blockwork inner leaf: cement mortar, plasterboard on battens and paint	806170022	A+	A+	A+	A	A	A+	A+	A+	A+	A+	A+	A+	A+	A+	60+	50	3.7	1	87
Reclaimed brickwork outer leaf, insulation:																				
aircrete blockwork inner leaf, cement mortar, plasterboard on battens, paint	806170617	A+	A+	A+	A+	A+	A+	A+	A+	A+	A+	A+	A+	A+	A+	60+	51	129	56	86
lightweight solid blockwork inner leaf, cement mortar, plasterboard on battens, paint	806170618	A+	A+	A+	A+	A	A+	A+	A+	A+	A+	A+	A+	A+	A	60+	57	129	46	87
Sandstone split faced outer leaf, insulation, dense solid blockwork inner leaf: cement mortar, plasterboard on battens, paint	806170039	A+	A+	A+	A	A	A+	A+	A+	A+	A	A+	A+	A+	A+	60+	51	3.7	1	87

Rendered or fairfaced blockwork cavity walls

All building types

	Element number	Summary Rating	Climate change	Water extraction	Mineral resource extraction	Stratospheric ozone depletion	Human toxicity	Ecotoxicity to freshwater	Nuclear waste (higher level)	Ecotoxicity to land	Waste disposal	Fossil fuel depletion	Eutrophication	Photochemical ozone creation	Acidification	Typical replacement interval	Embodied CO₂ (kg CO₂ eq.)	Recycled content (kg)	Recycled content (%)	Recycled currently at EOL (%)
Cement rendered aircrete blockwork cavity wall, insulation:																				
cement mortar, plaster, paint	806180024	A+	A	A+	A+	A	A+	A+	A+	A+	A+	A+	A+	A+	A+	50	72	0.7	0	81
cement mortar, plasterboard on battens, paint	806180035	A+	A	A+	A+	A	A+	A+	A+	A+	A+	A+	A+	A+	A	50	73	3.6	2	85
Cement rendered aircrete blockwork outer leaf, insulation:																				
dense solid blockwork inner leaf, cement mortar, plaster, paint	806180106	A+	A	A+	A+	A	A+	A+	A+	A+	A+	A+	A+	A+	A+	50	69	0.7	0	85
dense solid blockwork inner leaf, cement mortar, plasterboard on battens, paint	806180107	A+	A	A+	A+	A	A+	A+	A+	A+	A+	A+	A+	A+	A	50	71	3.6	1	87
medium density solid blockwork inner leaf, cement mortar, plaster, paint	806180114	A+	A	A+	A+	A	A+	A+	A+	A+	A+	A+	A+	A+	A+	50	77	0.7	0	84
medium density solid blockwork inner leaf, cement mortar, plasterboard on battens, paint	806180115	A+	A	A+	A+	A	A+	A+	A+	A+	A+	A+	A+	A+	A	50	78	3.6	1	87
superlightweight solid blockwork inner leaf, cement mortar, plaster, paint	806180122	A+	A	A+	A+	A	A+	A+	A+	A+	A+	A+	A+	A+	A+	50	78	0.7	0	83
superlightweight solid blockwork inner leaf, cement mortar, plasterboard on battens, paint	806180123	A+	A	A+	A+	A	A+	A+	A+	A+	A+	A+	A+	A+	A	50	80	3.6	2	86
Cement rendered dense solid blockwork cavity wall, insulation:																				
cement mortar, plaster, paint	806180029	A	A	A+	A	B	A+	A+	A+	A+	A	A+	A+	A+	A+	50	67	0.7	0	86
cement mortar, plasterboard on battens, paint	806180036	A	A	A+	A	B	A+	A+	A+	A+	A	A+	A+	A+	A	50	69	3.6	1	88
Cement rendered dense solid blockwork outer leaf, insulation:																				
aircrete concrete blockwork inner leaf, cement mortar, plaster, paint	806180025	A+	A	A+	A+	A	A+	A+	A+	A+	A+	A+	A+	A+	A+	50	69	0.7	0	85
aircrete concrete blockwork inner leaf, cement mortar, plasterboard on battens, paint	806180037	A+	A	A+	A+	A	A+	A+	A+	A+	A+	A+	A+	A+	A	50	71	3.6	1	87
medium density concrete solid blockwork inner leaf, cement mortar, plaster, paint	806180044	A	A	A+	A+	B	A+	A+	A+	A+	A	A+	A+	A+	A+	50	74	0.7	0	86

Cont'd . . . .

Rendered or fairfaced blockwork cavity walls

All building types

	Element number	Summary Rating	Climate change	Water extraction	Mineral resource extraction	Stratospheric ozone depletion	Human toxicity	Ecotoxicity to freshwater	Nuclear waste (higher level)	Ecotoxicity to land	Waste disposal	Fossil fuel depletion	Eutrophication	Photochemical ozone creation	Acidification	Typical replacement interval	Embodied CO_2 (kg CO_2 eq.)	Recycled content (kg)	Recycled content (%)	Recycled currently at EOL (%)
Cement rendered dense solid blockwork outer leaf, insulation (cont'd):																				
medium density concrete solid blockwork inner leaf, cement mortar, plasterboard on battens, paint	806180049	A+	A	A+	A+	B	A+	A+	A+	A+	A	A+	A+	A+	A	50	76	3.6	1	88
superlightweight concrete solid blockwork inner leaf, cement mortar, plaster, paint	806180150	A+	A	A+	A+	B	A+	A+	A+	A+	A	A+	A+	A+	A+	50	76	0.7	0	85
superlightweight concrete solid blockwork inner leaf, cement mortar, plasterboard on battens, paint	806180151	A+	A	A+	A+	B	A+	A+	A+	A+	A+	A+	A+	A+	A	50	78	3.6	1	87
Cement rendered lightweight solid blockwork cavity: insulation, cement mortar, plasterboard on battens, paint	806180597	A+	A	A+	A+	B	A+	A+	A+	A+	A+	A+	A+	A+	A	50	86	3.6	1	87
Cement rendered lightweight solid blockwork outer leaf: insulation, aircrete blockwork inner leaf, cement mortar, plasterboard on battens, paint	806180598	A+	A	A+	A+	A	A+	A+	A+	A+	A+	A+	A+	A+	A	50	80	3.6	2	86
Cement rendered medium density solid blockwork cavity wall, insulation:																				
cement mortar, plaster, paint	806180043	A+	A	A+	A+	B	A+	A+	A+	A+	A	A+	A+	A+	A+	50	82	0.7	0	85
cement mortar, plasterboard on battens, paint	806180042	A+	A	A+	A+	B	A+	A+	A+	A+	A+	A+	A	A+	A	50	84	3.6	1	88
Cement rendered medium density solid blockwork outer leaf, insulation:																				
aircrete blockwork inner leaf, cement mortar, plaster, paint	806180021	A+	A	A+	A+	A	A+	A+	A+	A+	A+	A+	A+	A+	A+	50	77	0.7	0	84
aircrete blockwork inner leaf, cement mortar, plasterboard on battens, paint	806180038	A+	A	A+	A+	A	A+	A+	A+	A+	A+	A+	A+	A+	A	50	79	3.6	1	87
dense solid blockwork inner leaf, cement mortar, plaster, paint	806180170	A	A	A+	A+	B	A+	A+	A+	A+	A	A+	A+	A+	A+	50	74	0.7	0	86

Rendered or fairfaced blockwork cavity walls

All building types

	Element number	Summary Rating	Climate change	Water extraction	Mineral resource extraction	Stratospheric ozone depletion	Human toxicity	Ecotoxicity to freshwater	Nuclear waste (higher level)	Ecotoxicity to land	Waste disposal	Fossil fuel depletion	Eutrophication	Photochemical ozone creation	Acidification	Typical replacement interval	Embodied CO_2 (kg CO_2 eq.)	Recycled content (kg)	Recycled content (%)	Recycled currently at EOL (%)
Cement rendered medium density solid blockwork outer leaf, insulation (cont'd):																				
dense solid blockwork inner leaf, cement mortar, plasterboard on battens, paint	806180171	A+	A	A+	A+	B	A+	A+	A+	A+	A	A+	A+	A+	A	50	76	3.6	1	88
lightweight solid blockwork inner leaf, cement mortar, plasterboard on battens, paint	806180595	A+	A	A+	A+	B	A+	A+	A+	A+	A+	A+	A	A+	A	50	85	3.6	1	87
superlightweight solid blockwork inner leaf, cement mortar, plaster, paint	806180180	A+	A	A+	A+	B	A+	A+	A+	A+	A+	A+	A+	A+	A+	50	83	0.7	0	85
superlightweight solid blockwork inner leaf, cement mortar, plasterboard on battens, paint	806180181	A+	A	A+	A+	B	A+	A+	A+	A+	A+	A+	A+	A+	A	50	85	3.6	1	87
Cement rendered superlightweight solid blockwork cavity wall, insulation:																				
cement mortar, plaster, paint	806180040	A+	A	A+	A+	B	A+	A+	A+	A+	A+	A+	A+	A+	A+	50	85	0.7	0	84
cement mortar, plasterboard on battens, paint	806180041	A+	A	A+	A+	B	A+	A+	A+	A+	A+	A+	A+	A+	A	50	86	3.9	2	85
Cement rendered superlightweight solid blockwork outer leaf, insulation:																				
aircrete blockwork inner leaf, cement mortar, plaster, paint	806180196	A+	A	A+	A+	A	A+	A+	A+	A+	A+	A+	A+	A+	A+	50	78	0.7	0	83
aircrete blockwork inner leaf, cement mortar, plasterboard on battens, paint	806180197	A+	A	A+	A+	A	A+	A+	A+	A+	A+	A+	A+	A+	A	50	80	3.6	2	86
dense solid blockwork inner leaf, cement mortar, plaster, paint	806180204	A+	A	A+	A+	B	A+	A+	A+	A+	A	A+	A+	A+	A+	50	76	0.7	0	85
dense solid blockwork inner leaf, cement mortar, plasterboard on battens, paint	806180205	A+	A	A+	A+	B	A+	A+	A+	A+	A+	A+	A+	A+	A	50	78	3.6	1	87
medium density solid blockwork inner leaf, cement mortar, plaster, paint	806180212	A+	A	A+	A+	B	A+	A+	A+	A+	A+	A+	A+	A+	A+	50	83	0.7	0	85
medium density solid blockwork inner leaf, cement mortar, plasterboard on battens, paint	806180213	A+	A	A+	A+	B	A+	A+	A+	A+	A+	A+	A+	A+	A	50	85	3.6	1	87

Rendered or fairfaced blockwork cavity walls

All building types

	Element number	Summary Rating	Climate change	Water extraction	Mineral resource extraction	Stratospheric ozone depletion	Human toxicity	Ecotoxicity to freshwater	Nuclear waste (higher level)	Ecotoxicity to land	Waste disposal	Fossil fuel depletion	Eutrophication	Photochemical ozone creation	Acidification	Typical replacement interval	Embodied CO2 (kg CO2 eq.)	Recycled content (kg)	Recycled content (%)	Recycled currently at EOL (%)
Cement:lime rendered aircrete blockwork cavity wall, insulation:																				
cement:lime mortar, plaster, paint	806180100	A+	A	A+	A+	A	A+	A+	A+	A+	A+	A+	A+	A+	A+	50	71	0.7	0	81
cement:lime mortar, plasterboard on battens, paint	806180101	A+	A	A+	A+	A	A+	A+	A+	A+	A+	A+	A+	A+	A+	50	72	3.6	2	85
Cement:lime rendered aircrete blockwork outer leaf, insulation:																				
dense solid blockwork inner leaf, cement:lime mortar, plaster, paint	806180104	A+	A	A+	A+	A	A+	A+	A+	A+	A+	A+	A+	A+	A+	50	68	0.7	0	85
dense solid blockwork inner leaf, cement:lime mortar, plasterboard on battens, paint	806180105	A+	A	A+	A+	A	A+	A+	A+	A+	A+	A+	A+	A+	A	50	70	3.6	1	87
medium density solid blockwork inner leaf, cement:lime mortar, plaster, paint	806180112	A+	A	A+	A+	A	A+	A+	A+	A+	A+	A+	A+	A+	A+	50	76	0.7	0	84
medium density solid blockwork inner leaf, cement:lime mortar, plasterboard on battens, paint	806180113	A+	A	A+	A+	A	A+	A+	A+	A+	A+	A+	A+	A+	A	50	77	3.6	1	87
superlightweight solid blockwork inner leaf, cement:lime mortar, plaster, paint	806180120	A+	A	A+	A+	A	A+	A+	A+	A+	A+	A+	A+	A+	A+	50	77	0.7	0	83
superlightweight solid blockwork inner leaf, cement:lime mortar, plasterboard on battens, paint	806180121	A+	A	A+	A+	A	A+	A+	A+	A+	A+	A+	A+	A+	A	50	79	3.6	2	86
Cement:lime rendered dense solid blockwork cavity wall, insulation:																				
cement:lime mortar, plaster, paint	806180062	A	A	A+	A	B	A+	A+	A+	A+	A	A+	A+	A+	A+	50	66	0.7	0	86
cement:lime mortar, plasterboard on battens, paint	806180069	A	A	A+	A	B	A+	A+	A+	A+	A	A+	A+	A+	A	50	68	3.6	1	88
Cement:lime rendered dense solid blockwork outer leaf, insulation:																				
aircrete concrete blockwork inner leaf, cement:lime mortar, plaster, paint	806180058	A+	A	A+	A+	A	A+	A+	A+	A+	A+	A+	A+	A+	A+	50	68	0.7	0	85
aircrete concrete blockwork inner leaf, cement:lime mortar, plasterboard on battens, paint	806180070	A+	A	A+	A+	A	A+	A+	A+	A+	A+	A+	A+	A+	A	50	70	3.6	1	87
medium density concrete solid blockwork inner leaf, cement:lime mortar, plaster, paint	806180082	A+	A	A+	A+	B	A+	A+	A+	A+	A	A+	A+	A+	A+	50	73	0.7	0	86

Cont'd . . . .

Rendered or fairfaced blockwork cavity walls

All building types

	Element number	Summary Rating	Climate change	Water extraction	Mineral resource extraction	Stratospheric ozone depletion	Human toxicity	Ecotoxicity to freshwater	Nuclear waste (higher level)	Ecotoxicity to land	Waste disposal	Fossil fuel depletion	Eutrophication	Photochemical ozone creation	Acidification	Typical replacement interval	Embodied CO2 (kg CO2 eq.)	Recycled content (kg)	Recycled content (%)	Recycled currently at EOL (%)
Cement:lime rendered dense solid blockwork outer leaf, insulation (cont'd):																				
medium density concrete solid blockwork inner leaf, cement:lime mortar, plasterboard on battens, paint	806180090	A+	A	A+	A+	B	A+	A+	A+	A+	A	A+	A+	A+	A	50	75	3.6	1	88
superlightweight concrete solid blockwork inner leaf, cement:lime mortar, plaster, paint	806180148	A+	A	A+	A+	B	A+	A+	A+	A+	A	A+	A+	A+	A+	50	75	0.7	0	85
superlightweight concrete solid blockwork inner leaf, cement:lime mortar, plasterboard on battens, paint	806180149	A+	A	A+	A+	B	A+	A+	A+	A+	A+	A+	A+	A+	A	50	77	3.6	1	87
Cement:lime rendered medium density solid blockwork cavity wall, insulation:																				
cement:lime mortar, plaster, paint	806180079	A+	A	A+	A+	B	A+	A+	A+	A+	A	A+	A+	A+	A+	50	81	0.7	0	85
cement:lime mortar, plasterboard on battens, paint	806180075	A+	A	A+	A+	B	A+	A+	A+	A+	A+	A+	A+	A+	A	50	82	3.6	1	88
Cement:lime rendered medium density solid blockwork outer leaf, insulation:																				
aircrete blockwork inner leaf, cement:lime mortar, plaster, paint	806180054	A+	A	A+	A+	A	A+	A+	A+	A+	A+	A+	A+	A+	A+	50	76	0.7	0	84
aircrete blockwork inner leaf, cement:lime mortar, plasterboard on battens, paint	806180071	A+	A	A+	A+	A	A+	A+	A+	A+	A+	A+	A+	A+	A	50	77	3.6	1	87
dense solid blockwork inner leaf, cement:lime mortar, plaster, paint	806180168	A+	A	A+	A+	B	A+	A+	A+	A+	A	A+	A+	A+	A+	50	73	0.7	0	86
dense solid blockwork inner leaf, cement:lime mortar, plasterboard on battens, paint	806180169	A+	A	A+	A+	B	A+	A+	A+	A+	A	A+	A+	A+	A	50	75	3.6	1	88
superlightweight solid blockwork inner leaf, cement:lime mortar, plaster, paint	806180178	A+	A	A+	A+	B	A+	A+	A+	A+	A+	A+	A+	A+	A+	50	82	0.7	0	85
superlightweight solid blockwork inner leaf, cement:lime mortar, plasterboard on battens, paint	806180179	A+	A	A+	A+	B	A+	A+	A+	A+	A+	A+	A+	A+	A	50	84	3.6	1	87

Rendered or fairfaced blockwork cavity walls

All building types

	Element number	Summary Rating	Climate change	Water extraction	Mineral resource extraction	Stratospheric ozone depletion	Human toxicity	Ecotoxicity to freshwater	Nuclear waste (higher level)	Ecotoxicity to land	Waste disposal	Fossil fuel depletion	Eutrophication	Photochemical ozone creation	Acidification	Typical replacement interval	Embodied CO2 (kg CO2 eq.)	Recycled content (kg)	Recycled content (%)	Recycled currently at EOL (%)
Cement:lime rendered superlightweight solid blockwork cavity wall, insulation:																				
cement:lime mortar, plaster, paint	806180073	A+	A	A+	A+	B	A+	A+	A+	A+	A+	A+	A+	A+	A+	50	84	0.7	0	84
cement:lime mortar, plasterboard on battens, paint	806180074	A+	A	A+	A+	B	A+	A+	A+	A+	A+	A+	A+	A+	A	50	85	3.9	2	85
Cement:lime rendered superlightweight solid blockwork outer leaf, insulation:																				
aircrete blockwork inner leaf, cement:lime mortar, plaster, paint	806180194	A+	A	A+	A+	A	A+	A+	A+	A+	A+	A+	A+	A+	A+	50	77	0.7	0	83
aircrete blockwork inner leaf, cement:lime mortar, plasterboard on battens, paint	806180195	A+	A	A+	A+	A	A+	A+	A+	A+	A+	A+	A+	A+	A	50	79	3.6	2	86
dense solid blockwork inner leaf, cement:lime mortar, plaster, paint	806180202	A+	A	A+	A+	B	A+	A+	A+	A+	A	A+	A+	A+	A+	50	75	0.7	0	85
dense solid blockwork inner leaf, cement:lime mortar, plasterboard on battens, paint	806180203	A+	A	A+	A+	B	A+	A+	A+	A+	A+	A+	A+	A+	A	50	77	3.6	1	87
medium density solid blockwork inner leaf, cement:lime mortar, plaster, paint	806180210	A+	A	A+	A+	B	A+	A+	A+	A+	A+	A+	A+	A+	A+	50	82	0.7	0	85
medium density solid blockwork inner leaf, cement:lime mortar, plasterboard on battens, paint	806180211	A+	A	A+	A+	B	A+	A+	A+	A+	A+	A+	A+	A+	A	50	84	3.6	1	87
Fairfaced solid blockwork outer leaf, insulation, aircrete blockwork inner leaf:																				
cement mortar, plaster, paint	806180232	A+	A	A+	A+	A	A+	A+	A+	A+	A+	A+	A+	A+	A+	60+	60	0.5	0	84
cement mortar, plasterboard on battens, paint	806180233	A+	A	A+	A+	A	A+	A+	A+	A+	A+	A+	A+	A+	A+	60+	62	3.4	1	87
cement:lime mortar, plaster, paint	806180230	A+	A	A+	A+	A	A+	A+	A+	A+	A+	A+	A+	A+	A+	60+	60	0.5	0	84
cement:lime mortar, plasterboard on battens, paint	806180231	A+	A	A+	A+	A	A+	A+	A+	A+	A+	A+	A+	A+	A+	60+	62	3.4	1	87

Rendered or fairfaced blockwork cavity walls

All building types

	Element number	Summary Rating	Climate change	Water extraction	Mineral resource extraction	Stratospheric ozone depletion	Human toxicity	Ecotoxicity to freshwater	Nuclear waste (higher level)	Ecotoxicity to land	Waste disposal	Fossil fuel depletion	Eutrophication	Photochemical ozone creation	Acidification	Typical replacement interval	Embodied CO2 (kg CO2 eq.)	Recycled content (kg)	Recycled content (%)	Recycled currently at EOL (%)
Fairfaced solid blockwork outer leaf, insulation, dense solid blockwork inner leaf:																				
cement mortar, plaster, paint	806180240	A+	A+	A+	A	A	A+	A+	A+	A+	A	A+	A+	A+	A+	60+	58	0.5	0	86
cement mortar, plasterboard on battens, paint	806180244	A+	A	A+	A+	A	A+	A+	A+	A+	A	A+	A+	A+	A+	60+	60	3.4	1	88
cement:lime mortar, plaster, paint	806180238	A+	A+	A+	A	A	A+	A+	A+	A+	A	A+	A+	A+	A+	60+	58	0.5	0	86
cement:lime mortar, plasterboard on battens, paint	806180239	A+	A	A+	A+	A	A+	A+	A+	A+	A	A+	A+	A+	A+	60+	60	3.4	1	88
Fairfaced solid blockwork outer leaf, insulation, medium density solid blockwork inner leaf:																				
cement mortar, plaster, paint	806180247	A+	A	A+	A+	A	A+	A+	A+	A+	A+	A+	A+	A+	A+	60+	65	0.5	0	86
cement mortar, plasterboard on battens, paint	806180248	A+	A	A+	A+	A	A+	A+	A+	A+	A+	A+	A+	A+	A	60+	67	3.4	1	88
cement:lime mortar, plaster, paint	806180245	A+	A	A+	A+	A	A+	A+	A+	A+	A+	A+	A+	A+	A+	60+	65	0.5	0	86
cement:lime mortar, plasterboard on battens, paint	806180246	A+	A	A+	A+	A	A+	A+	A+	A+	A+	A+	A+	A+	A	60+	67	3.4	1	88
Fairfaced solid blockwork outer leaf, insulation, superlightweight solid blockwork inner leaf:																				
cement mortar, plaster, paint	806180255	A+	A	A+	A+	A	A+	A+	A+	A+	A+	A+	A+	A+	A+	60+	67	0.5	0	85
cement mortar, plasterboard on battens, paint	806180256	A+	A	A+	A+	A	A+	A+	A+	A+	A+	A+	A+	A+	A	60+	69	3.4	1	87
cement:lime mortar, plaster, paint	806180253	A+	A	A+	A+	A	A+	A+	A+	A+	A+	A+	A+	A+	A+	60+	67	0.5	0	85
cement:lime mortar, plasterboard on battens, paint	806180254	A+	A	A+	A+	A	A+	A+	A+	A+	A+	A+	A+	A+	A	60+	69	3.4	1	87

Brick and light steel-framed construction

All building types

	Element number	Summary Rating	Climate change	Water extraction	Mineral resource extraction	Stratospheric ozone depletion	Human toxicity	Ecotoxicity to freshwater	Nuclear waste (higher level)	Ecotoxicity to land	Waste disposal	Fossil fuel depletion	Eutrophication	Photochemical ozone creation	Acidification	Typical replacement interval	Embodied CO2 (kg CO2 eq.)	Recycled content (kg)	Recycled content (%)	Recycled currently at EOL (%)
Brickwork, cement mortar:																				
cement-bonded particle board sheathing, insulation, light steel frame, vapour control layer, plasterboard on battens, paint	806470537	A+	A	A+	A+	A	A+	A+	A+	A+	A+	A+	A+	A+	A	60+	94	5	3	77
no sheathing, insulation, light steel frame, vapour control layer, plasterboard on battens, paint	806470091	A+	A	A+	A+	A+	A+	A+	A+	A+	A+	A+	A+	A+	A	60+	69	3.8	2	83
OSB/3 sheathing, insulation, light steel frame, vapour control layer, plasterboard on battens, paint	806470543	A+	A	A+	A+	A	A+	A+	A+	A+	A+	A+	A+	A+	A	60+	64	8.1	5	81
plywood (temperate EN 636-2) sheathing, insulation, light steel frame, vapour control layer, plasterboard on battens, paint	806470540	A+	A	A+	A+	A	A+	A+	A+	A	A+	A	A+	A+	A	60+	67	3.8	2	78
Brickwork, cement:lime mortar:																				
no sheathing, insulation, light steel frame, vapour control layer, plasterboard on battens, paint	806490046	A+	A	A+	A+	A+	A+	A+	A+	A+	A+	A+	A+	A+	A	60+	68	3.8	2	83
OSB/3 sheathing, insulation, light steel frame, vapour control layer, plasterboard on battens, paint	806470078	A+	A	A+	A+	A	A+	A+	A+	A+	A+	A+	A+	A+	A	60+	64	8.1	5	81
Reclaimed brickwork:																				
cement mortar, OSB/3 sheathing, insulation, light steel frame, vapour control layer, plasterboard on battens, paint	806470546	A+	A+	A+	A+	A+	A+	A+	A+	A+	A+	A+	A+	A+	A+	60+	40	134	72	80
plywood (temperate EN 636-2) sheathing, insulation, light steel frame, vapour control layer, plasterboard on battens, paint	806470050	A+	A+	A+	A+	A	A+	A+	A+	A	A+	A+	A+	A+	A+	60+	44	129	68	78

Brick and timber-framed construction

All building types

	Element number	Summary Rating	Climate change	Water extraction	Mineral resource extraction	Stratospheric ozone depletion	Human toxicity	Ecotoxicity to freshwater	Nuclear waste (higher level)	Ecotoxicity to land	Waste disposal	Fossil fuel depletion	Eutrophication	Photochemical ozone creation	Acidification	Typical replacement interval	Embodied CO_2 (kg CO_2 eq.)	Recycled content (kg)	Recycled content (%)	Recycled currently at EOL (%)
Brickwork, cement mortar:																				
cement-bonded particle board, timber frame with insulation, vapour control layer, plasterboard on battens, paint	806190536	A+	A	A+	A+	A	A+	A+	A+	A+	A+	A+	A+	A+	A	60+	82	5.7	3	73
OSB/3 sheathing, timber frame with insulation, vapour control layer, plasterboard on battens, paint	806190047	A+	A+	A+	A+	A	A+	A+	A+	A+	A+	A+	A+	A+	A	60+	52	8.8	5	76
plywood (temperate EN 636-2) sheathing, timber frame with insulation, vapour control layer, plasterboard on battens, paint	806190056	A+	A+	A+	A+	B	A+	A+	A	A	A+	A	A+	A	A	60+	55	4.1	2	75
Reclaimed brickwork:																				
cement mortar, OSB/3 sheathing, insulation, timber frame, vapour control layer, plasterboard on battens, paint	806190545	A+	A+	A+	A+	A	A+	A+	A+	A+	A+	A+	A+	A+	A+	60+	28	134	74	79
plywood (temperate EN 636-2) sheathing, timber frame with insulation, vapour control layer, plasterboard on battens, paint	806190051	A+	A+	A+	A+	A	A+	A+	A+	A	A+	A+	A+	A+	A+	60+	31	129	69	78

Rendered or fairfaced blockwork and light steel-framed construction

All building types

	Element number	Summary Rating	Climate change	Water extraction	Mineral resource extraction	Stratospheric ozone depletion	Human toxicity	Ecotoxicity to freshwater	Nuclear waste (higher level)	Ecotoxicity to land	Waste disposal	Fossil fuel depletion	Eutrophication	Photochemical ozone creation	Acidification	Typical replacement interval	Embodied CO_2 (kg CO_2 eq.)	Recycled content (kg)	Recycled content (%)	Recycled currently at EOL (%)
Cement render, aircrete blockwork outer leaf, cement mortar, insulation, light steel frame, vapour control layer, plasterboard on battens, paint	806480130	A+	A	A+	A+	A+	A+	A+	A+	A+	A+	A+	A+	A+	A+	50	68	3.9	3	80
Cement render, dense outer leaf, cement mortar, insulation, light steel frame, vapour control layer, plasterboard on battens, paint	806480158	A+	A	A+	A+	A	A+	A+	A+	A+	A+	A+	A+	A+	A+	50	66	3.9	2	85
Cement render, lightweight solid block outer leaf:																				
cement bonded particle board, insulation, light steel frame, vapour control layer, plasterboard on battens, paint	806480549	A+	A	A+	A+	A	A+	A+	A+	A+	A	A+	A+	A+	A	50	100	5.1	3	77
no sheathing, insulation, light steel frame, vapour control layer, plasterboard on battens, paint	806480550	A+	A	A+	A+	A	A+	A+	A+	A+	A+	A+	A+	A+	A	50	75	3.9	2	83
Cement render, medium density solid block outer leaf:																				
cement bonded particle board sheathing, insulation, light steel frame, vapour control layer, plasterboard on battens, paint	806480547	A+	A	A+	A+	A	A+	A+	A+	A+	A	A+	A+	A+	A	50	99	5.1	2	79
no sheathing, insulation, light steel frame, vapour control layer, plasterboard on battens, paint	806480548	A+	A	A+	A+	A	A+	A+	A+	A+	A+	A+	A+	A+	A	50	73	3.9	2	84
Cement render, superlightweight outer leaf, cement mortar, insulation, light steel frame, vapour control layer, plasterboard on battens, paint	806480229	A+	A	A+	A+	A	A+	A+	A+	A+	A+	A+	A+	A+	A	50	74	3.9	2	83
Cement:lime render, aircrete blockwork outer leaf, cement:lime mortar, insulation, light steel frame, vapour control layer, plasterboard on battens, paint	806480132	A+	A	A+	A+	A+	A+	A+	A+	A+	A+	A+	A+	A+	A+	50	67	3.9	3	80
Cement:lime render, dense outer leaf, cement:lime mortar, insulation, light steel frame, vapour control layer, plasterboard on battens, paint	806480156	A+	A	A+	A+	A	A+	A+	A+	A+	A+	A+	A+	A+	A+	50	64	3.9	2	85
Cement:lime render, lightweight outer leaf, cement:lime mortar, insulation, light steel frame, vapour control layer, plasterboard on battens, paint	806480186	A+	A	A+	A+	A	A+	A+	A+	A+	A+	A+	A+	A+	A	50	73	3.9	2	83

Rendered or fairfaced blockwork and light steel-framed construction

All building types

	Element number	Summary Rating	Climate change	Water extraction	Mineral resource extraction	Stratospheric ozone depletion	Human toxicity	Ecotoxicity to freshwater	Nuclear waste (higher level)	Ecotoxicity to land	Waste disposal	Fossil fuel depletion	Eutrophication	Photochemical ozone creation	Acidification	Typical replacement interval	Embodied CO$_2$ (kg CO$_2$ eq.)	Recycled content (kg)	Recycled content (%)	Recycled currently at EOL (%)
Cement:lime render, superlightweight outer leaf, cement:lime mortar, insulation, light steel frame, vapour control layer, plasterboard on battens, paint	806480226	A+	A	A+	A+	A	A+	A+	A+	A+	A+	A+	A+	A+	A	50	73	3.9	2	83
Fairfaced solid blockwork outer leaf, cement mortar, insulation, light steel frame, vapour control layer, plasterboard on battens, paint	806480267	A+	A+	A+	A+	A+	A+	A+	A+	A+	A+	A+	A+	A+	A+	60+	57	3.7	2	85

Rendered or fairfaced blockwork and timber-framed construction

All building types

	Element number	Summary Rating	Climate change	Water extraction	Mineral resource extraction	Stratospheric ozone depletion	Human toxicity	Ecotoxicity to freshwater	Nuclear waste (higher level)	Ecotoxicity to land	Waste disposal	Fossil fuel depletion	Eutrophication	Photochemical ozone creation	Acidification	Typical replacement interval	Embodied CO2 (kg CO2 eq.)	Recycled content (kg)	Recycled content (%)	Recycled currently at EOL (%)
Cement render, aircrete blockwork outer leaf, cement mortar, insulation, timber frame, vapour control layer, plasterboard on battens, paint	806480134	A+	A+	A+	A+	A	A+	A+	A+	A+	A+	A+	A+	A+	A+	50	55	4.2	3	75
Cement render, lightweight outer leaf, cement mortar, insulation, timber frame, vapour control layer, plasterboard on battens, paint	806480188	A+	A	A+	A+	B	A+	A+	A+	A+	A+	A+	A+	A+	A	50	62	4.2	2	79
Cement:lime render, aircrete blockwork outer leaf, cement:lime mortar, insulation, timber frame, vapour control layer, plasterboard on battens, paint	806480128	A+	A+	A+	A+	A	A+	A+	A+	A+	A+	A+	A+	A+	A+	50	54	4.2	3	75
Fairfaced solid blockwork outer leaf, insulation, timber frame, vapour control layer, plasterboard on battens, paint	806480265	A+	A+	A+	A+	A	A+	A+	A+	A+	A+	A+	A+	A+	A+	60+	44	4	2	82

Cladding on light steel-framed construction

All building types

	Element number	Summary Rating	Climate change	Water extraction	Mineral resource extraction	Stratospheric ozone depletion	Human toxicity	Ecotoxicity to freshwater	Nuclear waste (higher level)	Ecotoxicity to land	Waste disposal	Fossil fuel depletion	Eutrophication	Photochemical ozone creation	Acidification	Typical replacement interval	Embodied CO2 (kg CO2 eq.)	Recycled content (kg)	Recycled content (%)	Recycled currently at EOL (%)
Canadian cedar boarding on timber battens, breather membrane:																				
cement-bonded particle board sheathing, insulation, light steel frame, vapour control layer, plasterboard on battens, paint	806490593	A+	A+	A+	A+	A	A+	A+	A+	A+	A+	A+	A+	A	A	35	55	5.2	12	22
no sheathing, insulation, light steel frame, vapour control layer, plasterboard on battens, paint	806490594	A+	A+	A+	A+	A	A+	A+	A+	A+	A+	A+	A+	A+	A+	35	30	3.7	12	33
OSB/3 sheathing, insulation, light steel frame, vapour control layer, plasterboard on battens, paint	806490592	A+	A+	A+	A+	A	A+	A+	A+	A+	A+	A+	A+	A+	A	35	25	8.4	22	26
plywood sheathing, insulation, light steel frame, vapour control layer, plasterboard on battens, paint	806490591	A+	A+	A	A+	B	A+	A+	A+	A	A+	A+	A+	A	A	35	28	3.7	9	24
Clay tiles on timber battens, breather membrane:																				
cement-bonded particle board sheathing, insulation, light steel frame, vapour control layer, plasterboard on battens, paint	806490577	A	A	A	A+	B	A+	A+	A	A	A	B	A+	A	A	40	120	5.2	5	59
no sheathing, insulation, light steel frame, vapour control layer, plasterboard on battens, paint	806490578	A+	A	A+	A+	A	A+	A+	A	A+	A+	A	A+	A	A	40	91	3.7	4	70
OSB/3 sheathing, insulation, light steel frame, vapour control layer, plasterboard on battens, paint	806490576	A	A	A	A+	B	A+	A+	A	A+	A	A	A+	A	A	40	86	8.4	9	64
plywood (softwood) sheathing, insulation, light steel frame, vapour control layer, plasterboard on battens, paint	806490575	A	A	A	A+	B	A+	A+	B	B	A	B	A+	B	A	40	90	3.7	4	62
Concrete tiles on timber battens, breather membrane:																				
cement-bonded particle board sheathing, insulation, light steel frame, vapour control layer, plasterboard on battens, paint	806490581	A+	A	A+	A+	A	A+	A+	A+	A	A	A	A+	A	A	40	94	4.9	6	57
no sheathing, insulation, light steel frame, vapour control layer, plasterboard on battens, paint	806490582	A+	A	A+	A+	A	A+	A+	A+	A+	A+	A+	A+	A	A	40	68	3.7	5	69

Cont'd . . . .

Cladding on light steel-framed construction

All building types

	Element number	Summary Rating	Climate change	Water extraction	Mineral resource extraction	Stratospheric ozone depletion	Human toxicity	Ecotoxicity to freshwater	Nuclear waste (higher level)	Ecotoxicity to land	Waste disposal	Fossil fuel depletion	Eutrophication	Photochemical ozone creation	Acidification	Typical replacement interval	Embodied CO2 (kg CO2 eq.)	Recycled content (kg)	Recycled content (%)	Recycled currently at EOL (%)
Concrete tiles on timber battens, breather membrane (cont'd):																				
OSB/3 sheathing, insulation, light steel frame, vapour control layer, plasterboard on battens, paint	806490580	A+	A	A+	A+	A	A+	A+	A+	A+	A+	A+	A+	A	A	40	64	8.4	10	63
plywood (softwood) sheathing, insulation, light steel frame, vapour control layer, plasterboard on battens, paint	806490579	A+	A	A	A+	B	A+	A+	A	B	A+	A	A+	A	A	40	67	3.7	4	60
Angle seamed copper cladding with plywood backing on steel fixing rails, breather membrane, no sheathing, insulation, light steel frame, plasterboard on battens, paint	806490596	A	A+	C	A+	C	A+	A+	B	C	A	A	A	A	A	45	58	8.2	18	31
Glass reinforced plastic (GRP) cladding, aluminium fixing rails, insulation, light steel frame, vapour control layer, plasterboard on battens, paint	806490007	A	A	B	A+	A	B	A	B	E	A+	A	A+	A+	A	35	120	4.4	16	30
Glass reinforced composite (GRC) cladding with stainless steel support, insulation, edpm layer, light steel frame, plasterboard, paint	806491077	A+	A	A+	A+	A+	A+	A+	A+	A+	A+	A+	A+	A+	A+	60	91	7.2	29	44
Polymeric render system, breather membrane:																				
cement-bonded particle board sheathing, insulation, light steel frame, vapour control layer, plasterboard on battens, paint	806490573	A+	A	A+	A+	A+	A+	A+	A+	A+	A+	A+	A+	A+	A+	50	72	5.2	12	15
OSB/3 sheathing, insulation, light steel frame, vapour control layer, plasterboard on battens, paint	806490572	A+	A+	A+	A+	A+	A+	A+	A+	A+	A+	A+	A+	A+	A+	50	42	8.4	23	19
plywood (softwood) sheathing, insulation, light steel frame, vapour control layer, plasterboard on battens, paint	806490571	A+	A+	A+	A+	A+	A+	A+	A+	A	A+	A+	A+	A	A	50	45	3.7	9	17

Cladding on light steel-framed construction

All building types

	Element number	Summary Rating	Climate change	Water extraction	Mineral resource extraction	Stratospheric ozone depletion	Human toxicity	Ecotoxicity to freshwater	Nuclear waste (higher level)	Ecotoxicity to land	Waste disposal	Fossil fuel depletion	Eutrophication	Photochemical ozone creation	Acidification	Typical replacement interval	Embodied CO2 (kg CO2 eq.)	Recycled content (kg)	Recycled content (%)	Recycled currently at EOL (%)
Treated softwood boarding on timber battens, breather membrane:																				
cement-bonded particle board sheathing, insulation, light steel frame, vapour control layer, plasterboard on battens, paint	806490589	A+	A+	A+	A+	A	A+	A+	A+	A+	A	A+	A+	E	A+	30	40	5.2	11	18
no sheathing, insulation, light steel frame, vapour control layer, plasterboard on battens, paint	806490590	A+	A+	A+	A+	A	A+	A+	A+	A+	A+	A+	A+	E	A+	30	14	3.7	11	27
OSB/3 sheathing, insulation, light steel frame, vapour control layer, plasterboard on battens, paint	806490588	A+	A+	A+	A+	A	A+	A+	A+	A+	A	A+	A+	E	A+	30	9.5	8.4	21	22
plywood (softwood) sheathing, insulation, light steel frame, vapour control layer, plasterboard on battens, paint	806490587	A+	A+	A+	A+	B	A+	A+	A+	A	A	A+	A+	E	A+	30	13	3.7	8	20
UK produced natural slate on timber battens, breather membrane:																				
cement-bonded particle board sheathing, insulation, light steel frame, vapour control layer, plasterboard on battens, paint	806490585	A	A	A+	A	A	A+	A+	A+	A+	A+	A+	A+	A	A	60+	78	4.9	7	50
no sheathing, insulation, light steel frame, vapour control layer, plasterboard on battens, paint	806490586	A+	A+	A+	A	A	A+	A+	A+	A+	A+	A+	A+	A+	A	60+	52	3.7	6	65
OSB/3 sheathing, insulation, light steel frame, vapour control layer, plasterboard on battens, paint	806490584	A+	A+	A+	A	A	A+	A+	A+	A+	A+	A+	A+	A+	A	60+	47	8.4	12	58
plywood sheathing, insulation, light steel frame, vapour control layer, plasterboard on battens, paint	806490583	A	A+	A+	A	B	A+	A+	A	A	A+	A+	A	A	A	60+	51	3.7	5	55

Cladding on timber-framed construction

All building types

	Element number	Summary Rating	Climate change	Water extraction	Mineral resource extraction	Stratospheric ozone depletion	Human toxicity	Ecotoxicity to freshwater	Nuclear waste (higher level)	Ecotoxicity to land	Waste disposal	Fossil fuel depletion	Eutrophication	Photochemical ozone creation	Acidification	Typical replacement interval	Embodied CO2 (kg CO2 eq.)	Recycled content (kg)	Recycled content (%)	Recycled currently at EOL (%)
Angle seamed copper cladding on plywood (temperate EN 636-2) sheathing, breather membrane, timber frame with insulation, vapour control layer, plasterboard on timber battens, paint	806240451	A	A+	C	A+	C	A+	A+	B	C	A+	A	A	A	A	45	46	8.5	18	21
Canadian cedar weatherboarding:																				
breather membrane, plywood (temperate EN 636-2) sheathing, timber frame with insulation, vapour control layer, plasterboard on timber battens, paint	806210057	A+	A+	A	A+	B	A+	A+	A+	A	A+	A+	A+	A	A	35	17	4	9	13
breather membrane, OSB/3 sheathing, timber frame with insulation, vapour control layer, plasterboard on timber battens, paint	806210048	A+	A+	A+	A+	B	A+	A+	A+	A+	A+	A+	A+	A	A	35	14	8.7	21	14
Clay tiles on timber battens, breather membrane:																				
OSB/3 sheathing, timber frame with insulation, vapour control layer, plasterboard on timber battens, paint	806210570	A+	A	A	A+	B	A+	A+	A	A+	A+	A	A+	B	A	40	73	8.7	9	58
plywood (temperate EN 636-2) sheathing, timber frame with insulation, vapour control layer, plasterboard on timber battens, paint	806210058	A	A	A	A+	C	A+	A+	B	B	A	B	A+	B	A	40	76	4	4	55
Concrete tiles, battens, breather membrane:																				
OSB/3 sheathing, timber frame with insulation, vapour control layer, plasterboard on timber battens, paint	806210050	A+	A+	A+	A+	A	A+	A+	A+	A+	A+	A+	A+	A	A	40	50	8.7	10	55
plywood (temperate EN 636-2) sheathing, timber frame with insulation, vapour control layer, plasterboard on timber battens, paint	806210059	A+	A+	A	A+	B	A+	A+	A	B	A+	A	A+	A	A	40	53	4	5	53
Polymeric render system, breather membrane:																				
OSB/3 sheathing, timber frame with insulation, vapour control layer, plasterboard on timber battens, paint	806210554	A+	A+	A+	A+	A+	A+	A+	A+	A+	A+	A+	A+	A+	A+	50	29	8.7	22	7
plywood (temperate EN 636-2) sheathing, timber frame with insulation, vapour control layer, plasterboard on timber battens, paint	806210552	A+	A+	A+	A+	A	A+	A+	A+	A	A+	A+	A+	A	A	50	33	4	9	6

Cladding on timber-framed construction

All building types

	Element number	Summary Rating	Climate change	Water extraction	Mineral resource extraction	Stratospheric ozone depletion	Human toxicity	Ecotoxicity to freshwater	Nuclear waste (higher level)	Ecotoxicity to land	Waste disposal	Fossil fuel depletion	Eutrophication	Photochemical ozone creation	Acidification	Typical replacement interval	Embodied CO₂ (kg CO₂ eq.)	Recycled content (kg)	Recycled content (%)	Recycled currently at EOL (%)
Pre-treated softwood weatherboarding, breather membrane:																				
OSB/3 sheathing, timber frame with insulation, vapour control layer, plasterboard on timber battens, paint	806210051	A+	A+	A+	A+	B	A+	A+	A+	A+	A	A+	A+	E	A+	30	-3	8.7	20	11
plywood (temperate EN 636-2) sheathing, timber frame with insulation, vapour control layer, plasterboard on timber battens, paint	806210060	A+	A+	A+	A+	B	A+	A+	A+	A	A	A+	A+	E	A+	30	0.1	4	9	10
PVC weatherboarding, breather membrane:																				
OSB/3 sheathing, timber frame with insulation, vapour control layer, plasterboard on timber battens, paint	806210052	A+	A+	A+	A+	A	A+	A+	A	A+	A+	A+	A+	A+	A+	35	42	8.7	24	9
plywood (temperate EN 636-2) sheathing, timber frame with insulation, vapour control layer, plasterboard on timber battens, paint	806210061	A+	A+	A	A+	A	A+	A+	A	A	A+	A	A+	A	A	35	45	4	10	8
UK produced natural slate on timber battens, breather membrane:																				
OSB/3 sheathing, timber frame with insulation, vapour control layer, plasterboard on timber battens, paint	806210566	A+	A+	A+	A	A	A+	A+	A+	A+	A+	A+	A+	A	A	60+	35	8.7	12	49
plywood (temperate EN 636-2) sheathing, timber frame with insulation, vapour control layer, plasterboard on timber battens, paint	806210564	A	A+	A	A	B	A+	A+	A	A	A+	A+	A	A	A	60+	38	4	5	47

Cladding on loadbearing masonry

All building types

	Element number	Summary Rating	Climate change	Water extraction	Mineral resource extraction	Stratospheric ozone depletion	Human toxicity	Ecotoxicity to freshwater	Nuclear waste (higher level)	Ecotoxicity to land	Waste disposal	Fossil fuel depletion	Eutrophication	Photochemical ozone creation	Acidification	Typical replacement interval	Embodied CO$_2$ (kg CO$_2$ eq.)	Recycled content (kg)	Recycled content (%)	Recycled currently at EOL (%)
Autoclaved fibre cement (calcium silicate) cladding and steel support, insulation:																				
lightweight solid blockwork, plasterboard, paint	806220675	A+	A	A+	A+	A	A+	A+	A+	A+	A+	A+	A+	A+	A	35	82	3.7	2	78
medium density solid blockwork, plasterboard, paint	806220676	A+	A	A+	A+	A	A+	A+	A+	A+	A+	A+	A+	A+	A	35	81	3.7	2	80
aircrete blockwork, plasterboard, paint	806220701	A+	A	A+	A+	A+	A+	A+	A+	A+	A+	A+	A+	A+	A	35	73	3.7	3	70
Canadian Western red cedar cladding on timber battens, insulation:																				
lightweight solid blockwork, plasterboard, paint.	806220634	A+	A+	A+	A+	C	A+	A+	A+	A+	A+	A+	A+	A	A	35	54	3.7	2	81
medium density solid blockwork, plasterboard, paint	806220635	A+	A+	A+	A+	B	A+	A+	A+	A+	A+	A+	A+	A	A	35	52	3.7	2	83
aircrete blockwork, plasterboard, paint	806220692	A+	A+	A+	A+	B	A+	A+	A+	A+	A+	A+	A+	A	A	35	45	3.7	3	75
thin joint aircrete blockwork, plasterboard, paint	806220699	A+	A+	A+	A+	B	A+	A+	A+	A+	A+	A+	A+	A	A	35	44	3.7	4	74
Cement rendered:																				
lightweight solid blockwork with cement mortar, insulation, plasterboard on battens, paint	806220631	A+	A	A+	A+	A	A+	A+	A+	A+	A+	A+	A+	A+	A	50	70	3.9	2	84
medium density solid blockwork, insulation, plasterboard on battens, paint	806220007	A+	A	A+	A+	A	A+	A+	A+	A+	A+	A+	A+	A+	A	50	68	3.9	1	85
aircrete blockwork, insulation, plasterboard on battens, paint	806220693	A+	A	A+	A+	A+	A+	A+	A+	A+	A+	A+	A+	A+	A+	50	61	3.9	3	81
thin joint aircrete blockwork, insulation, plasterboard on battens, paint	806220694	A+	A	A+	A+	A+	A+	A+	A+	A+	A+	A+	A+	A+	A+	50	60	3.8	3	81
Cement:lime render:																				
lightweight solid blockwork with cement:lime mortar, insulation, plasterboard on battens, paint	806220626	A+	A	A+	A+	A	A+	A+	A+	A+	A+	A+	A+	A+	A	50	68	3.9	2	84
medium density solid blockwork with cement:lime mortar, insulation, plasterboard on battens, paint	806220620	A+	A+	A+	A+	A	A+	A+	A+	A+	A+	A+	A+	A+	A+	50	56	3.9	2	84
aircrete blockwork with cement:lime mortar, insulation, plasterboard on battens, paint	806220695	A+	A	A+	A+	A+	A+	A+	A+	A+	A+	A+	A+	A+	A+	50	60	3.9	3	81
thin joint aircrete blockwork, insulation, plasterboard on battens, paint	806220696	A+	A+	A+	A+	A+	A+	A+	A+	A+	A+	A+	A+	A+	A+	50	59	3.8	3	81

Cladding on loadbearing masonry

All building types

	Element number	Summary Rating	Climate change	Water extraction	Mineral resource extraction	Stratospheric ozone depletion	Human toxicity	Ecotoxicity to freshwater	Nuclear waste (higher level)	Ecotoxicity to land	Waste disposal	Fossil fuel depletion	Eutrophication	Photochemical ozone creation	Acidification	Typical replacement interval	Embodied CO₂ (kg CO₂ eq.)	Recycled content (kg)	Recycled content (%)	Recycled currently at EOL (%)
Clay tiles on timber battens:																				
lightweight solid blockwork with cement mortar, insulation, plasterboard on battens, paint	806220627	A	A	A+	A+	C	A+	A+	A	A+	A	B	A	B	A	40	110	3.7	2	83
medium density solid blockwork with cement mortar, insulation, plasterboard on battens, paint	806220621	A	A	A	A+	C	A+	A+	A	A+	A	B	A	B	A	40	110	3.7	1	84
aircrete blockwork with cement mortar, insulation, plasterboard on battens, paint	806220697	A	A	A+	A+	B	A+	A+	A	A+	A+	A	A+	A	A	40	100	3.7	2	80
thin joint aircrete blockwork with cement mortar, insulation, plasterboard on battens, paint	806220698	A	A	A+	A+	B	A+	A+	A	A+	A+	A	A+	A	A	40	100	3.7	2	80
Coated steel composite profiled panel with pentane blown PUR/PIR insulation and steel liner on steel support, breather membrane:																				
lightweight solid blockwork with cement mortar, plasterboard, paint	006300414	A	B	D	A+	B	A+	A+	A+	A	A	B	A	B	B	30	140	4.6	2	84
medium density solid blockwork with cement mortar, plasterboard, paint	806300413	A	B	D	A+	B	A+	A+	A+	A	A	B	A	B	B	30	140	4.6	2	85
aircrete blockwork with cement mortar, plasterboard, paint	806220700	A	B	D	A+	A	A+	A+	A+	A	A	B	A	B	A	30	130	4.6	4	80
Coated steel composite profiled panel with stone wool insulation and coated steel liner, breather membrane:																				
lightweight solid blockwork with cement mortar, plasterboard, paint	806300416	A	B	B	A+	A	A+	A+	A	A	B	B	A	A	B	30	150	12.9	7	80
medium density solid blockwork with cement mortar, plasterboard, paint	806300415	A	B	B	A+	A	A+	A+	A	A	B	B	A	A	B	30	150	12.9	5	82
aircrete blockwork with cement mortar, plasterboard, paint	806220702	A	B	B	A+	A+	A+	A+	A	A	A	A	A+	A	B	30	140	12.9	10	74

Cladding on loadbearing masonry

All building types

	Element number	Summary Rating	Climate change	Water extraction	Mineral resource extraction	Stratospheric ozone depletion	Human toxicity	Ecotoxicity to freshwater	Nuclear waste (higher level)	Ecotoxicity to land	Waste disposal	Fossil fuel depletion	Eutrophication	Photochemical ozone creation	Acidification	Typical replacement interval	Embodied CO2 (kg CO2 eq.)	Recycled content (kg)	Recycled content (%)	Recycled currently at EOL (%)
Coated steel profiled single sheet and steel support, breather membrane, insulation:																				
lightweight solid blockwork with cement mortar, plasterboard on battens, paint	806220412	A	B	B	A+	B	A+	A+	A	A	A	B	A	A	A	30	140	4.8	3	85
medium density solid blockwork with cement mortar, plasterboard on battens, paint	806220632	A	B	B	A+	A	A+	A+	A	A	A	B	A	A	A	30	130	4.8	2	86
aircrete blockwork with cement mortar, plasterboard on battens, paint	806220703	A	B	B	A+	A	A+	A+	A	A	A	A	A+	A	A	30	130	4.8	4	82
Concrete tiles on timber battens, spun bonded polyethylene sheet, insulation:																				
lightweight solid blockwork with cement mortar, plasterboard on battens, paint	806220408	A+	A	A+	A+	B	A+	A+	A+	A	A+	A	A	A	A	40	92	3.7	2	83
medium density solid blockwork with cement mortar, plasterboard on battens, paint	806220407	A	A	A+	A+	B	A+	A+	A+	A	A	A	A	A	A	40	90	3.7	1	85
aircrete blockwork with cement mortar, plasterboard on battens, paint	806220704	A+	A	A+	A+	A	A+	A+	A+	A	A+	A+	A+	A	A	40	83	3.7	2	80
Fibre cement sheet cladding on aluminium framework, insulation:																				
lightweight solid blockwork, plasterboard, paint	806220403	A	A	A+	A+	B	A	A	A	A	A+	A	A	A	B	30	110	4.1	2	79
medium density solid blockwork, plasterboard, paint	806220315	A	A	A+	A+	B	A	A	A	A	A+	A	A	A	A	30	110	4.1	2	82
aircrete blockwork, plasterboard, paint	806220705	A+	A	A+	A+	A	A	A	A	A+	A+	A	A	A+	A	30	100	4.1	4	73
Fibre reinforced plastic cladding on aluminium framework, insulation:																				
lightweight solid blockwork, plasterboard, paint	806220067	A	B	B	A+	C	B	A	B	E	A+	B	A	A	B	35	140	4.5	2	80
medium density solid blockwork, plasterboard, paint	806220298	A	B	B	A+	C	B	A	B	E	A+	B	A	A	B	35	140	4.1	2	86
Handset limestone cladding and support, insulation, lightweight solid blockwork, plasterboard and paint	806220034	A	B	B	A	B	A+	A+	A	A	A	B	B	A+	A	60+	150	8.8	3	87

Cladding on loadbearing masonry

All building types

	Element number	Summary Rating	Climate change	Water extraction	Mineral resource extraction	Stratospheric ozone depletion	Human toxicity	Ecotoxicity to freshwater	Nuclear waste (higher level)	Ecotoxicity to land	Waste disposal	Fossil fuel depletion	Eutrophication	Photochemical ozone creation	Acidification	Typical replacement interval	Embodied CO2 (kg CO2 eq.)	Recycled content (kg)	Recycled content (%)	Recycled currently at EOL (%)
High pressure laminate board with resin bonded cellulose core on timber battens, breather membrane, insulation:																				
lightweight solid blockwork, plasterboard, paint	806220026	A	A	C	A+	B	A	A+	A	A	A	B	A	A	A	40	91	3.7	2	78
medium density solid blockwork, plasterboard, paint	806220314	A	A	C	A+	B	A	A	A	A	A	B	A	A	A	40	90	3.7	2	80
aircrete blockwork, plasterboard, paint	806220706	A	A	C	A+	A	A	A+	A	A+	A+	B	A	A	A	40	82	3.7	3	70
Imported Chinese granite cladding and steel support, insulation:																				
lightweight solid blockwork, plasterboard, paint	806220088	B	B	A+	A	C	A+	A+	A+	A	A	B	B	A	B	60+	150	8.8	4	86
medium density solid blockwork, plasterboard, paint	806220677	B	B	A+	A	B	A+	A+	A+	A	A	B	B	A	B	60+	150	8.8	3	87
Imported Italian marble cladding, insulation and steel support:																				
lightweight solid blockwork, plasterboard, paint	806220048	B	B	A+	A	D	A+	A+	A+	A	A	B	B	A	B	60+	170	8.8	3	87
medium density solid blockwork, plasterboard on battens, paint	806220072	B	B	A	B	D	A+	A+	A+	A	A	B	B	A	B	60+	170	8.8	3	87
aircrete blockwork, plasterboard on battens, paint	806220708	B	B	A+	A	C	A+	A+	A+	A	A	B	B	A	A	60+	160	8.8	4	86
Limestone cladding and steel support, insulation, medium density solid blockwork, plasterboard on battens, paint	806220678	A	B	A	A+	B	A+	A+	A	A	A	A	A	A+	A	60+	140	8.8	3	87
PVC weatherboarding on timber battens, insulation:																				
lightweight solid blockwork wall, plasterboard, paint	806220059	A+	A	A+	A+	A	A+	A+	A	A+	A+	A	A+	A+	A	35	82	3.7	2	81
medium density solid blockwork wall, cement mortar, plasterboard, paint	806220045	A+	A	A+	A+	A	A+	A+	A+	A+	A+	A	A+	A+	A	35	80	3.7	2	83
aircrete blockwork wall, cement mortar, plasterboard, paint	806220707	A+	A	A+	A+	A+	A+	A+	A	A+	A+	A	A+	A+	A+	35	73	3.7	3	76

Cladding on loadbearing masonry

All building types

	Element number	Summary Rating	Climate change	Water extraction	Mineral resource extraction	Stratospheric ozone depletion	Human toxicity	Ecotoxicity to freshwater	Nuclear waste (higher level)	Ecotoxicity to land	Waste disposal	Fossil fuel depletion	Eutrophication	Photochemical ozone creation	Acidification	Typical replacement interval	Embodied CO_2 (kg CO_2 eq.)	Recycled content (kg)	Recycled content (%)	Recycled currently at EOL (%)
Sandstone rainscreen cladding and steel support, insulation:																				
lightweight solid blockwork, plasterboard and paint	806220083	B	B	A+	B	B	A+	A+	A+	A	A	A	A	A+	A	60+	140	8.8	3	87
medium density solid blockwork inner leaf, plasterboard and paint	806220055	B	B	A+	B	B	A+	A+	A+	A	A	A	A	A+	A	60+	130	8.8	3	88
Self supporting single skin copper cladding on steel fixing rails with insulation:																				
lightweight solid blockwork, plasterboard, paint	806220688	A	A	B	A	C	A+	A+	A	A+	A+	A	A	A+	A	45	110	9.2	5	85
medium density solid blockwork, plasterboard, paint	806220690	A	A	C	A	B	A+	A+	A	A+	A+	A	A	A+	A	45	100	9.2	4	86
Self supporting single skin copper rainscreen cladding on steel fixing rails with insulation:																				
medium density solid blockwork, plasterboard, paint	806220691	B	A	D	B	C	A+	A+	B	A+	A+	A	A	A+	A	45	120	12	5	87
vapour barrier, lightweight solid blockwork, plasterboard, paint	806220689	B	B	D	B	D	A+	A+	B	A+	A+	A	A	A+	A	45	120	12	7	86
Terracotta rainscreen cladding, aluminium framework, insulation:																				
lightweight solid blockwork wall, plasterboard and paint	806300077	A	A	A+	A+	B	A+	A	A	A+	A+	A	A+	A+	A	40	110	4.1	2	86
medium density solid blockwork wall, cement mortar, plasterboard and paint	806300055	A	A	A+	A+	B	A+	A	A	A+	A+	A	A+	A+	A	40	110	4.1	2	87
Treated softwood boarding on timber battens:																				
lightweight solid blockwork with cement mortar, insulation, plasterboard on battens, paint	806220629	A+	A+	A+	A+	C	A+	A+	A+	A+	A	A+	A+	E	A	30	37	3.7	2	79
medium density solid blockwork with cement mortar, insulation, plasterboard on battens, paint	806220623	A+	A+	A+	A+	B	A+	A+	A+	A+	A	A+	A+	E	A	30	35	3.7	2	82
UK produced natural slate on timber battens:																				
lightweight solid blockwork with cement mortar, insulation, plasterboard on battens, paint	806220628	A	A	A+	A	B	A+	A+	A+	A+	A+	A+	A	A	A	60+	75	3.7	2	83
medium density solid blockwork with cement mortar, insulation, plasterboard on battens, paint	806220622	A	A	A+	A	B	A+	A+	A+	A+	A+	A+	A	A	A	60+	73	3.7	1	84

Cladding on loadbearing masonry **All building types**	Element number	**Summary Rating**	Climate change	Water extraction	Mineral resource extraction	Stratospheric ozone depletion	Human toxicity	Ecotoxicity to freshwater	Nuclear waste (higher level)	Ecotoxicity to land	Waste disposal	Fossil fuel depletion	Eutrophication	Photochemical ozone creation	Acidification	Typical replacement interval	Embodied CO$_2$ (kg CO$_2$ eq.)	Recycled content (kg)	Recycled content (%)	Recycled currently at EOL (%)
UK slate rainscreen cladding and steel support, insulation:																				
lightweight aggregate solid blockwork inner leaf, plasterboard and paint	806220001	E	C	A	E	E	A	A	A	A	A	C	D	B	D	60+	190	9.2	3	86
medium density solid blockwork inner leaf, plasterboard and paint	806220002	E	B	A	E	E	A	A	A	A	A	C	D	B	D	60+	180	9.2	3	86

Insulated cladding on concrete frame with block infill

All building types

	Element number	Summary Rating	Climate change	Water extraction	Mineral resource extraction	Stratospheric ozone depletion	Human toxicity	Ecotoxicity to freshwater	Nuclear waste (higher level)	Ecotoxicity to land	Waste disposal	Fossil fuel depletion	Eutrophication	Photochemical ozone creation	Acidification	Typical replacement interval	Embodied CO2 (kg CO2 eq.)	Recycled content (kg)	Recycled content (%)	Recycled currently at EOL (%)
Coated aluminium composite profiled panel with pentane blown PUR/PIR insulation and steel liner on steel support:																				
structural concrete frame, lightweight solid blockwork with cement mortar, plasterboard on battens, paint	806370492	A	B	C	A+	B	A	A	A	B	A	B	A	B	B	35	140	11	6	84
structural concrete frame, medium solid blockwork with cement mortar, plasterboard on battens, paint	806370491	A	B	C	A+	B	A	A	A	B	A	B	A	B	B	35	140	11	5	85
structural concrete frame, aircrete blockwork with cement mortar, plasterboard on battens, paint	806370497	A	B	C	A+	A	A	A	A	B	A	A	A	A	A	35	130	11	9	81
Coated steel built up profiled panel with insulation and steel liner on steel support:																				
structural concrete frame, lightweight solid blockwork with cement mortar, plasterboard on battens, paint	806370490	A	B	B	A+	A	A+	A+	A	A	A	A	A	A	A	30	130	9.6	5	85
structural concrete frame, medium solid blockwork with cement mortar, plasterboard on battens, paint	806370489	A	B	B	A+	A	A+	A+	A	A	A	A	A	A	A	30	130	9.9	5	85
structural concrete frame, aircrete blockwork with cement mortar, plasterboard on battens, paint	806370496	A	A	B	A+	A	A+	A+	A	A	A	A	A+	A	A	30	120	9.6	8	83
Coated steel composite profiled panel with pentane blown PUR/PIR insulation and steel liner on steel support:																				
structural concrete frame, lightweight solid blockwork with cement mortar, plasterboard on battens, paint	806370488	A	B	D	A+	B	A+	A+	A+	A	A	B	A	B	B	30	130	9.5	5	84
structural concrete frame, medium solid blockwork with cement mortar, plasterboard on battens, paint	806370487	A	B	D	A+	B	A+	A+	A+	A	A	B	A	B	A	30	130	9.5	4	85
structural concrete frame, aircrete blockwork with cement mortar, plasterboard on battens, paint	806370495	A	B	D	A+	A	A+	A+	A+	A	A	B	A	B	A	30	130	9.5	7	82

Insulated cladding on concrete frame with block infill — All building types	Element number	Summary Rating	Climate change	Water extraction	Mineral resource extraction	Stratospheric ozone depletion	Human toxicity	Ecotoxicity to freshwater	Nuclear waste (higher level)	Ecotoxicity to land	Waste disposal	Fossil fuel depletion	Eutrophication	Photochemical ozone creation	Acidification	Typical replacement interval	Embodied CO_2 (kg CO_2 eq.)	Recycled content (kg)	Recycled content (%)	Recycled currently at EOL (%)
Mill finish aluminium composite profiled panel with pentane blown PUR/PIR insulation and steel liner on steel support:																				
structural concrete frame, lightweight solid blockwork with cement mortar, plasterboard on battens, paint	806370494	A	A	B	A+	A	A+	A+	A+	A	A+	A	A	A	A	50	110	11	6	84
structural concrete frame, medium solid blockwork with cement mortar, plasterboard on battens, paint	806370493	A	A	B	A+	A	A+	A+	A+	A	A+	A	A	A	A	50	110	11	5	85
structural concrete frame, aircrete blockwork with cement mortar, plasterboard on battens, paint	806370498	A+	A	B	A+	A	A+	A+	A+	A	A+	A	A+	A	A	50	100	11	9	81

Insulated cladding on concrete frame with metal stud infill — All building types	Element number	Summary Rating	Climate change	Water extraction	Mineral resource extraction	Stratospheric ozone depletion	Human toxicity	Ecotoxicity to freshwater	Nuclear waste (higher level)	Ecotoxicity to land	Waste disposal	Fossil fuel depletion	Eutrophication	Photochemical ozone creation	Acidification	Typical replacement interval	Embodied CO_2 (kg CO_2 eq.)	Recycled content (kg)	Recycled content (%)	Recycled currently at EOL (%)
Brick faced non-loadbearing precast concrete sandwich panel, reinforced concrete frame, light steel studwork, plasterboard, paint	806390025	D	E	B	B	E	A	A+	A	E	E	E	E	B	C	60+	350	33	4	89
Coated aluminium composite profiled panel with pentane blown PUR/PIR insulation and steel liner on steel support:																				
structural concrete frame, cement-bonded particle board, light steel frame, vapour control layer, plasterboard on battens, paint	806390499	A	B	C	A+	A	A	A	A	B	A	B	A	A	A	35	150	12.6	15	61
structural concrete frame, no sheathing, light steel frame, vapour control layer, plasterboard on battens, paint	806390508	A	A	C	A+	A	A	A	A	B	A	A	A+	A	A	35	120	11	16	75
structural concrete frame, OSB/3 sheathing board, light steel frame, vapour control layer, plasterboard on battens, paint	806390507	A	A	C	A+	A	A	A	A	B	A	A	A	A	A	35	120	15.7	21	67
structural concrete frame, sheathing ply, light steel frame, vapour control layer, plasterboard on battens, paint	806390500	A	A	C	A+	B	B	A	B	C	A	B	A	B	A	35	120	11	14	64
Coated steel built up profiled panel with insulation and steel liner on steel support:																				
structural concrete frame, cement-bonded particle board, light steel frame, vapour control layer, plasterboard on battens, paint	806390497	A	B	B	A+	A+	A+	A+	A	A	A	A	A+	A	A	30	140	11.4	13	61
structural concrete frame, no sheathing board, light steel frame, vapour control layer, plasterboard on battens, paint	806390506	A	A	B	A+	A+	A+	A+	A	A	A	A	A+	A+	A	30	110	9.9	14	74
structural concrete frame, OSB/3 sheathing board, light steel frame, vapour control layer, plasterboard on battens, paint	806390505	A	A	B	A+	A+	A+	A+	A	A	A	A	A+	A	A	30	110	14.6	18	67
structural concrete frame, sheathing ply, light steel frame, vapour control layer, plasterboard on battens, paint	806390498	A	A	C	A+	A	A+	A+	A	B	A	A	A+	A	A	30	110	9.9	12	64

Insulated cladding on concrete frame with metal stud infill

All building types

	Element number	Summary Rating	Climate change	Water extraction	Mineral resource extraction	Stratospheric ozone depletion	Human toxicity	Ecotoxicity to freshwater	Nuclear waste (higher level)	Ecotoxicity to land	Waste disposal	Fossil fuel depletion	Eutrophication	Photochemical ozone creation	Acidification	Typical replacement interval	Embodied CO_2 (kg CO_2 eq.)	Recycled content (kg)	Recycled content (%)	Recycled currently at EOL (%)
Coated steel composite profiled panel with pentane blown PUR/PIR insulation and steel liner on steel support:																				
structural concrete frame, cement-bonded particle board, light steel frame, vapour control layer, plasterboard on battens, paint	806390495	A	B	D	A+	A	A+	A+	A+	A	A	B	A	B	A	30	140	11	13	62
structural concrete frame, no sheathing board, light steel frame, vapour control layer, plasterboard on battens, paint	806390504	A	A	D	A+	A	A+	A+	A+	A	A	A	A+	A	A	30	120	9.5	13	75
structural concrete frame, OSB/3 sheathing board, light steel frame, vapour control layer, plasterboard on battens, paint	806390503	A	A	D	A+	A	A+	A+	A+	A	A	A	A	B	A	30	110	14.2	18	68
structural concrete frame, sheathing ply, light steel frame, vapour control layer, plasterboard on battens, paint	806390496	A	A	D	A+	B	A+	A+	A	C	A	B	A	B	A	30	120	9.5	12	64
Mill finish aluminium composite profiled panel with pentane blown PUR/PIR insulation and steel liner on steel support:																				
structural concrete frame, cement-bonded particle board, light steel frame, vapour control layer, plasterboard on battens, paint	806390501	A	A	B	A+	A	A+	A+	A+	A	A	A	A+	A	A	50	120	12.5	15	61
structural concrete frame, no sheathing, light steel frame, vapour control layer, plasterboard on battens, paint	806390510	A+	A	B	A+	A+	A+	A+	A+	A	A+	A	A+	A	A	50	93	10.9	16	75
structural concrete frame, OSB/3 sheathing board, light steel frame, vapour control layer, plasterboard on battens, paint	806390509	A+	A	B	A+	A+	A+	A+	A+	A	A+	A	A+	A	A	50	89	15.6	20	67
structural concrete frame, sheathing ply, light steel frame, vapour control layer, plasterboard on battens, paint	806390502	A	A	B	A+	A	A+	A	A	B	A	A	A+	A	A	50	92	10.9	14	64
Sandstone faced non-loadbearing precast concrete sandwich panel, concrete frame, light steel studwork, plasterboard, paint	806390024	E	E	B	C	E	A	A+	A	E	E	E	E	B	C	60+	350	33	4	89

Insulated cladding on steel frame with block infill

All building types

	Element number	Summary Rating	Climate change	Water extraction	Mineral resource extraction	Stratospheric ozone depletion	Human toxicity	Ecotoxicity to freshwater	Nuclear waste (higher level)	Ecotoxicity to land	Waste disposal	Fossil fuel depletion	Eutrophication	Photochemical ozone creation	Acidification	Typical replacement interval	Embodied CO2 (kg CO2 eq.)	Recycled content (kg)	Recycled content (%)	Recycled currently at EOL (%)
Coated aluminium composite profiled panel with pentane blown PUR/PIR insulation and steel liner on steel support:																				
structural steel frame, lightweight solid blockwork with cement mortar, plasterboard on battens, paint	806340532	A	B	C	A+	B	A	A	A	B	A	B	A	B	B	35	160	19.8	12	84
structural steel frame, medium solid blockwork with cement mortar, plasterboard on battens, paint	806340531	A	B	C	A+	B	A	A	A	C	A	B	A	B	B	35	160	20	10	85
Coated steel built up profiled panel with insulation and steel liner on steel support:																				
structural steel frame, lightweight solid blockwork with cement mortar, plasterboard on battens, paint	806340530	A	B	B	A+	A	A+	A+	A	A	A	B	A	A	A	30	150	18.6	11	83
structural steel frame, medium solid blockwork with cement mortar, plasterboard on battens, paint	806340529	A	B	B	A+	A	A+	A+	A	A	A	B	A	A	A	30	150	18	9	86
Coated steel composite profiled panel with pentane blown PUR/PIR insulation and steel liner on steel support:																				
structural steel frame, lightweight solid blockwork with cement mortar, plasterboard on battens, paint	806340528	A	B	C	A+	B	A+	A+	A	B	A	B	A	B	B	30	160	18.2	11	84
structural steel frame, medium solid blockwork with cement mortar, plasterboard on battens, paint	806340527	A	B	D	A+	B	A+	A+	A	B	A	B	A	B	B	30	150	18	9	85
Copper composite profiled panel with stone wool insulation and steel liner on steel support, structural steel frame, medium solid blockwork with cement mortar, plasterboard on battens, paint	806340687	C	C	D	A	B	A+	A+	C	B	C	C	B	A	B	45	230	30.4	14	81
Mill finish aluminium composite profiled panel with pentane blown PUR/PIR insulation and steel liner on steel support:																				
structural steel frame, lightweight solid blockwork with cement mortar, plasterboard on battens, paint	806340534	A	B	B	A+	B	A+	A+	A	A	A+	A	A	A	A	50	130	19.7	12	84
structural steel frame, medium solid blockwork with cement mortar, plasterboard on battens, paint	806340533	A	B	B	A+	A	A+	A+	A	A	A	A	A	A	A	50	130	20	10	85

Insulated cladding on steel frame with block infill — All building types	Element number	Summary Rating	Climate change	Water extraction	Mineral resource extraction	Stratospheric ozone depletion	Human toxicity	Ecotoxicity to freshwater	Nuclear waste (higher level)	Ecotoxicity to land	Waste disposal	Fossil fuel depletion	Eutrophication	Photochemical ozone creation	Acidification	Typical replacement interval	Embodied CO₂ (kg CO₂ eq.)	Recycled content (kg)	Recycled content (%)	Recycled currently at EOL (%)
Stainless steel built up profiled panel with insulation and steel liner on steel support, structural steel frame, medium solid blockwork with cement mortar, plasterboard on battens, paint	806340686	B	C	B	A+	A	A+	A+	A	C	C	C	B	A+	A	30	220	22.1	10	83
Stainless steel composite profiled panel with pentane blown PUR/PIR insulation and steel liner:																				
insulation on steel support, structural steel frame, medium solid blockwork with cement mortar, plaster, paint	806340685	B	C	B	A+	A	A+	A+	A+	C	C	C	B	A	A	50	220	22	10	83
insulation on steel support, structural steel frame, medium solid blockwork with cement mortar, plasterboard on battens, paint	806340684	B	C	C	A+	A	A+	A+	A+	C	C	C	B	A	A	50	220	25	12	85

Insulated cladding on steel frame with metal stud infill

All building types

	Element number	Summary Rating	Climate change	Water extraction	Mineral resource extraction	Stratospheric ozone depletion	Human toxicity	Ecotoxicity to freshwater	Nuclear waste (higher level)	Ecotoxicity to land	Waste disposal	Fossil fuel depletion	Eutrophication	Photochemical ozone creation	Acidification	Typical replacement interval	Embodied CO2 (kg CO2 eq.)	Recycled content (kg)	Recycled content (%)	Recycled currently at EOL (%)
Brick faced non-loadbearing precast concrete sandwich panel, structural steel frame, light steel studwork, plasterboard, paint	806360031	E	E	B	B	E	A	A+	B	E	E	E	E	C	D	60+	370	42	6	89
Coated aluminium composite profiled panel with pentane blown PUR/PIR insulation and steel liner on steel support:																				
structural steel frame, cement-bonded particle board, light steel frame, vapour control layer, plasterboard on battens, paint	806360515	A	B	C	A+	A	A	A	B	C	A	B	A	B	B	35	170	21.3	33	54
structural steel frame, OSB/3 sheathing, light steel frame, vapour control layer, plasterboard on battens, paint	806360524	A	B	C	A+	A	A	A	A	B	A	B	A	A	A	35	140	24.4	42	61
structural steel frame, sheathing ply, light steel frame, vapour control layer, plasterboard on battens, paint	806360523	A	B	C	A+	B	B	A	B	D	A	B	A	B	B	35	140	19.7	32	57
Coated steel built up profiled panel with insulation and steel liner on steel support:																				
structural steel frame, cement-bonded particle board, light steel frame, vapour control layer, plasterboard on battens, paint	806360514	A	B	B	A+	A	A+	A+	A	A	B	B	A	A	A	30	160	20.1	29	54
structural steel frame, OSB/3 sheathing, light steel frame, vapour control layer, plasterboard on battens, paint	806360522	A	B	B	A+	A+	A+	A+	A	A	A	A	A+	A	A	30	130	23.3	38	61
structural steel frame, sheathing ply, light steel frame, vapour control layer, plasterboard on battens, paint	806360521	A	B	C	A+	A	A+	A+	B	B	A	B	A	A	A	30	130	18.6	29	58
Coated steel composite profiled panel with pentane blown PUR/PIR insulation and steel liner on steel support:																				
structural steel frame, cement-bonded particle board, light steel frame, vapour control layer, plasterboard on battens, paint	806360511	A	B	D	A+	A	A+	A+	A	B	B	B	A	B	A	30	160	19.7	29	55
structural steel frame, light steel frame, vapour control layer, plasterboard on battens, paint	806490009	A	B	C	A+	A	A+	A+	A	B	A	B	A	B	A	30	140	18.2	35	71

Cont'd . . . .

Insulated cladding on steel frame with metal stud infill

All building types

	Element number	Summary Rating	Climate change	Water extraction	Mineral resource extraction	Stratospheric ozone depletion	Human toxicity	Ecotoxicity to freshwater	Nuclear waste (higher level)	Ecotoxicity to land	Waste disposal	Fossil fuel depletion	Eutrophication	Photochemical ozone creation	Acidification	Typical replacement interval	Embodied CO$_2$ (kg CO$_2$ eq.)	Recycled content (kg)	Recycled content (%)	Recycled currently at EOL (%)
Coated steel composite profiled panel with pentane blown PUR/PIR insulation and steel liner on steel support (cont'd):																				
structural steel frame, OSB/3 sheathing, light steel frame, vapour control layer, plasterboard on battens, paint	806360520	A	B	D	A+	A	A+	A+	A	B	A	B	A	B	A	30	130	22.9	39	62
structural steel frame, sheathing ply, light steel frame, vapour control layer, plasterboard on battens, paint	806360519	A	B	D	A+	B	A+	A+	A	C	A	B	A	B	A	30	140	18.2	29	58
Copper built up profiled cladding panel with insulation and coated steel liner on steel support:																				
structural steel frame, cement particle sheathing, light steel frame, vapour control layer, plasterboard on battens, paint	806360691	A	B	C	A	B	A+	A+	B	A	A	B	A	A	A	30	150	24	33	56
structural steel frame, OSB/3 sheathing, light steel frame, vapour control layer, plasterboard on battens, paint	806360689	A	A	C	A	B	A+	A+	B	A	A	A	A+	A+	A	30	120	27.2	42	63
structural steel frame, sheathing ply, light steel frame, vapour control layer, plasterboard on battens, paint	806360690	A	B	D	A	B	A+	A+	B	B	A	B	A	A	A	30	130	22.5	33	59
Copper composite profiled panel with stone wool insulation and steel liner on steel support, structural steel frame, light steel frame, vapour control layer, plasterboard on battens, paint	806360688	A	B	B	A	A	A+	A+	B	A	A	A	A+	A+	A	45	130	30.4	47	60
Mill finish aluminium composite profiled panel with pentane blown PUR/PIR insulation and steel liner on steel support:																				
structural steel frame, cement-bonded particle board, light steel frame, vapour control layer, plasterboard on battens, paint	806360518	A	B	B	A+	A	A+	A+	A	A	A	A	A+	A	A	50	140	21.2	32	54
structural steel frame, light steel frame, vapour control layer, plasterboard on battens, paint	806360517	A	A	B	A+	A+	A+	A+	A	A	A+	A	A+	A	A	50	110	19.6	39	70

Cont'd . . . .

Insulated cladding on steel frame with metal stud infill — All building types	Element number	Summary Rating	Climate change	Water extraction	Mineral resource extraction	Stratospheric ozone depletion	Human toxicity	Ecotoxicity to freshwater	Nuclear waste (higher level)	Ecotoxicity to land	Waste disposal	Fossil fuel depletion	Eutrophication	Photochemical ozone creation	Acidification	Typical replacement interval	Embodied CO2 (kg CO2 eq.)	Recycled content (kg)	Recycled content (%)	Recycled currently at EOL (%)
Mill finish aluminium composite profiled panel with pentane blown PUR/PIR insulation and steel liner on steel support (cont'd):																				
structural steel frame, OSB/3 sheathing, light steel frame, vapour control layer, plasterboard on battens, paint	806360526	A	A	B	A+	A	A+	A+	A	A	A+	A	A+	A	A	50	110	24.3	42	61
structural steel frame, sheathing ply, light steel frame, vapour control layer, plasterboard on battens, paint	806360525	A	A	B	A+	A	A+	A	A	C	A	A	A	A	A	50	110	19.6	32	57
Sandstone faced non-loadbearing precast concrete sandwich panel, structural steel frame, light steel studwork, plasterboard, paint	806360030	E	E	B	C	E	A	A+	B	E	E	E	E	C	C	60+	370	42	6	89
Stainless steel built up profiled panel with insulation and steel liner on steel support, structural steel frame, light steel frame, vapour control layer, plasterboard on battens, paint	806360687	B	C	B	A+	A+	A+	A+	A	B	B	B	B	A+	A	30	210	25.3	43	72
Stainless steel composite profiled panel with pentane blown PUR/PIR insulation and steel liner, insulation on steel support, structural steel frame, light steel frame, vapour control layer, plasterboard on battens, paint	806360683	A	C	B	A+	A+	A+	A+	A+	C	B	B	B	A	A	50	210	24.9	44	73

Insulated cladding on steel frame with no internal finish

All building types

	Element number	Summary Rating	Climate change	Water extraction	Mineral resource extraction	Stratospheric ozone depletion	Human toxicity	Ecotoxicity to freshwater	Nuclear waste (higher level)	Ecotoxicity to land	Waste disposal	Fossil fuel depletion	Eutrophication	Photochemical ozone creation	Acidification	Typical replacement interval	Embodied CO2 (kg CO2 eq.)	Recycled content (kg)	Recycled content (%)	Recycled currently at EOL (%)
Coated aluminium composite profiled panel with pentane blown PUR/PIR insulation and steel liner on steel support, structural steel frame with no internal finish	806600003	A	A	B	A+	A	A	A+	A	B	A+	A	A+	A	A+	35	120	16.5	48	87
Coated steel:																				
built up profiled panel with insulation and steel liner on steel support, structural steel frame with no internal finish	806600002	A+	A	B	A+	A+	A+	A+	A	A	A+	A	A+	A+	A+	30	110	15.3	40	85
composite profiled panel with pentane blown PUR/PIR insulation and steel liner on steel support, structural steel frame with no internal finish	806600001	A+	A	C	A+	A+	A+	A+	A+	A	A+	A	A+	A	A+	30	120	14.9	41	87
Mill finish aluminium composite profiled panel with pentane blown PUR/PIR insulation and steel liner on steel support, structural steel frame with no internal finish	806600004	A+	A	A	A+	A+	A+	A+	A+	A	A+	A+	A+	A+	A+	50	94	16.4	47	87
Stainless steel:																				
built up profiled panel with insulation and steel liner on steel support, structural steel frame with no internal finish	806600006	A	C	A	A+	A+	A+	A+	A+	B	B	B	B	A+	A+	30	190	22	51	86
composite profiled panel with pentane blown PUR/PIR insulation and steel liner on steel support, structural steel frame with no internal finish	806600005	A	C	B	A+	A+	A+	A+	A+	B	B	B	B	A+	A+	50	190	21.6	52	88

Rainscreen cladding on concrete frame with block infill

All building types

	Element number	Summary Rating	Climate change	Water extraction	Mineral resource extraction	Stratospheric ozone depletion	Human toxicity	Ecotoxicity to freshwater	Nuclear waste (higher level)	Ecotoxicity to land	Waste disposal	Fossil fuel depletion	Eutrophication	Photochemical ozone creation	Acidification	Typical replacement interval	Embodied CO2 (kg CO2 eq.)	Recycled content (kg)	Recycled content (%)	Recycled currently at EOL (%)
Autoclaved fibre cement single sheet and timber battens, breather membrane, insulation, structural concrete frame:																				
lightweight solid blockwork with cement mortar, plasterboard on battens, paint	806260456	A+	A	A+	A+	A	A+	A+	A+	A+	A+	A+	A+	A	A	35	66	8.3	5	78
medium density solid blockwork with cement mortar, plasterboard on battens, paint	806260457	A+	A	A+	A+	A	A+	A+	A+	A+	A+	A+	A+	A	A	35	65	8.3	4	80
Coated aluminium profiled single sheet and metal support, breather membrane, insulation, structural concrete frame:																				
lightweight solid blockwork with cement mortar, plasterboard on battens, paint	806260454	A	A	A	A+	A	B	A	A	A	A+	A	A+	A+	A	35	120	11	6	85
medium density solid blockwork with cement mortar, plasterboard on battens, paint	806260455	A	A	A	A+	A	B	A	A	A	A	A	A+	A+	A	35	120	11	5	86
Coated steel profiled single sheet and metal support, breather membrane, insulation, structural concrete frame:																				
lightweight solid blockwork with cement mortar, plasterboard on battens, paint	806260452	A	B	B	A+	A	A+	A+	A	A	A	B	A	A	A	30	130	9.8	6	85
medium density solid blockwork with cement mortar, plasterboard on battens, paint	806260453	A	B	B	A+	A	A+	A+	A	A	A	B	A	A	A	30	130	9.8	5	86
Precast concrete panel (non-loadbearing) with 'reconstructed stone' and support system, structural concrete frame, breather membrane, insulation, medium density solid blockwork with cement mortar, plasterboard on battens, paint	806260465	C	D	A	A	C	A	A+	A+	C	D	C	C	A	B	60+	250	27	5	89
Precast concrete panel (non-loadbearing) with imported Chinese granite facing panels and support system, breather membrane, insulation, structural concrete frame, medium density solid blockwork with cement mortar, plasterboard on battens, paint	806260461	D	D	B	C	E	A	A+	A	D	D	D	E	B	D	60+	290	27	4	89

Rainscreen cladding on concrete frame with block infill All building types	Element number	Summary Rating	Climate change	Water extraction	Mineral resource extraction	Stratospheric ozone depletion	Human toxicity	Ecotoxicity to freshwater	Nuclear waste (higher level)	Ecotoxicity to land	Waste disposal	Fossil fuel depletion	Eutrophication	Photochemical ozone creation	Acidification	Typical replacement interval	Embodied CO₂ (kg CO₂ eq.)	Recycled content (kg)	Recycled content (%)	Recycled currently at EOL (%)
Precast concrete panel with 50 mm natural limestone facing panels and support system, structural concrete frame, breather membrane, insulation, medium density solid blockwork with cement mortar, plasterboard on battens, paint	806260463	D	D	B	B	D	A	A+	A	D	D	D	D	A	C	60+	270	27	4	89
Precast concrete panel with sandstone finish and support system, structural concrete frame, breather membrane, insulation, medium density solid blockwork with cement mortar, plasterboard on battens, paint	806260686	D	D	B	C	D	A	A+	A	D	D	D	D	B	C	60+	270	27	4	89
UK limestone cladding panel and support system, breather membrane, insulation, structural concrete frame:																				
lightweight solid blockwork with cement mortar, plasterboard on battens, paint	806260458	A	B	A	A+	A	A+	A+	A	A	A	A	A	A+	A	60+	140	14	5	87
medium density solid blockwork with cement mortar, plasterboard on battens, paint	806260459	A	B	A	A+	A	A+	A+	A	A	A	A	A	A+	A	60+	140	14	4	87

Rainscreen cladding on concrete frame with metal stud infill

All building types

	Element number	Summary Rating	Climate change	Water extraction	Mineral resource extraction	Stratospheric ozone depletion	Human toxicity	Ecotoxicity to freshwater	Nuclear waste (higher level)	Ecotoxicity to land	Waste disposal	Fossil fuel depletion	Eutrophication	Photochemical ozone creation	Acidification	Typical replacement interval	Embodied CO2 (kg CO2 eq.)	Recycled content (kg)	Recycled content (%)	Recycled currently at EOL (%)
Autoclaved fibre cement single sheet and timber battens, breather membrane, insulation, structural concrete frame:																				
cement-bonded particle board, light steel frame, polyethylene sheet VCL, plasterboard on battens, paint	806280480	A+	A	A+	A+	A+	A+	A+	A+	A+	A+	A+	A+	A	A	35	76	10.2	11	48
OSB/3 sheathing board, light steel frame, polyethylene sheet VCL, plasterboard on battens, paint	806280482	A+	A+	A+	A+	A+	A+	A+	A+	A+	A+	A+	A+	A	A+	35	45	13.4	16	52
sheathing ply, light steel frame, polyethylene sheet VCL, plasterboard on battens, paint	806280481	A+	A+	A+	A+	A	A+	A+	A	A	A+	A+	A+	A	A	35	48	8.6	10	50
Coated aluminium profiled single sheet and metal support, breather membrane, insulation, structural concrete frame:																				
cement-bonded particle board, light steel frame, polyethylene sheet VCL, plasterboard on battens, paint	806280473	A	B	A	A+	A	B	A	A	B	A	A	A+	A+	A	35	130	12.8	15	59
OSB/3 sheathing board, light steel frame, polyethylene sheet VCL, plasterboard on battens, paint	806280475	A	A	A	A+	A	B	A	A	A	A+	A	A+	A+	A	35	96	15.9	21	65
sheathing ply, light steel frame, polyethylene sheet VCL, plasterboard on battens, paint	806280474	A	A	A	A+	A	B	A	B	C	A	A	A+	A	A	35	99	11.2	14	62
Coated steel profiled single sheet and metal support, breather membrane, insulation, structural concrete frame:																				
cement-bonded particle board, light steel frame, polyethylene sheet VCL, plasterboard on battens, paint	806280466	A	B	B	A+	A	A+	A+	A	A	B	A	A+	A	A	30	140	11.7	13	61
OSB/3 sheathing board, light steel frame, polyethylene sheet VCL, plasterboard on battens, paint	806280468	A	A	B	A+	A+	A+	A+	A	A	A	A	A+	A	A	30	110	14.8	18	67
sheathing ply, light steel frame, polyethylene sheet VCL, plasterboard on battens, paint	806280467	A	A	C	A+	A	A+	A+	B	B	A	B	A	A	A	30	110	10.1	12	64
Imported Italian marble rainscreen cladding on stainless steel supports, breather membrane, insulation, structural concrete frame, cement-bonded particle board, light steel frame, polyethylene sheet VCL, plasterboard on battens, paint	806280299	B	B	A+	A	B	A+	A+	A+	A	B	A	B	A+	A	60+	160	15	9	77

Rainscreen cladding on concrete frame with metal stud infill

All building types

	Element number	Summary Rating	Climate change	Water extraction	Mineral resource extraction	Stratospheric ozone depletion	Human toxicity	Ecotoxicity to freshwater	Nuclear waste (higher level)	Ecotoxicity to land	Waste disposal	Fossil fuel depletion	Eutrophication	Photochemical ozone creation	Acidification	Typical replacement interval	Embodied CO₂ (kg CO₂ eq.)	Recycled content (kg)	Recycled content (%)	Recycled currently at EOL (%)
Precast concrete panel (non-loadbearing) with 'reconstructed stone' and support system, structural concrete frame, breather membrane, insulation, light steel frame with plasterboard on battens, paint	806260464	B	C	A	A	B	A	A+	A+	C	C	C	C	A	B	60+	240	27	6	88
Precast concrete panel (non-loadbearing) with 50 mm limestone facing panels, support system, structural concrete frame, breather membrane, insulation, light steel frame with plasterboard on battens, paint	806260462	D	D	B	C	D	A	A+	A	D	C	D	D	B	D	60+	270	27	5	88
Precast concrete panel (non-loadbearing) with imported Chinese granite facing panels and support system, breather membrane, insulation, structural concrete frame, light steel frame with plasterboard on battens, paint	806260460	D	D	B	C	D	A	A+	A	D	C	D	D	B	D	60+	270	27	5	88
Precast concrete panel with brick finish and support system, structural concrete frame, breather membrane, insulation, light steel frame with plasterboard on battens, paint	806230682	C	D	A	A	C	A	A+	A+	C	D	C	C	A	B	60+	260	27	5	89
Precast concrete panel with sandstone finish and support system, structural concrete frame, breather membrane, insulation, steel stud infill with plasterboard on battens, paint	806260685	D	D	B	C	C	A	A+	A	C	D	C	C	A	B	60+	260	27	5	89

Rainscreen cladding on concrete frame with timber stud infill

All building types

	Element number	Summary Rating	Climate change	Water extraction	Mineral resource extraction	Stratospheric ozone depletion	Human toxicity	Ecotoxicity to freshwater	Nuclear waste (higher level)	Ecotoxicity to land	Waste disposal	Fossil fuel depletion	Eutrophication	Photochemical ozone creation	Acidification	Typical replacement interval	Embodied CO2 (kg CO2 eq.)	Recycled content (kg)	Recycled content (%)	Recycled currently at EOL (%)
Autoclaved fibre cement single sheet and timber battens, breather membrane, structural concrete frame:																				
insulation, sheathing ply, timber stud with insulation, polyethylene sheet VCL, plasterboard on battens, paint	806270483	A+	A+	A	A+	A	A+	A+	A	A	A+	A+	A+	A	A	35	43	9	10	45
OSB/3 sheathing board, timber stud with insulation, polyethylene sheet VCL, plasterboard on battens, paint	806270484	A+	A+	A+	A+	A	A+	A+	A+	A+	A+	A+	A+	A	A+	35	41	13.7	16	47
Coated aluminium profiled single sheet and metal support, breather membrane, insulation, structural concrete frame:																				
OSB/3 sheathing board, timber stud, polyethylene sheet VCL, plasterboard on battens, paint	806270477	A	A	A	A+	A	B	A	A	A	A+	A	A+	A+	A	35	82	16	23	64
sheathing ply, timber stud, polyethylene sheet VCL, plasterboard on battens, paint	806270476	A	A	A	A+	A	B	A	B	C	A	A	A+	A+	A	35	85	11	15	60
Coated steel profiled single sheet and metal support, breather membrane, insulation, structural concrete frame:																				
OSB/3 sheathing board, timber stud, polyethylene sheet VCL, plasterboard on battens, paint	806270470	A	A	B	A+	A+	A+	A+	A	A	A	A	A+	A	A	30	96	14	20	66
sheathing ply, timber stud, polyethylene sheet VCL, plasterboard on battens, paint	806270469	A	A	C	A+	A	A+	A+	A	B	A	A	A+	A	A	30	99	10.1	12	61

Rainscreen cladding on steel frame with block infill **All building types**	Element number	Summary Rating	Climate change	Water extraction	Mineral resource extraction	Stratospheric ozone depletion	Human toxicity	Ecotoxicity to freshwater	Nuclear waste (higher level)	Ecotoxicity to land	Waste disposal	Fossil fuel depletion	Eutrophication	Photochemical ozone creation	Acidification	Typical replacement interval	Embodied CO_2 (kg CO_2 eq.)	Recycled content (kg)	Recycled content (%)	Recycled currently at EOL (%)
Autoclaved fibre cement single sheet and timber battens, breather membrane, insulation, structural steel frame:																				
medium density solid blockwork with cement mortar, plasterboard on battens, paint	806230421	A+	A	A+	A+	A	A+	A+	A+	A	A+	A	A+	A	A	35	85	17	8	80
lightweight solid blockwork with cement mortar, plasterboard on battens, paint	806230422	A+	A	A+	A+	A	A+	A+	A+	A	A+	A	A+	A	A	35	87	17	10	77
Coated aluminium profiled single sheet and steel support, breather membrane, insulation, structural steel frame:																				
lightweight solid blockwork with cement mortar, plasterboard on battens, paint	806230420	A	B	A	A+	B	B	A	B	B	A	A	A	A	A	35	140	20	13	85
medium density solid blockwork with cement mortar, plasterboard on battens, paint	806230419	A	B	A	A+	A	B	A	B	B	A	A	A	A	A	35	140	20	10	86
Coated steel profiled single sheet and steel support, breather membrane, insulation, structural steel frame:																				
lightweight solid blockwork with cement mortar, plasterboard on battens, paint	806230418	A	B	B	A+	A	A+	A+	A	A	B	A	A	A	A	30	150	19	12	85
medium density solid blockwork with cement mortar, plasterboard on battens, paint	806230417	A	B	B	A+	A	A+	A+	A	A	B	A	A	A	A	30	150	19	9	86
Precast concrete panel (non-loadbearing) with 'reconstructed stone' finish and support system, structural steel frame, breather membrane, insulation, medium density solid blockwork with cement mortar, plasterboard on battens, paint	806230429	C	D	A	A	C	A	A+	A	D	D	C	C	A	B	60+	270	35	6	89
Precast concrete panel (non-loadbearing) with imported Chinese granite facing panels and support system, breather membrane, insulation, structural steel frame, medium density solid blockwork with cement mortar, plasterboard on battens, paint	806230425	D	E	B	C	E	A	A+	A	D	D	D	E	B	D	60+	310	35.8	6	88

Rainscreen cladding on steel frame with block infill

All building types

	Element number	Summary Rating	Climate change	Water extraction	Mineral resource extraction	Stratospheric ozone depletion	Human toxicity	Ecotoxicity to freshwater	Nuclear waste (higher level)	Ecotoxicity to land	Waste disposal	Fossil fuel depletion	Eutrophication	Photochemical ozone creation	Acidification	Typical replacement interval	Embodied CO₂ (kg CO₂ eq.)	Recycled content (kg)	Recycled content (%)	Recycled currently at EOL (%)
Precast concrete panel (non-loadbearing) with limestone facing panels, support system, breather membrane, insulation, structural steel frame, medium density solid blockwork with cement mortar, plasterboard on battens, paint	806230427	D	E	B	C	E	A	A+	A	D	D	D	E	B	D	60+	310	35.8	6	88
Precast concrete panel with brick finish and support system: structural steel frame, breather membrane, insulation, medium density solid blockwork with cement mortar, plasterboard on battens, paint	806230680	C	D	A	A	D	A	A+	A	D	D	D	D	B	C	60+	290	35	6	89
Precast concrete panel with sandstone finish and support system, structural steel frame, breather membrane, insulation, medium density solid blockwork with cement mortar, plasterboard on battens, paint	806230683	D	D	B	C	D	A	A+	B	D	D	D	D	B	C	60+	300	35	5	89
UK limestone cladding panel and support system, breather membrane, insulation, structural steel frame:																				
medium density solid blockwork with cement mortar, plasterboard on battens, paint	806230423	A	B	A	A+	A	A+	A+	A	B	A	B	A	A+	A	60+	160	23	8	87
lightweight solid blockwork with cement mortar, plasterboard on battens, paint	806230424	A	B	A	A+	B	A+	A+	A	B	A	B	A	A+	A	60+	160	23	9	87

Rainscreen cladding on steel frame with metal stud infill

All building types

	Element number	Summary Rating	Climate change	Water extraction	Mineral resource extraction	Stratospheric ozone depletion	Human toxicity	Ecotoxicity to freshwater	Nuclear waste (higher level)	Ecotoxicity to land	Waste disposal	Fossil fuel depletion	Eutrophication	Photochemical ozone creation	Acidification	Typical replacement interval	Embodied CO_2 (kg CO_2 eq.)	Recycled content (kg)	Recycled content (%)	Recycled currently at EOL (%)
Autoclaved fibre cement single sheet and timber battens, breather membrane, insulation, structural steel frame:																				
cement-bonded particle board, light steel frame, plasterboard on battens, paint	806250445	A+	A	A+	A+	A+	A+	A+	A	A	A+	A+	A+	A	A	35	95	18.9	26	37
OSB/3 sheathing board, light steel frame, plasterboard on battens, paint	806250451	A+	A	A+	A+	A+	A+	A+	A	A+	A+	A+	A+	A	A	35	65	22.1	34	42
sheathing ply, light steel frame, plasterboard on battens, paint	806250448	A+	A	A+	A+	A	A+	A+	A	B	A+	A	A+	A	A	35	68	17.4	26	40
Coated aluminium profiled single sheet and metal support, breather membrane, insulation, structural steel frame:																				
cement-bonded particle board, light steel frame, plasterboard on battens, paint	806250438	A	B	A	A+	A	B	A	B	B	A	A	A+	A+	A	35	150	21.5	34	51
OSB/3 sheathing board, light steel frame, plasterboard on battens, paint	806250444	A	A	A	A+	A	B	A	B	B	A	A	A+	A+	A	35	120	24.6	44	58
sheathing ply, light steel frame, plasterboard on battens, paint	806250441	A	A	A	A+	A	B	A	B	C	A	B	A	A	A	35	120	19.9	33	54
Coated steel profiled single sheet and metal support, breather membrane, insulation, structural steel frame:																				
cement-bonded particle board, light steel frame, plasterboard on battens, paint	806250431	A	B	B	A+	A	A+	A+	A	A	B	B	A	A	A	30	160	20.4	29	55
OSB/3 sheathing board, light steel frame, plasterboard on battens, paint	806250437	A	B	B	A+	A+	A+	A+	A	A	A	B	A+	A	A	30	130	23.5	38	62
sheathing ply, light steel frame, plasterboard on battens, paint	806250434	A	B	C	A+	A	A+	A+	B	C	B	B	A	A	A	30	130	18.8	29	58
Precast concrete panel (non-loadbearing) with 50 mm limestone facing panels, support system, breather membrane, insulation, structural steel frame, light steel frame with plasterboard on battens, paint	806230428	D	D	B	C	D	A	A+	A	D	D	D	D	B	D	60+	290	35	7	89

Rainscreen cladding on steel frame with metal stud infill All building types	Element number	Summary Rating	Climate change	Water extraction	Mineral resource extraction	Stratospheric ozone depletion	Human toxicity	Ecotoxicity to freshwater	Nuclear waste (higher level)	Ecotoxicity to land	Waste disposal	Fossil fuel depletion	Eutrophication	Photochemical ozone creation	Acidification	Typical replacement interval	Embodied CO2 (kg CO2 eq.)	Recycled content (kg)	Recycled content (%)	Recycled currently at EOL (%)
Precast concrete panel (non-loadbearing) with imported Chinese granite facing panels and support system, breather membrane, insulation, structural steel frame, light steel frame with plasterboard on battens, paint	806230426	D	D	B	C	D	A	A+	A	D	D	D	D	B	D	60+	290	35	7	89
Precast concrete panel with brick finish and support system, breather membrane, insulation, structural steel frame, light steel frame with plasterboard, paint	806230681	C	D	A	A	C	A	A+	A	D	D	C	C	A	C	60+	280	35	7	89
Precast concrete panel with exposed aggregate finish and support system, breather membrane, insulation, structural steel frame, light steel frame with plasterboard, paint	806230430	C	D	A	A	B	A	A+	A	D	C	C	C	A	B	60+	260	35.7	8	88
Precast concrete panel with sandstone finish and support system, breather membrane, insulation, structural steel frame, steel stud infill with plasterboard on battens, paint	806230684	D	D	B	C	D	A	A+	A	D	D	D	C	B	B	60+	280	35	7	89

Rainscreen cladding on steel frame with timber stud infill

All building types

	Element number	Summary Rating	Climate change	Water extraction	Mineral resource extraction	Stratospheric ozone depletion	Human toxicity	Ecotoxicity to freshwater	Nuclear waste (higher level)	Ecotoxicity to land	Waste disposal	Fossil fuel depletion	Eutrophication	Photochemical ozone creation	Acidification	Typical replacement interval	Embodied CO2 (kg CO2 eq.)	Recycled content (kg)	Recycled content (%)	Recycled currently at EOL (%)
Autoclaved fibre cement single sheet and timber battens, breather membrane, insulation, structural steel frame:																				
sheathing ply, timber stud, plasterboard on battens, paint	806240447	A+	A	A+	A+	A	A+	A+	A	B	A+	A	A+	A	A	35	63	17.7	25	33
OSB/3 sheathing board, timber stud with insulation, plasterboard on battens, paint	806240450	A+	A	A+	A+	A	A+	A+	A	A+	A+	A+	A+	A	A	35	60	22.4	34	35
Coated aluminium profiled single sheet and metal support, breather membrane, insulation, structural steel frame:																				
OSB/3 sheathing board, timber stud, plasterboard on battens, paint	806240443	A	A	A	A+	A	B	A	B	B	A+	A	A+	A+	A	35	100	24.6	45	53
sheathing ply, timber stud, plasterboard on battens, paint	806240440	A	A	A	A+	A	B	A	B	C	A	A	A+	A	A	35	100	19.9	34	49
Coated steel profiled single sheet and metal support, breather membrane, insulation, structural steel frame:																				
OSB/3 sheathing board, timber stud, plasterboard on battens, paint	806240436	A	A	B	A+	A	A+	A+	A	A	A	A	A+	A	A	30	120	23.5	39	57
sheathing ply, timber stud, plasterboard on battens, paint	806240433	A	A	C	A+	A	A+	A+	B	B	A	B	A	A	A	30	120	18.8	29	54

Rainscreen cladding on loadbearing single-leaf blockwork walls with metal stud infill All building types	Element number	Summary Rating	Climate change	Water extraction	Mineral resource extraction	Stratospheric ozone depletion	Human toxicity	Ecotoxicity to freshwater	Nuclear waste (higher level)	Ecotoxicity to land	Waste disposal	Fossil fuel depletion	Eutrophication	Photochemical ozone creation	Acidification	Typical replacement interval	Embodied CO2 (kg CO2 eq.)	Recycled content (kg)	Recycled content (%)	Recycled currently at EOL (%)
Clay tiles on timber battens:																				
lightweight solid block outer, light steel frame (with insulation), polyethylene sheet, plasterboard on battens, paint	806320669	A	A	A	A+	B	A+	A+	A	A+	A	B	A+	B	A	40	110	3.7	2	82
medium density solid block outer, light steel frame (with insulation), polyethylene sheet, plasterboard on battens, paint	806320670	A	A	A	A+	B	A+	A+	A	A+	A	B	A+	B	A	40	110	3.7	2	83
Treated softwood boarding on timber battens:																				
lightweight solid block outer, light steel frame (with insulation), polyethylene sheet, plasterboard on battens, paint	806320673	A+	A+	A+	A+	B	A+	A+	A+	A+	A	A+	A+	E	A	30	37	3.7	3	76
medium density solid block outer, light steel frame (with insulation), polyethylene sheet, plasterboard on battens, paint	806320674	A+	A+	A+	A+	B	A+	A+	A+	A+	A	A+	A+	E	A	30	35	3.7	2	79
UK produced natural slate on timber battens:																				
lightweight solid block outer, light steel frame (with insulation), polyethylene sheet, plasterboard on battens, paint	806320671	A	A	A+	A	B	A+	A+	A+	A+	A+	A+	A	A	A	60+	75	3.7	2	81
medium density solid block outer, light steel frame (with insulation), polyethylene sheet, plasterboard on battens, paint	806320672	A	A	A+	A	B	A+	A+	A+	A+	A+	A+	A	A	A	60+	74	3.7	2	83

Rainscreen cladding on loadbearing single-leaf blockwork walls with timber stud infill

All building types

	Element number	Summary Rating	Climate change	Water extraction	Mineral resource extraction	Stratospheric ozone depletion	Human toxicity	Ecotoxicity to freshwater	Nuclear waste (higher level)	Ecotoxicity to land	Waste disposal	Fossil fuel depletion	Eutrophication	Photochemical ozone creation	Acidification	Typical replacement interval	Embodied CO2 (kg CO2 eq.)	Recycled content (kg)	Recycled content (%)	Recycled currently at EOL (%)
Clay tiles on timber battens:																				
lightweight solid block outer, timber stud with insulation, polyethylene sheet, plasterboard on battens, paint	806310663	A	A	A	A+	C	A+	A+	A	A+	A+	B	A	B	A	40	110	4	2	79
medium density solid block outer, timber stud with insulation, polyethylene sheet, plasterboard on battens, paint	806310664	A	A	A	A+	C	A+	A+	A	A+	A	B	A	B	A	40	110	4	2	81
Treated softwood boarding on timber battens:																				
lightweight solid block outer, timber stud with insulation, polyethylene sheet, plasterboard on battens, paint	806310667	A+	A+	A+	A+	C	A+	A+	A+	A+	A	A+	A+	E	A	30	31	4	3	73
medium density solid block outer, timber stud with insulation, polyethylene sheet, plasterboard on battens, paint	806310668	A+	A+	A+	A+	B	A+	A+	A+	A+	A	A+	A+	E	A	30	30	4	2	76
UK produced natural slate on timber battens:																				
lightweight solid block outer, timber stud with insulation, polyethylene sheet, plasterboard on battens, paint	806310665	A	A	A+	A	B	A+	A+	A+	A+	A+	A	A	A	A	60+	70	4	2	79
medium density solid block outer, timber stud with insulation, polyethylene sheet, plasterboard on battens, paint	806310666	A	A	A+	A	B	A+	A+	A+	A+	A+	A	A	A	A	60+	69	4	2	81

Rainscreen cladding on loadbearing masonry cavity walls

All building types

	Element number	Summary Rating	Climate change	Water extraction	Mineral resource extraction	Stratospheric ozone depletion	Human toxicity	Ecotoxicity to freshwater	Nuclear waste (higher level)	Ecotoxicity to land	Waste disposal	Fossil fuel depletion	Eutrophication	Photochemical ozone creation	Acidification	Typical replacement interval	Embodied CO2 (kg CO2 eq.)	Recycled content (kg)	Recycled content (%)	Recycled currently at EOL (%)
Clay tiles on timber battens:																				
lightweight solid blockwork cavity wall, insulation, plasterboard on battens, paint	806290605	A	B	A	A	D	A+	A+	A	A	A	B	A	B	A	40	130	3.4	1	86
lightweight solid blockwork outer, insulation, aircrete blockwork inner, plasterboard on battens, paint	806290606	A	B	A	A+	C	A+	A+	A	A+	A	B	A	B	A	40	120	3.4	1	85
medium density solid blockwork outer, insulation, aircrete blockwork inner, plasterboard on battens, paint	806290604	A	A	A	A+	C	A+	A+	A	A	A	B	A	B	A	40	120	3.4	1	86
medium density solid blockwork outer, insulation, lightweight solid blockwork inner, plasterboard on battens, paint	806290603	A	B	A	A	C	A+	A+	A	A	A	B	A	B	A	40	130	3.4	1	86
aircrete blockwork cavity wall, insulation, plasterboard on battens, paint	806290615	A	A	A	A+	B	A+	A+	A	A+	A+	B	A+	B	A	40	120	3.4	2	84
thin joint aircrete blockwork cavity wall, insulation, plasterboard on battens, paint	806290616	A	A	A	A+	B	A+	A+	A	A+	A+	B	A+	B	A	40	120	3.7	2	82
Treated softwood boarding on timber battens:																				
lightweight solid blockwork outer, insulation, aircrete blockwork inner, plasterboard on battens, paint	806290614	A+	A+	A+	A+	C	A+	A+	A+	A+	A	A+	A+	E	A	30	47	3.4	2	82
lightweight solid blockwork cavity wall, insulation, plasterboard on battens, paint	806290613	A+	A+	A+	A+	C	A+	A+	A+	A+	A	A+	A	E	A	30	53	3.4	1	83
medium density solid blockwork outer, insulation, aircrete block inner, plasterboard on battens, paint	806290612	A+	A+	A+	A+	B	A+	A+	A+	A+	A	A+	A+	E	A	30	45	3.7	2	82
medium density solid blockwork outer, insulation, lightweight solid block inner, plasterboard on battens, paint	806290611	A+	A+	A+	A+	C	A+	A+	A+	A+	A	A+	A	E	A	30	52	3.4	1	84
aircrete blockwork cavity wall, insulation, plasterboard on battens, paint	806290617	A+	A+	A+	A+	B	A+	A+	A+	A+	A	A+	A+	E	A+	30	40	3.4	2	79
thin joint aircrete blockwork cavity wall, insulation, plasterboard on battens, paint	806290618	A+	A+	A+	A+	B	A+	A+	A+	A+	A+	A+	A+	E	A+	30	39	3.7	3	76

Rainscreen cladding on loadbearing masonry cavity walls

All building types

	Element number	Summary Rating	Climate change	Water extraction	Mineral resource extraction	Stratospheric ozone depletion	Human toxicity	Ecotoxicity to freshwater	Nuclear waste (higher level)	Ecotoxicity to land	Waste disposal	Fossil fuel depletion	Eutrophication	Photochemical ozone creation	Acidification	Typical replacement interval	Embodied CO_2 (kg CO_2 eq.)	Recycled content (kg)	Recycled content (%)	Recycled currently at EOL (%)
UK produced natural slate on timber battens:																				
lightweight solid blockwork outer, insulation, aircrete blockwork inner, plasterboard on battens, paint	806290610	A	A	A+	A	B	A+	A+	A+	A+	A+	A	A	A	A	60+	85	3.7	2	84
lightweight solid blockwork cavity, insulation, plasterboard on battens, paint	806290609	A	A	A+	A	C	A+	A+	A+	A+	A+	A	A	A	B	60+	91	3.4	1	86
medium density solid blockwork outer, insulation, aircrete blockwork inner, plasterboard on battens, paint	806290608	A	A	A+	A	B	A+	A+	A+	A+	A+	A	A	A	A	60+	84	3.4	1	86
medium density solid blockwork outer, insulation, lightweight solid blockwork inner, plasterboard on battens, paint	806290607	A	A	A+	A	C	A+	A+	A+	A+	A+	A	A	A	B	60+	90	3.4	1	86

Insulated render systems on loadbearing single-leaf blockwork walls

All building types

	Element number	Summary Rating	Climate change	Water extraction	Mineral resource extraction	Stratospheric ozone depletion	Human toxicity	Ecotoxicity to freshwater	Nuclear waste (higher level)	Ecotoxicity to land	Waste disposal	Fossil fuel depletion	Eutrophication	Photochemical ozone creation	Acidification	Typical replacement interval	Embodied CO$_2$ (kg CO$_2$ eq.)	Recycled content (kg)	Recycled content (%)	Recycled currently at EOL (%)
Cement rendered medium density solid blockwork wall (blocks laid flat), insulation, plaster, paint	806450008	A+	A	A+	A+	B	A+	A+	A+	A+	A	A	A	A+	A	50	89	4	1	87
Insulated polymeric render system:																				
140 mm lightweight solid blockwork with cement mortar, plasterboard on battens, paint	806450630	A+	A	A	A+	C	A+	A+	A+	A+	A+	B	A+	C	A	50	98	3.4	2	79
140 mm medium density solid blockwork with cement mortar, plasterboard on battens, paint	806450624	A+	A	A	A+	B	A+	A+	A+	A+	A+	B	A+	B	A	50	96	3.4	1	82
215 mm lightweight solid blockwork with cement mortar, insulation, plasterboard on battens, paint	806450636	A	A	A	A+	C	A+	A+	A+	A+	A	B	A	C	B	50	120	3.4	1	83
215 mm aircrete blockwork with cement mortar, insulation, plasterboard on battens, paint	806450637	A+	A	A	A+	B	A+	A+	A+	A+	A+	B	A+	B	A	50	110	3.4	2	78
spun bonded polyethylene sheet, insulation, 140 mm lightweight solid blockwork with cement mortar, plasterboard on battens, paint	806450401	A+	A	A	A+	C	A+	A+	A+	A+	A+	B	A+	C	A	50	98	3.4	2	79
spun bonded polyethylene sheet, insulation, 140 mm medium density solid blockwork with cement mortar, plasterboard on battens, paint	806450400	A+	A	A	A+	B	A+	A+	A+	A+	A+	B	A+	B	A	50	96	3.4	1	82

Aluminium curtain walling systems

All building types

	Element number	Summary Rating	Climate change	Water extraction	Mineral resource extraction	Stratospheric ozone depletion	Human toxicity	Ecotoxicity to freshwater	Nuclear waste (higher level)	Ecotoxicity to land	Waste disposal	Fossil fuel depletion	Eutrophication	Photochemical ozone creation	Acidification	Typical replacement interval	Embodied CO_2 (kg CO_2 eq.)	Recycled content (kg)	Recycled content (%)	Recycled currently at EOL (%)
Extruded aluminium stick type curtain wall: 1 transom per floor:																				
laminated sealed glass unit, coated aluminium spandrel panel with pentane blown PUR/PIR insulation	806510649	C	D	D	A+	C	E	E	E	D	A	D	B	B	D	25	260	12	26	77
laminated sealed glass unit, glue bonded insulation, medium density concrete solid blockwork, plasterboard on dabs, paint	806510001	B	C	C	A+	C	A	B	C	A	B	C	B	A	D	25	200	7.8	4	82
laminated sealed glass, coated aluminium spandrel panel with pentane blown PUR/PIR insulation, medium density concrete solid blockwork, plasterboard on dabs, paint	806510004	D	D	E	A+	D	E	E	E	D	B	E	C	C	E	25	300	15	7	82
Extruded aluminium stick type curtain wall: 2 transoms per floor:																				
laminated sealed glass unit, coated aluminium spandrel panel with pentane blown PUR/PIR insulation	806510648	C	D	D	A+	C	E	D	E	D	A	D	B	B	D	25	260	12	26	77
laminated sealed glass unit, glue bonded insulation, medium density concrete solid blockwork, plasterboard on dabs, paint	806510002	B	C	C	A+	C	A	A	B	A	A	C	B	A	D	25	200	7.7	4	82
laminated sealed glass, coated aluminium spandrel panel with pentane blown PUR/PIR insulation, medium density concrete solid blockwork, plasterboard on dabs, paint	806510003	D	D	E	A+	D	E	E	E	D	B	E	C	C	E	25	300	15	7	81
Extruded aluminium stick type curtain wall: 3 transoms per floor:																				
laminated sealed glass unit, coated aluminium spandrel panel with pentane blown PUR/PIR insulation	806510650	C	D	D	A+	C	E	E	E	D	A	D	C	B	D	25	270	13	27	77
laminated sealed glass unit, glue bonded insulation, medium density concrete solid blockwork, plasterboard on dabs, paint	806510651	B	C	C	A+	C	B	B	C	B	B	C	B	A	D	25	210	8.2	4	82
laminated sealed glass, coated aluminium spandrel panel with pentane blown PUR/PIR insulation, medium density concrete solid blockwork, plasterboard on dabs, paint	806510653	D	D	E	A+	D	E	E	E	D	B	E	C	C	F	25	310	16	7	82

Timber curtain walling systems

All building types

	Element number	Summary Rating	Climate change	Water extraction	Mineral resource extraction	Stratospheric ozone depletion	Human toxicity	Ecotoxicity to freshwater	Nuclear waste (higher level)	Ecotoxicity to land	Waste disposal	Fossil fuel depletion	Eutrophication	Photochemical ozone creation	Acidification	Typical replacement interval	Embodied CO$_2$ (kg CO$_2$ eq.)	Recycled content (kg)	Recycled content (%)	Recycled currently at EOL (%)
Laminated timber stick type curtain wall: 1 transom per floor:																				
laminated sealed glass unit, coated aluminium spandrel panel with pentane blown PUR/PIR insulation	806520658	C	D	E	A+	C	E	D	E	D	A	D	C	B	D	25	260	11	23	69
laminated sealed glass unit, coated aluminium spandrel panel with pentane blown PUR/PIR insulation, medium density solid blockwork, plasterboard on dabs	806520661	D	D	E	A+	E	E	E	E	E	C	E	D	C	E	25	300	14	7	80
laminated sealed glass unit, glue bonded insulation, medium density concrete solid blockwork, plasterboard on dabs, paint	806520660	B	C	D	A+	D	A	A	C	B	B	D	C	B	D	25	200	7.4	4	77
Laminated timber stick type curtain wall: 2 transoms per floor:																				
laminated sealed glass unit, coated aluminium spandrel panel with pentane blown PUR/PIR insulation, medium density concrete solid blockwork, plasterboard on dabs, paint	806520657	D	D	E	A+	E	E	E	E	E	C	E	D	C	E	25	310	15	7	80
laminated sealed glass unit, coated spandrel panel with pentane blown PUR/PIR insulation	806520659	C	D	E	A+	C	E	E	E	D	A	D	C	B	D	25	270	11	23	70
laminated sealed glass unit, glue bonded insulation, medium density concrete solid blockwork, plasterboard on dabs, paint	806520662	B	C	C	A+	C	A	A	B	A	B	C	B	A	D	25	190	7.2	4	79

Loadbearing precast concrete systems

All building types

	Element number	Summary Rating	Climate change	Water extraction	Mineral resource extraction	Stratospheric ozone depletion	Human toxicity	Ecotoxicity to freshwater	Nuclear waste (higher level)	Ecotoxicity to land	Waste disposal	Fossil fuel depletion	Eutrophication	Photochemical ozone creation	Acidification	Typical replacement interval	Embodied CO2 (kg CO2 eq.)	Recycled content (kg)	Recycled content (%)	Recycled currently at EOL (%)
Brick faced precast concrete cladding panel, insulation:																				
light steel studwork, plasterboard, paint	806230679	C	D	A	A	C	A	A+	A	C	D	C	C	A	B	60+	260	27	5	88
medium density solid blockwork, plasterboard, paint	806230687	C	D	B	A	D	A	A+	A	D	D	D	D	B	C	60+	280	27	4	89
Brick faced precast concrete sandwich panel, plaster skim, paint	806530294	D	E	B	B	D	A	A+	A	E	E	D	D	B	B	60+	330	30	4	90
Imported Chinese granite faced precast concrete cladding panel, insulation:																				
light steel studwork, plasterboard, paint	806230688	D	D	A	C	D	A	A+	A	D	C	C	D	B	C	60+	270	27	6	88
medium density solid blockwork, plasterboard, paint	806530022	D	D	B	C	E	A	A+	A	D	D	D	E	B	D	60+	290	27	4	89
Imported Chinese granite faced precast concrete sandwich panel, plaster skim, paint	806530295	E	E	B	C	E	A	A+	A	E	E	E	E	B	C	60+	340	30	5	90
Limestone faced precast concrete cladding panel, insulation:																				
light steel studwork, plasterboard, paint	806260690	C	D	B	A	C	A	A+	B	D	C	C	C	A	B	60+	260	27	5	88
medium density solid blockwork, plasterboard, paint	806530021	D	D	C	B	D	A	A+	B	D	D	D	D	B	C	60+	280	27	4	89
Limestone faced precast concrete sandwich panel, plaster skim, paint	806530296	D	E	C	B	D	A	A+	B	E	E	D	E	B	B	60+	330	30	4	90
Reconstructed stone faced precast concrete cladding panel, insulation:																				
medium density solid blockwork, plasterboard, paint	806000023	C	D	A	A	C	A	A+	A+	C	C	C	C	A	B	60+	250	27	5	89
light steel studwork, plasterboard, paint	806260689	B	C	A	A	B	A	A+	A+	C	C	B	C	A	B	60+	230	27	7	88
Reconstructed stone faced precast concrete sandwich panel, plaster skim, paint	806530293	C	D	A	A	C	A	A+	A+	D	D	D	D	A	B	60+	310	30	5	90

Loadbearing precast concrete systems / All building types	Element number	Summary Rating	Climate change	Water extraction	Mineral resource extraction	Stratospheric ozone depletion	Human toxicity	Ecotoxicity to freshwater	Nuclear waste (higher level)	Ecotoxicity to land	Waste disposal	Fossil fuel depletion	Eutrophication	Photochemical ozone creation	Acidification	Typical replacement interval	Embodied CO2 (kg CO2 eq.)	Recycled content (kg)	Recycled content (%)	Recycled currently at EOL (%)
Sandstone faced precast concrete cladding panel, insulation:																				
light steel studwork, plasterboard, paint	806530031	D	C	A	C	C	A	A+	A	C	C	C	C	A	A	60+	250	23	5	90
medium density solid blockwork, plasterboard, paint	806530020	D	D	B	C	D	A	A+	A	D	D	D	D	B	C	60+	270	27	4	89
Sandstone faced precast concrete sandwich panel, plaster skim, paint	806530297	E	E	B	C	E	A	A+	A	E	E	D	E	B	B	60+	330	30	4	90

6.6 WINDOWS AND CURTAIN WALLING

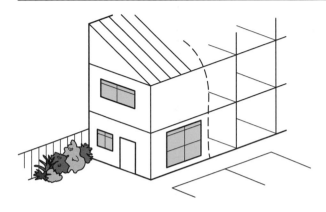

Functional unit for windows and curtain walling:

Non-domestic:

1 m² of double-glazed fixed pane window or clear-glazed curtain walling, to satisfy Building Regulations in England & Wales, and in particular, a U-value of 1.8 W/m²K. To include any repair, refurbishment or replacement over the 60-year study period.

Domestic:

Double-glazed window based on the BFRC domestic window model (1.48 m high × 1.23 m wide with a central mullion and one opening light[42], to satisfy Building Regulations in England & Wales, and, in particular, a U-value of 1.8 W/m²K. To include any repair, refurbishment or replacement over the 60-year study period.

Two sets of window ratings are provided and are categorised into Domestic and Non-domestic buildings. Please refer to the latest guidance on application of these ratings given on *The Green Guide to Specification Online* website[8].

The main environmental impact of windows is from the heat loss through them. Attention is drawn to the large number of credits available in BREEAM, The Code for Sustainable Homes and EcoHomes for reducing fabric heat loss and improving operational CO_2 emissions compared with the small number available for materials specification.

The embodied impact of windows should be taken into account only as a small part of the decision, with the main emphasis being to choose a window that will reduce operational energy usage.

Windows are one of the elements with a less important role in the overall embodied impact of buildings.

However, the narrower the plan depth, as with external walls, the greater the impact as the surface area of the building increases relative to the floor area.

Although at a glazing ratio of 30%, windows may not seem to represent a significant proportion of the building impact, it is possible for a high percentage of the façade to consist of glazed areas, particularly in commercial developments with glazed curtain walling. In such cases, the choice of window specification can make a significant contribution to the reduction of the building's overall embodied impact.

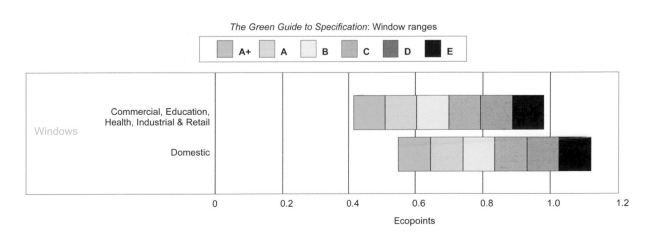

The Green Guide to Specification: Window ranges

A+ A B C D E

Windows

Commercial, Education, Health, Industrial & Retail

Domestic

Ecopoints

Windows and curtain walling — Commercial, Education, Health, Industrial & Retail	Element number	Summary Rating	Climate change	Water extraction	Mineral resource extraction	Stratospheric ozone depletion	Human toxicity	Ecotoxicity to freshwater	Nuclear waste (higher level)	Ecotoxicity to land	Waste disposal	Fossil fuel depletion	Eutrophication	Photochemical ozone creation	Acidification	Typical replacement interval	Embodied CO_2 (kg CO_2 eq.)	Recycled content (kg)	Recycled content (%)	Recycled currently at EOL (%)
Powder coated aluminium curtain walling system	831500016	D	E	B	E	A	B	C	C	A+	C	D	E	A+	E	40	170	5.3	15	76
Powder coated aluminium window:																				
profile <1.2 kg/m, redwood timber internal frame, water based stain to timber, double glazed	831500021	C	C	A	B	C	C	C	E	A	A	D	C	A+	C	40	140	3.7	14	66
profile >1.2 kg/m, redwood timber internal frame, water based stain to timber, double glazed	831500003	D	C	A	B	C	C	D	E	A	A	D	D	A+	C	40	140	3.9	14	66
profile <0.9 kg/m, double glazed	831500023	A	B	A+	A+	A+	B	B	A	A+	A+	A+	A+	A+	A	40	120	3.2	15	72
profile <1.25 kg/m, double glazed	831500018	B	C	A+	A	A+	C	C	B	A+	A+	A	A+	A+	B	40	140	3.6	16	73
profile <1.5 kg/m, double glazed	831500017	C	D	A+	B	A+	D	D	C	A+	A+	C	A	A+	C	40	150	4.1	17	74
profile <1.75 kg/m, double glazed	831500020	D	E	A+	B	A+	E	E	D	A+	A+	D	B	A+	D	40	170	4.6	19	75
profile >1.75 kg/m, double glazed	831500006	E	E	A+	C	A	E	E	E	A+	A+	E	D	A+	E	40	180	5.1	20	75
redwood timber internal frame, solvent borne gloss paint to timber, double glazed	831500004	D	C	A	B	C	C	D	E	A	A	D	D	B	C	40	140	3.9	14	66
Durable hardwood window:																				
solvent borne gloss painted inside and out (TWAS), double glazed	831500008	A+	A+	A+	A+	D	A+	A+	A+	A+	B	A+	B	C	A+	35	77	1.7	7	56
solvent borne gloss painted inside and out (non-TWAS), double glazed	831500009	A+	A	A	A	E	A+	A+	A	A+	C	B	D	C	A	30	100	1.7	7	58
water based stain inside and out (non-TWAS), double glazed	831500012	A+	A	A	A	E	A+	A+	A	A+	C	B	D	A+	A	30	100	1.7	7	58
water based stained inside and out (TWAS), double glazed	831500011	A+	A+	A+	A+	D	A+	A+	A+	A+	B	A+	B	A+	A+	35	76	1.7	7	56
Laminated timber curtain walling system	831500015	C	C	B	D	C	A	B	B	A+	E	D	E	A+	E	30	140	4	10	60

Note: TWAS = Timber Window Accreditation Scheme.

Windows and curtain walling

Commercial, Education, Health, Industrial & Retail

	Element number	Summary Rating	Climate change	Water extraction	Mineral resource extraction	Stratospheric ozone depletion	Human toxicity	Ecotoxicity to freshwater	Nuclear waste (higher level)	Ecotoxicity to land	Waste disposal	Fossil fuel depletion	Eutrophication	Photochemical ozone creation	Acidification	Typical replacement interval	Embodied CO$_2$ (kg CO$_2$ eq.)	Recycled content (kg)	Recycled content (%)	Recycled currently at EOL (%)
Pre-treated softwood timber window:																				
solvent borne gloss painted inside and out (non-TWAS), double glazed	831500007	A	A	A	A	E	A+	A+	A	A+	C	B	B	E	A	30	110	1.7	7	58
solvent borne gloss painted inside and out (TWAS), double glazed	831500010	A+	A+	A	A+	E	A+	A+	B	A+	B	A	B	E	A+	35	90	1.7	7	57
water based stained inside and out (non-TWAS), double glazed	831500014	A	A	A	A	E	A+	A+	A	A+	C	B	B	B	A+	30	100	1.7	7	58
water based stained inside and out (TWAS), double glazed	831500013	A+	A+	A	A+	E	A+	A+	B	A+	B	A+	A	C	A+	35	88	1.7	7	57
PVC-U window, steel reinforcement, double glazed	831500001	A+	B	B	A+	B	A+	A+	A	A+	A+	C	A+	A+	A+	35	120	1.9	8	66
Steel (cold formed) window, double glazed	831500002	B	D	E	D	C	A+	A+	A+	A+	E	D	D	A+	A	35	160	3.3	11	74
Steel (hot rolled) window, double glazed	831500005	B	D	B	E	D	A+	A+	A+	E	A	C	C	A+	A	35	150	1.8	6	74

Note: TWAS = Timber Window Accreditation Scheme.

Windows and curtain walling

Domestic

	Element number	Summary Rating	Climate change	Water extraction	Mineral resource extraction	Stratospheric ozone depletion	Human toxicity	Ecotoxicity to freshwater	Nuclear waste (higher level)	Ecotoxicity to land	Waste disposal	Fossil fuel depletion	Eutrophication	Photochemical ozone creation	Acidification	Typical replacement interval	Embodied CO_2 (kg CO_2 eq.)	Recycled content (kg)	Recycled content (%)	Recycled currently at EOL (%)
Durable hardwood window:																				
double glazed, solvent borne gloss paint (non-TWAS)	813100013	A+	B	B	A+	E	A+	A+	A	A+	D	C	E	C	B	30	220	2.9	6	48
double glazed, solvent borne gloss paint (TWAS)	813100004	A+	A+	A	A+	E	A+	A+	A	A+	E	A+	E	C	A	35	150	2.9	5	45
double glazed, water based stain (non-TWAS)	813100016	A+	A	B	A+	D	A+	A+	A	A+	D	B	E	A+	A	30	210	2.9	6	48
double glazed, water based stain (TWAS)	813100005	A+	A+	A	A+	D	A+	A+	A	A+	E	A+	E	A+	A	35	140	2.9	5	45
Powder coated aluminium clad softwood window:																				
double glazed, solvent borne gloss paint internally	813100018	D	D	C	A	C	C	C	E	A	D	D	E	B	E	40	320	7.2	13	62
double glazed, water based stain internally	813100003	D	D	B	A	C	C	C	E	A	D	C	E	A+	D	40	310	7.2	13	63
Powder coated aluminium window:																				
profile < 0.88 kg/m, double glazed	813100001	B	D	A+	A	A+	D	C	A	A+	A+	A+	A+	A+	B	40	300	7.7	17	74
profile < 1.08 kg/m, double glazed	813100007	C	E	A+	A	A+	D	D	B	A+	A+	A	A+	A+	C	40	330	8.4	18	74
profile > 1.08 kg/m, double glazed	813100030	D	E	A+	A	A+	E	E	C	A+	A+	A	A	A+	D	40	350	9.2	18	75
softwood internal frame, double glazed, solvent borne gloss paint internally	813100010	E	E	B	B	B	E	E	E	A	B	D	E	B	E	40	350	9.7	17	70
softwood internal frame, double glazed, water based stain internally	813100002	E	E	A	B	A	E	E	E	A	B	C	E	A+	E	40	350	9.7	17	71
Powder coated galvanised hot rolled steel window, double glazed	813100011	B	D	C	E	A+	A+	A+	A+	E	E	A+	A+	A+	A	35	310	3.8	6	82
Preservative pre-treated softwood window:																				
double glazed, solvent borne gloss paint (Non-TWAS)	813100017	A	B	B	A+	E	A+	A+	B	A+	E	B	B	E	A+	30	220	2.9	6	48
double glazed, water based stain (Non-TWAS)	813100019	A	A	B	A+	D	A+	A+	B	A+	E	B	B	B	A+	30	220	2.9	6	48
double glazed, water based stain (TWAS)	813100020	A+	A	B	A+	E	A+	A+	C	A	E	A	D	C	A+	35	190	2.9	5	47
doubled glazed, solvent borne gloss paint (TWAS)	813100006	A	A	C	A+	E	A+	A+	C	A	E	B	D	E	A+	35	200	2.9	5	46
PVC-U window with steel reinforcement, double glazed	813100009	A	D	E	A	B	A+	A+	B	A	C	E	B	A+	A	35	310	4.4	8	65

Note: TWAS = Timber Window Accreditation Scheme.

6.7 INTERNAL WALLS

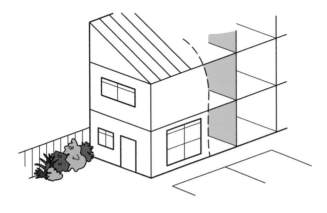

Functional unit for internal walls:

1 m² of internal wall or partitioning, to satisfy Building Regulations in England & Wales, and to include any repair, refurbishment or replacement over a 60-year study period.

Variation for education:

Walls adjoining classrooms: 1 m² of internal wall or partitioning between classrooms, to satisfy Building Regulations in England & Wales, in particular minimum 45 $D_{nT\,(T_{mf,max}),w}$ (dB) airborne sound insulation (Source: BB93[40]) and mid-frequency reverberation time, T_{mf}, in classroom not to exceed 0.6 seconds (Source: BB93[40]). Wall to be specified to Severe Duty (SD) as per BS 5234-2[43]. To include any repair, refurbishment or replacement over the 60-year study period.

In low-rise construction, the domestic and non-domestic ratings apply to all internal walls except separating walls between dwellings. For any building of four storeys or more, only non-loadbearing walls throughout the building need to be assessed. However, please refer to the latest guidance on application of the ratings on *The Green Guide to Specification Online* website[8].

The functional unit has been left intentionally undefined. Internal walls and partitioning may be transparent, translucent or opaque, and may achieve particular fire resistance or compartmentation standards.

The exception to this rule is education buildings where a functional unit based on a minimum acoustic performance and level of robustness has been used. The functional unit is based on the UK Government's Department for Children, Schools and Families (dcfs) standard specifications documents[40,44,45] and

partition type B which are all classed as having acoustic performance greater than 45 R_w dB and severe duty robustness ratings; these documents give example specifications which are deemed compliant with the functional unit.

Division of internal walls into subsections

Internal wall specifications have been arranged into subsections for ease of use by designers. However, ratings have been arrived at through comparison of all internal wall types shown across all subsections. The subsections are:

- Framed partitions,
- Masonry partitions,
- Demountable and proprietary partitions.

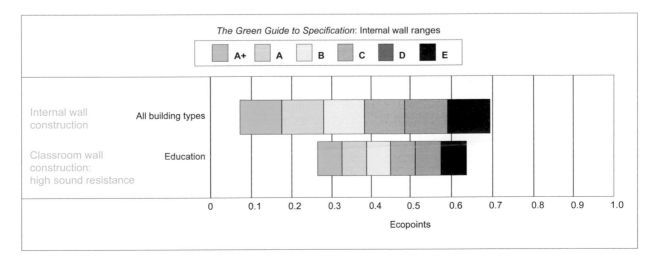

The Green Guide to Specification: Internal wall ranges

A+   A   B   C   D   E

Internal wall construction — All building types

Classroom wall construction: high sound resistance — Education

Ecopoints

Note: where descriptions refer to, say 100% RCA this refers to 100% of the coarse aggregate in the concrete being replaced with Recycled Concrete Aggregate.

Concrete block solid densities are as follows:
- Dense block/blockwork ($\approx$ 1950 kg/m^3),
- Medium density block/blockwork ($\approx$ 1450 kg/m^3),
- Lightweight blockwork ($\approx$ 1100 kg/m^3),
- Superlightweight block/blockwork ($\approx$ 850 kg/m^3).

Framed partitions

All building types

	Element number	Summary Rating	Climate change	Water extraction	Mineral resource extraction	Stratospheric ozone depletion	Human toxicity	Ecotoxicity to freshwater	Nuclear waste (higher level)	Ecotoxicity to land	Waste disposal	Fossil fuel depletion	Eutrophication	Photochemical ozone creation	Acidification	Typical replacement interval	Embodied CO_2 (kg CO_2 eq.)	Recycled content (kg)	Recycled content (%)	Recycled currently at EOL (%)
Galvanised steel jumbo studwork, plasterboard, paint	809760012	A	B	B	A+	A+	A	C	A	A+	A	A	A+	A+	C	60+	35	6.5	25	28
Galvanised steel studwork, plasterboard, paint	809760002	A	A	A	A+	A+	A	C	A+	A+	A	A+	A+	A+	C	60+	28	6.5	28	19
Hardwood veneered MDF framed glazed partitioning, double glazed	809760009	A	B	C	A+	A	A+	A+	A	A	A+	B	A+	A+	A	30	45	5.6	16	57
Softwood framed:																				
single glazed partition, safety glass	809760001	A+	B	B	A+	A	A+	A+	B	A+	A+	A	A+	A+	A	30	34	1.3	6	53
double glazed partition, safety glass	809760010	A	B	C	A+	A	A+	A+	B	A+	A+	B	A+	A+	A	30	51	2.6	8	62
Timber cassette internal wall panel with plywood (softwood) sheathing, plasterboard and paint	809760054	A	A+	A	A+	A	A	D	A	B	A	A	A+	A+	C	60+	13	6.5	20	3
Timber studwork:																				
OSB/3 facing, paint	809760025	A+	A+	A	A+	A+	A+	C	A+	A+	A+	A+	A+	A+	A+	60+	-1	6.8	46	7
plasterboard, paint	809760003	A+	A	A	A+	A+	A	C	A+	A+	A	A+	A+	A+	C	60+	15	6.5	30	5
plywood (softwood), unpainted	809760024	A+	A+	A+	A+	A	A+	A	A	B	A+	A+	A+	A+	A+	60+	-7	0	0	6
t&g softwood boarding, gloss paint	809760004	A+	A+	A	A+	C	A+	C	A	A+	A+	A+	A	E	A+	60+	-5	0	0	35

Masonry partitions
All building types

	Element number	Summary Rating	Climate change	Water extraction	Mineral resource extraction	Stratospheric ozone depletion	Human toxicity	Ecotoxicity to freshwater	Nuclear waste (higher level)	Ecotoxicity to land	Waste disposal	Fossil fuel depletion	Eutrophication	Photochemical ozone creation	Acidification	Typical replacement interval	Embodied CO2 (kg CO2 eq.)	Recycled content (kg)	Recycled content (%)	Recycled currently at EOL (%)
Aircrete blockwork:																				
cement:lime mortar, painted finish only	809180038	A+	A	A	A+	A+	A+	C	A+	A+	A+	A+	A+	A+	A+	60+	30	0.1	0	89
cement:lime mortar, plaster, paint	809180034	A	B	A	A	A	A+	C	A	A+	A	A+	A+	A+	A+	60+	35	0.1	0	62
cement:lime mortar, plasterboard, paint	809180015	B	B	C	A+	A	A	D	A	A+	A	A	A+	A+	D	60+	48	6.6	7	64
plaster, paint	809180021	A	B	A	A	A	A+	C	A	A+	A	A+	A+	A+	A+	60+	34	0.1	0	62
thin joint mortar, plaster, paint	809180022	A	B	A	A	A+	A+	C	A	A+	A	A+	A+	A+	A+	60+	34	0	0	60
thin joint mortar, plasterboard, paint	809180050	B	B	C	A+	A	A	D	A	A+	A	A	A+	A+	D	60+	48	6.5	8	61
painted finish only	809180037	A+	A	A	A+	A+	A+	C	A+	A+	A+	A+	A+	A+	A+	60+	30	0.1	0	89
plasterboard, paint	809180003	B	B	C	A+	A	A	D	A	A	A	A	A+	A+	D	60+	48	6.6	7	64
Brickwork:																				
cement:lime mortar, plaster, paint	809180033	B	B	A	C	B	B	C	A	A+	B	A	A+	A+	A	60+	47	0.2	0	76
cement:lime mortar, plasterboard, paint	809180016	C	C	C	C	B	C	D	B	A+	B	B	A+	A+	E	60+	61	6.7	4	77
plaster, paint	809180023	B	B	A	C	B	B	C	A	A+	B	A	A+	A+	A	60+	47	0.2	0	76
plasterboard, paint	809180004	C	C	C	B	B	C	D	B	A	B	B	A+	A+	E	60+	60	6.7	4	77
Dense solid blockwork:																				
cement:lime mortar, painted finish only	809180012	A	A	A	C	A	A+	C	A+	A+	A	A+	A+	A+	A+	60+	28	0.1	0	90
cement:lime mortar, plaster, paint	809180035	B	A	A	C	B	A+	C	A	A+	B	A+	A+	A+	A+	60+	32	0.1	0	79
cement:lime mortar, plasterboard, paint	809180014	C	B	B	C	B	A	D	A	A	B	A	A+	A+	D	60+	46	6.6	3	79
plaster, paint	809180019	B	A	A	C	B	A+	C	A	A+	B	A+	A+	A+	A+	60+	32	0.1	0	79
painted finish only	809180001	A	A	A	C	A	A+	C	A+	A+	A	A+	A+	A+	A+	60+	28	0.1	0	90
plasterboard, paint	809180002	C	B	B	C	B	A	D	A	A	B	A	A+	A+	D	60+	46	6.6	3	79
Fairfaced brickwork	809180010	A	B	A+	B	A	B	A+	A+	A+	A+	A	A+	A+	A	60+	33	0.2	0	90
Fairfaced brickwork, cement:lime mortar	809180017	A	B	A+	B	A	B	A+	A+	A+	A+	A	A+	A+	A	60+	33	0.2	0	90

Masonry partitions
All building types

	Element number	Summary Rating	Climate change	Water extraction	Mineral resource extraction	Stratospheric ozone depletion	Human toxicity	Ecotoxicity to freshwater	Nuclear waste (higher level)	Ecotoxicity to land	Waste disposal	Fossil fuel depletion	Eutrophication	Photochemical ozone creation	Acidification	Typical replacement interval	Embodied CO2 (kg CO2 eq.)	Recycled content (kg)	Recycled content (%)	Recycled currently at EOL (%)
Fairfaced non-reinforced concrete	809180056	A	A	A	C	A+	A+	A+	A+	A+	A+	A+	A+	A+	A+	60+	28	1.3	1	90
Fairfaced reclaimed brickwork:																				
cement mortar	809180049	A+	A+	A+	A+	A+	A+	A+	A+	A+	A+	A+	A+	A+	A+	60+	11	126	80	90
cement:lime mortar	809180011	A+	A+	A+	A+	A+	A+	A+	A+	A+	A+	A+	A+	A+	A+	60+	7.8	145	82	90
Fairfaced reinforced concrete	809180006	A	B	A	C	A+	A+	A+	A+	A	A	A+	A+	A+	A+	60+	43	14	6	90
Fairfaced solid blockwork	809180009	A	A	A	B	A	A+	A+	A+	A+	A+	A+	A+	A+	A+	60+	22	0.1	0	90
Fairfaced solid blockwork, cement:lime mortar	809180013	A	A	A	C	A	A+	A+	A+	A+	A+	A+	A+	A+	A+	60+	22	0.1	0	90
Glass blockwork:																				
100 mm thick	809180054	A+	A	A+	A+	A+	A+	A+	A+	A+	A	A+	A+	A+	A+	60+	29	1.8	2	78
50 mm thick	809180007	A+	A	A+	A+	A+	A+	A+	A+	A+	A+	A+	A+	A+	A+	60+	22	1.7	3	78
Lightweight solid blockwork:																				
cement:lime mortar, painted	809180040	A	B	A	A	A	A+	C	A+	A+	A+	A	A+	A+	A+	60+	35	0.1	0	90
cement:lime mortar, plaster, paint	809180036	B	B	A	B	B	A+	C	A	A+	B	A	A+	A+	A	60+	40	0.1	0	76
cement:lime mortar, plasterboard, paint	809180018	B	C	C	A	B	A	D	A	A	B	B	A	A+	D	60+	54	6.6	4	77
plaster, paint	809180020	B	B	A	B	B	A+	C	A	A+	B	A	A+	A+	A	60+	40	0.1	0	76
painted finish only	809180039	A	B	A	A	A	A+	C	A+	A+	A+	A	A+	A+	A+	60+	35	0.1	0	90
Medium density solid blockwork, plasterboard, paint	809180008	B	C	C	A	B	A	D	A	A	B	B	A	A+	D	60+	53	6.6	4	77
Non-loadbearing precast concrete wall panel:																				
100 mm, painted	809180029	C	C	B	C	B	A	D	A	A	A	A	A	A+	A	60+	66	6.6	3	90
150 mm, painted	809180052	D	E	B	E	C	A	D	B	B	B	B	A	A+	B	60+	94	7.9	2	90
75 mm, painted	809180028	B	B	A	B	A	A+	C	A	A	A	A	A	A+	A	60+	52	6.6	4	90
Non-loadbearing, precast fibre reinforced concrete wall panel, painted	809180030	D	D	D	D	C	E	E	C	D	B	B	A	A+	B	60+	83	0	0	88

Masonry partitions

All building types

	Element number	Summary Rating	Climate change	Water extraction	Mineral resource extraction	Stratospheric ozone depletion	Human toxicity	Ecotoxicity to freshwater	Nuclear waste (higher level)	Ecotoxicity to land	Waste disposal	Fossil fuel depletion	Eutrophication	Photochemical ozone creation	Acidification	Typical replacement interval	Embodied CO$_2$ (kg CO$_2$ eq.)	Recycled content (kg)	Recycled content (%)	Recycled currently at EOL (%)
Non-reinforced concrete, plasterboard, paint	809180055	C	C	C	C	A	A	D	A	A	B	A	A+	A+	D	60+	55	7.8	3	81
Precast concrete panel (non-loadbearing, 150 mm), plasterboard, paint	809180026	E	E	D	E	D	B	E	C	B	D	C	B	A	E	60+	110	14	4	84
Precast, permanent formwork system, two panels joined by a lattice girder, ready mix between	809180053	C	D	B	E	C	A	A	A	B	B	B	A	A+	B	60+	85	7.9	2	90
Reinforced concrete, plasterboard, paint	809180024	C	C	D	C	A	A	D	B	B	C	B	A	A+	D	60+	70	21	7	82
Superlightweight solid blockwork:																				
cement mortar, plasterboard, paint	809180046	B	C	B	A	B	A	D	A	A	B	B	A	A+	D	60+	55	6.6	5	71
cement:lime mortar, plaster, paint	809180043	B	B	A	A	B	A+	C	A	A+	B	A	A+	A+	A	60+	41	0.1	0	70
cement:lime mortar, plasterboard, paint	809180044	B	C	B	A	B	A	D	A	A	B	B	A	A+	D	60+	55	6.6	5	71
painted finish only	809180041	A	B	A	A	A	A+	C	A+	A+	A+	A	A+	A+	A	60+	37	0.1	0	90
cement mortar, plaster, paint	809180045	B	B	A	A	B	A+	C	A	A+	B	A	A+	A+	A	60+	41	0.1	0	70
cement:lime mortar, painted	809180042	A	B	A	A	A	A+	C	A+	A+	A+	A	A+	A+	A	60+	37	0.1	0	90

Proprietary and demountable partitions All building types	Element number	Summary Rating	Climate change	Water extraction	Mineral resource extraction	Stratospheric ozone depletion	Human toxicity	Ecotoxicity to freshwater	Nuclear waste (higher level)	Ecotoxicity to land	Waste disposal	Fossil fuel depletion	Eutrophication	Photochemical ozone creation	Acidification	Typical replacement interval	Embodied CO$_2$ (kg CO$_2$ eq.)	Recycled content (kg)	Recycled content (%)	Recycled currently at EOL (%)
Aluminium framed partitioning system, plasterboard panels with cardboard honeycomb core, paint	809750008	A	B	B	A+	A+	D	E	B	A+	A	A	A+	A+	D	30	38	7.7	34	11
Aluminium proprietary glazed partitioning system:																				
double glazed, safety glass	809750001	A	C	C	A+	A	C	C	B	A	A+	B	A+	A+	B	30	63	4.2	12	72
single glazed, safety glass	809750002	A	B	B	A+	A+	C	C	B	A+	A+	A	A+	A+	A	30	43	2.1	15	69
Enamelled steel partition: mineral wool core	809750005	B	C	E	A+	A+	A+	A	E	A	A	A	A+	A+	A	60	64	5.6	23	81
Frameless glazed partitioning system, silicon jointed, aluminium base channel	809760022	A+	B	B	A+	A+	A+	A+	A	A+	A+	A+	A+	A+	A	60+	40	3.2	10	75
Vinyl finish chipboard panels with flaxboard core, aluminium framing	809750009	D	A	E	A+	E	E	E	E	E	E	E	E	A	C	15	25	13	48	9

Classroom wall construction: high sound resistance

Education

	Element number	Summary Rating	Climate change	Water extraction	Mineral resource extraction	Stratospheric ozone depletion	Human toxicity	Ecotoxicity to freshwater	Nuclear waste (higher level)	Ecotoxicity to land	Waste disposal	Fossil fuel depletion	Eutrophication	Photochemical ozone creation	Acidification	Typical replacement interval	Embodied CO2 (kg CO2 eq.)	Recycled content (kg)	Recycled content (%)	Recycled currently at EOL (%)
140 mm solid blockwork (density 1450 kg/m³):																				
cement mortar, paint to each side	816110010	A+	A	A+	A	B	A+	A+	A+	A+	A+	A	B	A+	A+	60+	46	0.1	0	90
cement mortar, plaster and paint to each side	816110028	A	B	A	A	B	A+	A+	A	A	B	B	B	A+	A+	60+	50	0.1	0	79
cement mortar, plasterboard and paint to each side	816110029	A	C	B	A	B	A	B	A	B	A	C	C	A	A	60+	55	6.6	3	83
cement:lime mortar, plasterboard and paint to each side	816110030	A+	A	A+	A	A	A	A	A+	A+	A	A	A	A	A	60+	45	6.6	4	80
210 mm dense solid blockwork:																				
cement mortar, paint to each side	816110011	C	B	A+	D	D	A+	A	B	A	A	A	C	A+	A+	60+	49	0.1	0	90
cement mortar, plaster and paint to each side	816110032	D	B	A+	E	D	A+	B	D	B	D	B	D	A+	A+	60+	53	0.1	0	84
cement:lime mortar, plasterboard and paint to each side	816110031	E	E	B	E	E	B	D	E	E	D	E	E	B	A	60+	68	6.6	2	86
Staggered 60 mm metal studs with insulation in cavity (total width 178 mm), two layers of taped and filled plasterboard and paint to each side	816110019	A	D	E	A+	A+	B	B	E	E	B	D	A	B	B	60+	58	13.4	27	18
Steel C studs (70 mm) with 50 mm mineral wool insulation of density 12.9 kg/m³, 15 mm high density plasterboard and 13 mm high density plasterboard with glass fibre additives, and paint, to each side	816110027	C	D	E	A+	A	E	E	E	E	E	B	E	E	E	60	62	20.3	33	7
Steel C studs (75 mm) with 60 mm mineral wool insulation within cavity, 12.5 mm gypsum fibreboard and paint to each side	816110026	A+	A+	A	A+	A+	A	A+	B	A+	A	A+	A+	A	A	60+	39	12.1	32	12

6.8 SEPARATING WALLS

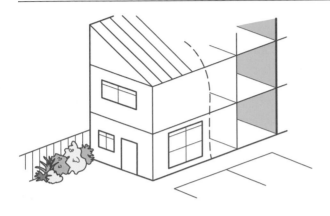

Functional unit for separating walls (party walls):

1 m² of separating wall to satisfy England & Wales Building Regulations, in particular the provision of minimum airborne sound insulation $D_{nT,w} + C_{tr}$ of 45 dB (Source: Approved Document E 2003 incorporating amendments 2004[41]). To include any repair, refurbishment or replacement over the 60-year study period.

Note: where descriptions refer to, say 100% RCA this refers to 100% of the coarse aggregate in the concrete being replaced with Recycled Concrete Aggregate.

Where specifications state 'proprietary' products please refer to *Robust Details*[44] as only products designated by them can be used.

Concrete block solid densities are as follows unless otherwise stated:
- Dense block/blockwork ($\approx$ 1950 kg/m³),
- Medium density block/blockwork ($\approx$ 1450 kg/m³),
- Lightweight blockwork ($\approx$ 1100 kg/m³),
- Superlightweight block/blockwork ($\approx$ 850 kg/m³).

Division of separating walls into subsections
Separating wall specifications have been arranged into subsections for ease of use by designers. However, ratings have been arrived at through comparison of all separating wall types shown across all subsections. The subsections are:
- Masonry walls,
- Steel framed walls,
- Timber framed walls.

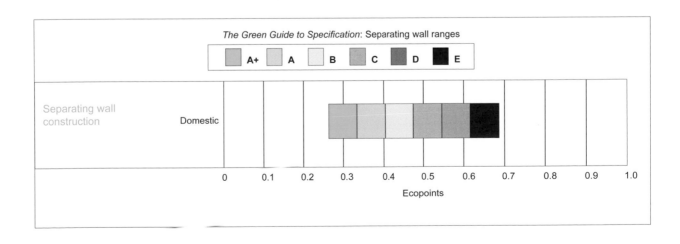

The Green Guide to Specification: Separating wall ranges

A+ | A | B | C | D | E

Separating wall construction — Domestic

Ecopoints: 0 0.1 0.2 0.3 0.4 0.5 0.6 0.7 0.8 0.9 1.0

Separating walls: masonry construction

Domestic

	Element number	Summary Rating	Climate change	Water extraction	Mineral resource extraction	Stratospheric ozone depletion	Human toxicity	Ecotoxicity to freshwater	Nuclear waste (higher level)	Ecotoxicity to land	Waste disposal	Fossil fuel depletion	Eutrophication	Photochemical ozone creation	Acidification	Typical replacement interval	Embodied CO₂ (kg CO₂ eq.)	Recycled content (kg)	Recycled content (%)	Recycled currently at EOL (%)
Approved Document E Wall Type 1.1: 215 mm solid dense blockwork laid flat, 13 mm lightweight plaster (min. 10 kg/m²) and paint on both faces. Meets overall minimum mass of 415 kg/m²	818190052	C	A	A+	E	C	A+	C	A	A+	A	A+	B	A+	A+	60+	53	0.2	0	86
Approved Document E Wall Type 1.2:																				
non-reinforced dense concrete cast in situ 190 mm (at density 2200 kg/m³), 13 mm lightweight plaster (min. 10 kg/m²) and paint on both faces. Overall minimum mass of 415 kg/m²	818190065	D	B	C	E	A+	A+	C	A	A+	B	A+	B	A+	A+	60+	68	2.5	1	86
reinforced dense concrete cast in situ 190 mm (at density 2200 kg/m³), 13 mm lightweight plaster (min. 10 kg/m²) and paint on both faces. Overall minimum mass of 415 kg/m²	818190066	E	D	D	E	A	A+	D	A	C	B	B	C	A+	A+	60+	97	27.2	5	87
Approved Document E Wall Type 1.3: 215 mm solid brickwork wall, 13 mm lightweight plaster (min. 10 kg/m²) and paint on both faces. Overall minimum mass of 375 kg/m²	818190054	D	C	A	D	C	D	C	B	A+	A	C	A	A+	A+	60+	82	0.3	0	85
Approved Document E Wall Type 2.1: 100 mm Solid dense blockwork cavity wall (cavity minimum 50 mm), 13 mm lightweight plaster (min. 10 kg/m²) and paint on both faces. Overall minimum mass of 415 kg/m²	818190055	C	A	A+	D	B	A+	C	A	A+	A	A+	B	A+	A+	60+	50	0.1	0	86
Approved Document E Wall Type 2.2: 100 mm solid medium dense aggregate blockwork cavity wall (min. 75 mm), 13 mm lightweight plaster (min. 10 kg/m²) and paint on both faces. Overall minimum mass of 300 kg/m²	818190056	B	B	B	B	B	A+	C	A+	A+	A	A	B	A+	A+	60+	65	0.1	0	84
Approved Document E Wall Type 2.3: 100 mm solid medium dense aggregate blockwork (1350–1600 kg/m³) cavity wall (min. 75 mm), plasterboard (min. 10 kg/m²) and paint on both faces. Overall minimum mass 290 kg/m²	818190057	C	C	C	B	B	A	D	A	A	A	B	C	A	A	60+	74	7.3	2	84

Separating walls: masonry construction

Domestic

	Element number	Summary Rating	Climate change	Water extraction	Mineral resource extraction	Stratospheric ozone depletion	Human toxicity	Ecotoxicity to freshwater	Nuclear waste (higher level)	Ecotoxicity to land	Waste disposal	Fossil fuel depletion	Eutrophication	Photochemical ozone creation	Acidification	Typical replacement interval	Embodied CO2 (kg CO2 eq.)	Recycled content (kg)	Recycled content (%)	Recycled currently at EOL (%)
Approved Document E Wall Type 2.4: aircrete blockwork cavity wall, minimum 75 mm cavity, 1 sheet plasterboard (min. 10 kg/m²) and paint to each side (min. mass including finishes 150 kg/m²)	818190008	A	B	A	A	A	A+	C	A	A+	A+	A	A	A+	A	60+	64	7.3	5	77
Approved Document E Wall Type 3.1: 140 mm solid dense blockwork (2200 kg/m³) (min. 300 kg/m²) with independent panels comprising 2 sheets of plasterboard (min. 20 kg/m²) and paint to each side	818190058	C	B	A	C	B	B	D	A	A+	B	A	B	B	B	60+	57	15	5	79
Robust Detail E-WM-1:																				
twin-leaf 100 mm solid dense aggregate blocks (1850–2300 kg/m³) with 75 mm min. cavity, type A wall ties, 13 mm plaster (min. 10 kg/m²) and paint to each side	818190045	C	A	A+	D	B	A+	C	A	A+	A	A+	B	A+	A+	60+	50	0.1	0	86
twin-leaf 100 mm solid dense aggregate blocks (1850–2300 kg/m³) with 75 mm min. cavity, type A wall ties, sand:cement render with plaster skim (min. 10 kg/m²) and paint to each side	818190015	C	A	A+	E	C	A+	C	A+	A+	A	A+	B	A+	A+	60+	53	0.3	0	88
Robust Detail E-WM-10: twin-leaf 100 mm solid aircrete blocks (600–800 kg/m³), thin joint system, with 75 mm min. cavity, proprietary wall ties, 8 mm sand:cement render, gypsum based board (8 kg/m²) on dabs and paint to each side	818190023	B	D	D	A	B	A	D	C	A	A+	C	B	A	A	60+	88	6.7	3	78
Robust Detail E-WM-11:																				
twin-leaf 100 mm medium dense concrete blocks, with 100 mm min. cavity, type A wall ties, 8 mm proprietary gypsum based render, gypsum based board (8 kg/m²) on dabs with paint to each side	818190002	D	C	E	B	C	A	D	B	A	B	C	C	A	A	60+	82	6.6	2	79
twin-leaf 100 mm medium dense concrete blocks, with 100 mm min. cavity, type A wall ties, 8 mm sand:cement render, gypsum based board (8 kg/m²) on dabs with paint to each side	818190031	D	D	E	C	C	A	D	B	A	A	D	D	A	A	60+	85	6.8	2	83

Separating walls: masonry construction

Domestic

	Element number	Summary Rating	Climate change	Water extraction	Mineral resource extraction	Stratospheric ozone depletion	Human toxicity	Ecotoxicity to freshwater	Nuclear waste (higher level)	Ecotoxicity to land	Waste disposal	Fossil fuel depletion	Eutrophication	Photochemical ozone creation	Acidification	Typical replacement interval	Embodied CO2 (kg CO2 eq.)	Recycled content (kg)	Recycled content (%)	Recycled currently at EOL (%)
Robust Detail E-WM-12:																				
twin-leaf 100 mm proprietary lightweight blocks (block density 1050 kg/m³), Type A cavity wall ties, 75 mm min. cavity, 8 mm cement: sand render with gypsum based board (8 kg/m²) mounted on dabs and paint to each side	818190061	C	D	C	B	D	A	D	B	A	A	C	C	A	A	60+	86	6.8	2	81
twin-leaf 100 mm proprietary lightweight blocks (block density 1050 kg/m³), Type A cavity wall ties, 75 mm min. cavity, 8 mm gypsum based render with gypsum based board (8 kg/m²) mounted on dabs and paint to each side.	818190064	C	C	C	B	C	A	D	B	A	B	C	C	A	A	60+	82	6.6	3	75
Robust Detail E-WM-13: twin-leaf 100 mm solid aircrete blocks (600–800 kg/m³), thin joint system, no wall ties, 75 mm min. cavity, 8 mm cement:sand render with gypsum based board (8 kg/m²) on dabs with paint to each side	818190062	B	C	C	A	A	A+	D	B	A	A+	B	A	A	A	60+	75	6.7	4	75
Robust Detail E-WM-2:																				
twin-leaf 100 mm solid medium dense aggregate blocks (1350–1600 kg/m³) with 75 mm min. cavity, type A wall ties, 13 mm plaster (min. 10 kg/m²) and paint to each side.	818190029	B	B	B	B	B	A+	C	A+	A+	A	A	B	A+	A+	60+	65	0.1	0	84
twin-leaf 100 mm solid medium dense aggregate blocks (1350–1600 kg/m³) with 75 mm min. cavity, type A wall ties, sand:cement render with plaster skim (min. 10 kg/m²) and paint to each side.	818190016	D	D	B	D	E	A+	D	A	A	A+	D	E	A	A+	60+	97	0.3	0	87
Robust Detail E-WM-3:																				
twin-leaf 100 mm solid dense aggregate blocks (1850–2300 kg/m³) with 75 mm min. cavity, type A wall ties, 8 mm proprietary gypsum based internal render, gypsum based board (8 kg/m²) on dabs and paint to each side	818190024	E	B	C	E	C	A	D	C	A	C	B	C	A	A	60+	67	6.6	2	81
twin-leaf 100 mm solid dense aggregate blocks (1850–2300 kg/m³) with 75 mm min. cavity, type A wall ties, 8 mm sand:cement render, gypsum based board (8 kg/m²) on dabs and paint to each side	818190017	D	C	C	E	C	A	D	C	A	B	B	C	A	A	60+	70	6.8	2	85

Separating walls: masonry construction

Domestic

	Element number	Summary Rating	Climate change	Water extraction	Mineral resource extraction	Stratospheric ozone depletion	Human toxicity	Ecotoxicity to freshwater	Nuclear waste (higher level)	Ecotoxicity to land	Waste disposal	Fossil fuel depletion	Eutrophication	Photochemical ozone creation	Acidification	Typical replacement interval	Embodied CO₂ (kg CO₂ eq.)	Recycled content (kg)	Recycled content (%)	Recycled currently at EOL (%)
Robust Detail E-WM-4:																				
twin-leaf 100 mm solid medium dense aggregate blocks (1350–1600 kg/m³) with 75 mm min. cavity, type A wall ties, 8 mm proprietary gypsum based internal render, gypsum based board (8 kg/m²) on dabs and paint to each side	818190028	D	C	E	B	C	A	D	B	A	B	C	C	A	A	60+	82	6.6	2	79
twin-leaf 100 mm solid medium dense aggregate blocks (1350–1600 kg/m³) with 75 mm min. cavity, type A wall ties, 8 mm sand:cement render, gypsum based board (8 kg/m²) on dabs and paint to each side	818190018	D	D	E	C	C	A	D	B	A	A	D	D	A	A	60+	85	6.8	2	83
Robust Detail E-WM-5:																				
twin-leaf 100 mm proprietary dense aggregate cellular blocks, with 75 mm min. cavity, type A wall ties, 8 mm proprietary gypsum based render, gypsum based board (8 kg/m²) on dabs with paint to each side	818190019	D	B	C	D	B	A	D	B	A	B	B	B	A	A	60+	62	6.7	2	79
twin-leaf 100 mm proprietary dense aggregate cellular blocks, with 75 mm min. cavity, type A wall ties, 8 mm sand:cement render, gypsum based board (8 kg/m²) on dabs with paint to each side	818190030	C	B	C	D	C	A	D	A	A	B	B	A	A	60+	65	6.9	2	83
Robust Detail E-WM-6: twin-leaf 100 mm solid aircrete blocks (600–800 kg/m³), with 75 mm min. cavity, Type A wall ties, 8 mm cement:sand render and gypsum based board (8 kg/m²) on dabs with paint, to each side	818190020	C	D	D	A	B	A	D	C	A	A+	C	B	A	A	60+	88	6.8	3	79
Robust Detail E-WM-8: twin-leaf 100 mm solid medium dense blocks (1350–1600 kg/m³), with 75 mm min. cavity including proprietary foil faced glass wool acoustic batts, type A wall ties, with gypsum based board (9.8 kg/m²) on dabs with paint to each side	818190021	E	E	E	C	E	A	E	D	B	A	E	B	A	60+	110	7.6	2	82
Robust Detail E-WM-9: single-leaf 215 mm proprietary solid dense aggregate blocks (1850–2300 kg/m³) laid flat, 13 mm (min.) cement:sand render and gypsum based board (12.5 kg/m²) on dabs with paint to each side	818190022	E	C	B	E	D	B	D	B	A	C	B	D	B	A	60+	73	11	2	85

Separating walls: steel construction Domestic	Element number	Summary Rating	Climate change	Water extraction	Mineral resource extraction	Stratospheric ozone depletion	Human toxicity	Ecotoxicity to freshwater	Nuclear waste (higher level)	Ecotoxicity to land	Waste disposal	Fossil fuel depletion	Eutrophication	Photochemical ozone creation	Acidification	Typical replacement interval	Embodied CO2 (kg CO2 eq.)	Recycled content (kg)	Recycled content (%)	Recycled currently at EOL (%)
Robust Detail E-WS-1:																				
twin lightweight steel frames, 200 mm min. between wall linings, 25 mm mineral wool quilt on each side (10 kg/m³ min.), 2 layers staggered gypsum based board (22 kg/m²) and paint on each side	818580066	A	A	B	A+	A+	A	C	A	A+	A	A+	A+	A	B	60+	51	14.8	29	18
twin lightweight steel frames, 200 mm min. between wall linings, 50 mm mineral wool batts between frames or 25 mm mineral wool batts on each side (33–60 kg/m³), 2 layers staggered gypsum based board (22 kg/m²) and paint on each side	818580013	A	A	B	A+	A+	A	C	A	A+	A	A	A+	A	B	60+	52	15.5	30	17
Robust Detail E-WS-3:																				
modular build twin light steel frames 'C' or 'I' studs (100 mm) with 12.5 mm OSB sheathing (min. 7.5 kg/m²) & 40 mm min. cavity between, 75 mm mineral wool batts (45 kg/m³) between studs & 2 layers gypsum based board (24 kg/m²) and paint on each side	818580067	B	B	E	A+	A+	B	D	C	A	C	B	A	B	B	60+	57	28.8	36	15
modular build twin light steel frames 'C' or 'I' studs (100 mm) with 12 mm ply sheathing (min 7.5 kg/m²) & 40 mm min. cavity between, 75 mm mineral wool batts (45 kg/m³) between studs & 2 layers gypsum based board (24 kg/m²) and paint on each side	818580068	C	B	E	A+	B	B	E	E	E	C	C	B	C	B	60+	62	19.4	24	15
modular build twin light steel frames 'C' or 'I' studs (75 mm) with 12.5 mm ply sheathing (min. 7.5 kg/m²) & 40 mm min. cavity between, 75 mm mineral wool batts (45 kg/m³) between studs & 2 layers gypsum based board (32 kg/m²) and paint on each side	818580064	B	A	D	A+	A	C	A+	D	E	C	B	B	C	C	60+	53	25.2	27	10
Robust Detail E-WS-2: twin proprietary steel frames, 190 mm min. between wall linings, 100 mm min. proprietary glass wool quilt between frames, 2 layers proprietary plasterboard and paint on each side	818580044	D	C	E	A+	A	E	A+	B	A	E	C	A	E	E	35	81	18.9	31	15

Separating walls: timber construction

Domestic

	Element number	Summary Rating	Climate change	Water extraction	Mineral resource extraction	Stratospheric ozone depletion	Human toxicity	Ecotoxicity to freshwater	Nuclear waste (higher level)	Ecotoxicity to land	Waste disposal	Fossil fuel depletion	Eutrophication	Photochemical ozone creation	Acidification	Typical replacement interval	Embodied CO_2 (kg CO_2 eq.)	Recycled content (kg)	Recycled content (%)	Recycled currently at EOL (%)
Approved Document E Wall Type 4.1: timber frame cavity wall (min. 200 mm) filled with 50 mm mineral wool insulation with composite panels comprising 2 sheets of plasterboard (min. 20 kg/m²) and paint on each side	818570061	A+	A+	A+	A+	A+	A	C	A+	A+	A+	A+	A+	A	A	60+	26	15.5	32	4
Robust Detail E-WT-2:																				
twin timber frames with 50 mm min. between sheathing & 240 mm min. between wall linings; to each side 9 mm plywood sheathing, 60 mm mineral wool (10–60 kg/m³) between studs, 2 or more layers gypsum based board (22 kg/m²) and emulsion paint	818570063	A	A+	B	A+	A	B	E	C	C	A	A	A	B	B	60+	30	17	27	3
twin timber frames with 50 mm min. between sheathing and 240 mm min. between wall linings; to each side 9 mm OSB sheathing, 60 mm mineral wool (10–60 kg/m³) between studs, 2 or more layers gypsum based board (22 kg/m²) and emulsion paint	818570065	A+	A+	B	A+	A+	B	D	A	A+	A	A	A	A	B	60+	26	23.7	38	3
Robust Detail E-WT-1: twin timber frames without sheathing board, 240 mm min. between wall linings, wall ties where necessary, to each side, 60 mm min. mineral wool between studs, 2 or more layers of gypsum based board (22 kg/m²) and paint	818570062	A+	A+	A	A+	A+	A	C	A+	A+	A+	A+	A+	A	A	60+	33	17	34	4

6.9 INSULATION

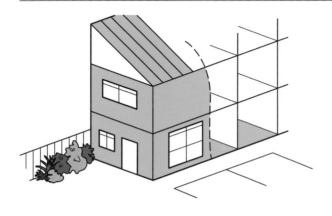

Thermal insulation is generally a low density material and only relatively small masses are needed to provide high levels of thermal resistance. Nevertheless, as Building Regulations have improved, and low U-values have become more common, the environmental impact of the insulation compared with the impact of the construction element in which it is used has grown.

Notwithstanding this, the use of insulation in the building fabric will significantly reduce the operational impact of the building over its lifetime. Therefore, the benefit of using any of the insulations listed in *The Green Guide to Specification* will outweigh the embodied environmental impact of their manufacture, installation and end-of-life disposal over the life cycle. This is illustrated by the large number of credits available in BREEAM and the Code for Sustainable Homes for

Functional unit for insulation:

1 m² of insulation with sufficient thickness to provide a thermal resistance value of 3 m²K/W, equivalent to approximately 100 mm of insulation with a conductivity (k value) of 0.033 W/mK. To include any repair, refurbishment or replacement over the 60-year study period.

reducing operational CO_2 emissions and the single credit available for insulation specification.

The basis of the comparison used here is a common thermal resistance so that all the insulations included can be compared on an equal footing, as they would all transmit the same amount of heat if they were used in the same construction. The insulation materials have different conductivities so they are able to provide the same thermal resistance with different thicknesses of material. All insulations have been compared on the basis of the same 60-year study period.

How insulation is assessed within BREEAM 2008
BREEAM 2008 has a materials credit for the use of insulation with low environmental impact within construction elements.

The Green Guide to Specification assesses the impact of insulation in construction elements on the basis of a typical 'generic' insulation, except where the insulation provides a significant additional function. In such cases, the insulation is named, for example, a beam

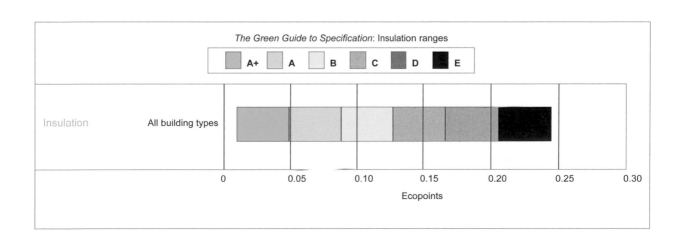

The Green Guide to Specification: Insulation ranges

| A+ | A | B | C | D | E |

| Insulation | All building types |

0   0.05   0.10   0.15   0.20   0.25   0.30

Ecopoints

and expanded polystyrene block floor. In this case, the insulation also provides a structural function. Additional situations are where the insulation is incorporated into the construction offsite, for example in a composite insulated cladding panel. In these cases, the specific insulation is listed in the element description and its specific impact is assessed for the element. Where this occurs, the insulation should be assumed to be A+ to calculate the *BREEAM 2008*[3] insulation credit.

Insulation

All building types

	Element number	Summary Rating	Climate change	Water extraction	Mineral resource extraction	Stratospheric ozone depletion	Human toxicity	Ecotoxicity to freshwater	Nuclear waste (higher level)	Ecotoxicity to land	Waste disposal	Fossil fuel depletion	Eutrophication	Photochemical ozone creation	Acidification	Typical replacement interval	Embodied CO_2 (kg CO_2 eq.)	Recycled content (kg)	Recycled content (%)	Recycled currently at EOL (%)
Cavity blown glass wool insulation: density 17 kg/m³	815320036	A+	B	A+	A+	A+	A+	A+	A+	E	A+	A+	A+	A+	A+	60+	4.2	1.2	61	0
Cavity blown stone wool insulation: density 30 kg/m³	815320037	A+	B	A+	A	A+	A+	A+	A+	E	A+	A+	A+	A+	A	60+	5.2	2.5	64	0
Cellular glass insulation:																				
density 105 kg/m³	815320019	C	B	A	A	A	D	A	D	E	A+	B	A+	A	A	60+	23	9.7	81	0
density 120 kg/m³	815320020	D	C	A	B	A	E	A	E	E	A+	C	A+	A	B	60+	28	12.2	81	0
Corkboard insulation: density 120 kg/m³	815320021	A	A	A	A+	A	C	A	B	E	A+	B	A+	B	C	60+	-5	0	0	0
Dry blown recycled cellulose insulation: density 24 kg/m³	815320035	A+	B	A+	C	A+	A+	A+	A+	E	A+	A+	A+	A+	A+	60+	-2	3.9	80	0
Expanded polystyrene (EPS):																				
density 15 kg/m³	815320022	A+	B	A+	A+	A+	A+	A+	A+	E	A+	A	A+	C	A	60+	6.9	0	0	0
density 20 kg/m³	815320023	A+	B	A+	A+	A	A+	A+	A+	E	A+	A	A+	D	A	60+	8.7	0	0	0
density 25 kg/m³	815320024	A+	B	A+	A+	A	A+	A+	A+	E	A+	B	A+	E	B	60+	11	0	0	0
density 30 kg/m³	815320025	A+	B	A+	A+	A	A+	A+	A+	E	A+	B	A+	E	B	60+	12	0	0	0
Extruded polystyrene (XPS): HFC blown, density 35 kg/m³	815320027	E	E	A	A+	E	A+	A+	A	E	A+	C	A+	B	B	60+	110	0	0	0
Glass wool insulation:																				
density 10 kg/m³	815320005	A+	B	A+	A+	A+	A+	A+	A+	E	A+	A+	A+	A+	A+	60+	2	0.6	61	0
density 12 kg/m³	815320001	A+	B	A+	A+	A+	A+	A+	A+	E	A+	A+	A+	A+	A+	60+	3.1	0.9	61	0
density 24 kg/m³	815320002	A+	B	A+	A+	A+	A+	A+	A+	E	A+	A+	A+	A+	A+	60+	5.4	1.5	61	0
density 32 kg/m³	815320003	A+	B	A+	A+	A+	A+	A+	A+	E	A+	A+	A+	A+	A+	60+	7.1	2	61	0
density 48 kg/m³	815320004	A+	B	A+	A+	A+	A	A+	A+	E	A+	A	A+	A+	A	60+	10	2.8	61	0
Rigid urethane (pentane blown): density 32 kg/m³	815320017	A	B	B	A+	A	A+	A+	A+	E	A+	A	A+	D	B	60+	12	0	0	0
Sheep's wool insulation: density 25 kg/m³	815320033	A	B	E	A+	A+	A+	A+	A+	E	A+	A+	C	A+	E	60+	11	0	0	0

Insulation

All building types

	Element number	Summary Rating	Climate change	Water extraction	Mineral resource extraction	Stratospheric ozone depletion	Human toxicity	Ecotoxicity to freshwater	Nuclear waste (higher level)	Ecotoxicity to land	Waste disposal	Fossil fuel depletion	Eutrophication	Photochemical ozone creation	Acidification	Typical replacement interval	Embodied CO_2 (kg CO_2 eq.)	Recycled content (kg)	Recycled content (%)	Recycled currently at EOL (%)
Stone wool insulation:																				
density 100 kg/m³	815320011	A	B	A+	C	A+	A	A+	A+	E	A+	A	A+	A	C	60+	15	6.7	64	0
density 128 kg/m³	815320012	B	B	A+	D	A+	B	A+	A+	E	A+	B	A+	A	D	60+	19	8.5	64	0
density 140 kg/m³	815320013	B	B	A+	D	A+	B	A+	A+	E	A+	B	A+	A	D	60+	20	9.3	64	0
density 160 kg/m³	815320014	C	B	A+	E	A+	C	A+	A+	E	A	B	A+	B	E	60+	25	11.3	64	0
density 33 kg/m³	815320007	A+	B	A+	A	A+	A+	A+	A+	E	A+	A+	A+	A+	A+	60+	5.1	2.3	64	0
density 45 kg/m³	815320008	A+	B	A+	A	A+	A+	A+	A+	E	A+	A+	A+	A+	A	60+	6.6	3	64	0
density 60 kg/m³	815320009	A+	B	A+	B	A+	A+	A+	A+	E	A+	A+	A+	A+	A	60+	8.8	4	64	0
density 80 kg/m³	815320010	A	B	A+	B	A+	A	A+	A+	E	A+	A	A+	A+	B	60+	12	5.3	64	0
Straw bale used as insulation	815320029	A	A+	A+	A+	A	C	E	A+	A	C	A+	C	B	B	60+	-53	0	0	0
Strawboard thermal insulation: density 420 kg/m³	815320034	C	A+	A+	A+	C	E	A	A+	A+	E	C	E	E	E	60+	-63	0	0	0
Wet blown recycled cellulose insulation: density 45 kg/m³	815320039	A+	B	A+	C	A+	A+	A+	A+	E	A+	A+	A+	A+	A+	60+	-2	3.9	80	0

6.10   LANDSCAPING

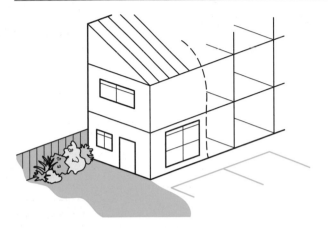

Surfacing for pedestrian areas only

This section provides ratings for landscape surfacing specifications for areas exposed to pedestrian traffic only, which includes public and private spaces. Examples of private spaces include domestic patios and enclosed garden areas. These areas are not expected to support vehicle loadings. All the specifications are expected to achieve standard disabled access requirements.

Where soft landscaping solutions can be used, such as wood chippings or grass turf, these achieve the highest rating band possible of A+.

Hard surfacing (Car)

1 m² of hard surfacing, suitable for the parking of cars, to satisfy Building Regulations in England & Wales, and to include any repair, refurbishment or replacement over the 60-year study period.

Variation for Hard surfacing (Heavy Goods Vehicle):

As above but able to take HGV.

Variation for Hard surfacing (Pedestrian only):

As above for pedestrian traffic only.

Boundary protection

1 m² of boundary protection or balustrading up to 2 m high.

Sustainable Urban Drainage Systems (SUDS), such as permeable precast concrete block paving or permeable asphalt systems, can be considered to have the same ratings as their conventional equivalents. The additional material that may be necessary for SUDS is discounted as the benefit it provides is for facilitating drainage and therefore sits outside the scope of the functional unit.

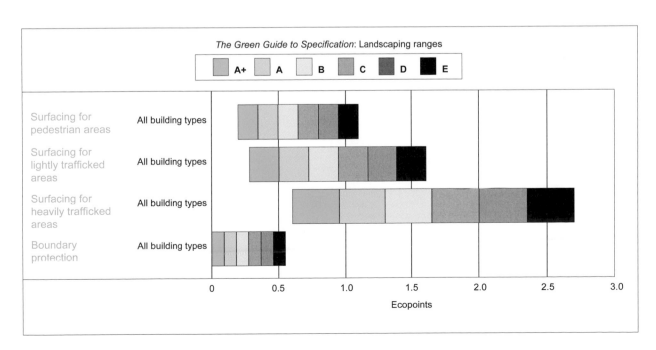

The Green Guide to Specification: Landscaping ranges

A+ | A | B | C | D | E

Surfacing for lightly trafficked areas*

Lightly trafficked areas are not expected to withstand a lot of heavy vehicle traffic movements. They are not likely to be overridden by more than occasional heavier vehicular traffic[†]. These areas include car parking spaces and with ratios of nine car parking spaces to every 10 occupants or one space per 25 m² of gross floor area still common for office developments, hard surfacing can be around 80% of the floor area of the building.

---

* Assumed approximate mechanical strength of sub-grades to be California Bearing Ratio (CBR) of 4–5%.

[†] Informed by British Standards for lightly trafficked pavements, BS 7533-2:2001[46].

Surfacing for heavily trafficked areas‡

Heavily trafficked areas are expected to withstand heavy vehicles and/or repetitive lighter traffic.

Boundary protection

The perimeter of an 'out-of-town' site is often long enough for the boundary protection to be significant compared with the area of the external wall of the building it surrounds. Boundary protection can therefore make a significant contribution to the overall impacts of out-of-town large-scale developments.

---

‡ Informed by British Standards for heavy duty pavements, BS 7533-1:2001[46] and assumes a CBR of 5–10% and 0.5–1.5 million standard axles (MSA) durability.

Surfacing for pedestrian areas	Element number	Summary Rating	Climate change	Water extraction	Mineral resource extraction	Stratospheric ozone depletion	Human toxicity	Ecotoxicity to freshwater	Nuclear waste (higher level)	Ecotoxicity to land	Waste disposal	Fossil fuel depletion	Eutrophication	Photochemical ozone creation	Acidification	Typical replacement interval	Embodied CO2 (kg CO2 eq.)	Recycled content (kg)	Recycled content (%)	Recycled currently at EOL (%)
Asphalt paving (75 mm):																				
over prepared recycled sub-base	824130029	A	A	A+	A+	C	A+	A	A	A	C	E	A	A+	A+	35	41	227	59	53
over prepared sub-base	824130001	B	A	A+	B	B	A+	A	A	A	C	E	A	A+	A+	35	41	6.7	2	53
Cement mortar wet laid clay setts (50 mm):																				
over prepared recycled sub-base	824130027	C	D	A+	A+	B	D	C	C	C	E	C	A	A+	A	50	85	221	55	90
over prepared sub-base	824130014	C	D	A+	B	B	D	C	C	C	E	C	A	A+	A	50	85	0.6	0	90
Cement mortar wet laid imported Chinese granite setts (100 mm), no sub-base	824130023	E	E	A+	E	E	C	E	C	E	E	E	E	A	E	50	120	0.6	0	90
Cement mortar wet laid imported Indian sandstone riven paving flags (29 mm), no sub-base	824130058	B	B	A+	B	D	A	B	B	B	A	B	B	A+	A	50	55	0.2	0	90
Cement mortar wet laid reclaimed stone setts (100 mm), no sub-base	824130013	B	B	A+	A+	C	A+	C	A	B	E	B	A	A+	A+	40	58	215	64	90
Cement mortar wet laid UK sandstone paving flags (29 mm), no sub-base	824130012	A	A+	A+	A	A+	A+	A	A	A	A	A+	A+	A+	A+	50	27	0.2	0	90
Cement mortar wet laid wet cast replica sandstone (35 mm), no sub-base	824130020	A	B	A+	A+	A	A+	C	B	B	A	A	A	A+	A+	50	46	4	2	90
Clay pavers (50 mm), no sub-base	824130002	A	B	A+	A	A	E	A	C	A	A+	B	A+	A+	A	60	61	0	0	90
Concrete block pavers (CBP) (50 mm), no sub-base	824130005	A	A	A+	A	A+	A+	B	B	A	A+	A	A+	A+	A+	60	41	5.5	2	90
Concrete paving flags (35 mm), no sub-base	824130006	A+	A+	A+	A+	A+	A+	A	A+	A+	A+	A+	A+	A+	A+	60	23	4	3	90
Pre-treated softwood timber decking on concrete foundations	824130010	B	A	A+	A	C	A	E	D	D	D	B	A	E	A	20	33	2	1	86
Proprietary grass concrete paving (100 mm), no sub-base	824130011	B	B	E	A+	A+	A+	B	E	B	A+	A	A+	A+	A+	30	52	6.5	1	31
Reclaimed clay pavers (50 mm), no sub-base	824130025	A+	A+	A+	A+	A+	A+	A+	A+	A+	A	A+	A+	A+	A+	50	8.7	110	49	90
Reinforced concrete laid in situ (100 mm):																				
over prepared recycled sub-base	824130028	B	C	A+	A	A	A+	C	B	C	C	B	A	A+	A	50	77	224	49	90
over prepared sub-base	824130004	C	C	A+	C	A+	A+	C	B	C	C	B	A	A+	A	50	76	4.2	1	90

Surfacing for lightly trafficked areas

	Element number	Summary Rating	Climate change	Water extraction	Mineral resource extraction	Stratospheric ozone depletion	Human toxicity	Ecotoxicity to freshwater	Nuclear waste (higher level)	Ecotoxicity to land	Waste disposal	Fossil fuel depletion	Eutrophication	Photochemical ozone creation	Acidification	Typical replacement interval	Embodied CO2 (kg CO2 eq.)	Recycled content (kg)	Recycled content (%)	Recycled currently at EOL (%)
Asphalt (85 mm):																				
over prepared recycled sub-base	830120020	A+	A	A+	A+	B	A+	A	A	A+	A	D	A+	A	A+	35	46	228	56	51
over prepared sub-base	830120001	A	A	A+	B	B	A+	A	A	A+	A	D	A+	A	A+	35	45	7.5	2	51
Cement mortar wet laid clay setts (50 mm):																				
over prepared recycled sub-base	830120030	B	D	A+	A	B	D	D	D	C	D	C	A	B	A	50	120	221	45	90
over prepared sub-base	830120014	C	D	A+	B	B	D	D	D	C	D	C	A	B	A	50	120	1	0	90
Cement mortar wet laid imported Chinese granite setts (100 mm):																				
over prepared recycled sub-base	830120027	E	E	A+	D	E	D	E	D	E	E	E	E	E	E	50	160	221	34	90
over prepared sub-base	830120008	E	E	A+	E	E	D	E	E	E	E	E	E	E	E	50	160	1.1	0	90
Cement mortar wet laid imported Indian sandstone riven setts (50 mm):																				
over prepared recycled sub-base	830120052	B	C	A+	B	E	B	C	C	B	B	C	B	D	B	50	94	220	72	90
over prepared sub-base	830120051	B	C	A+	C	E	B	C	C	B	B	C	B	C	B	50	93	0.4	0	90
Cement mortar wet laid reclaimed stone setts (100 mm):																				
over prepared recycled sub-base	830120029	B	C	A+	A+	C	A	D	B	C	E	C	B	B	A	40	99	436	67	90
over prepared sub-base	830120013	C	C	A+	A	C	A	D	B	C	E	C	B	B	A	40	99	216	33	90
Cement mortar wet laid UK sandstone setts (50 mm):																				
over prepared recycled sub-base	830120032	A	A	A+	A	A	A+	A	A	A	A	A+	A+	A+	A+	50	42	220	51	90
over prepared sub-base	830120019	B	A	A+	C	A+	A+	A	A	A	A	A+	A+	A+	A+	50	42	0.3	0	90
Clay pavers (50 mm):																				
over prepared recycled sub-base	830120021	A	B	A+	A+	A	E	A	C	A	B	A+	A	A+	A+	60	70	220	50	90
over prepared sub-base	830120002	A	B	A+	B	A	E	A	C	A	B	A+	A	A+	A+	60	70	0	0	90
Concrete block pavers (CBP) (60 mm):																				
over prepared recycled sub-base	830120025	A+	A	A+	A+	A	A+	B	B	A	A	A	A+	A	A+	60	57	227	49	90
over prepared sub-base	830120005	A	A	A+	B	A+	A+	B	B	A	A	A	A+	A+	A+	60	57	6.6	1	90

Surfacing for lightly trafficked areas

	Element number	Summary Rating	Climate change	Water extraction	Mineral resource extraction	Stratospheric ozone depletion	Human toxicity	Ecotoxicity to freshwater	Nuclear waste (higher level)	Ecotoxicity to land	Waste disposal	Fossil fuel depletion	Eutrophication	Photochemical ozone creation	Acidification	Typical replacement interval	Embodied CO₂ (kg CO₂ eq.)	Recycled content (kg)	Recycled content (%)	Recycled currently at EOL (%)
Concrete paving flags (60 mm):																				
over prepared recycled sub-base	830120026	A+	A	A+	A+	A+	A+	A	A	A	A	A+	A+	A+	A+	60	47	227	54	90
over prepared sub-base	830120006	A	A	A+	A	A+	A+	A	A	A	A	A+	A+	A+	A+	60	47	6.8	2	90
Gravel:																				
over prepared recycled sub-base	830120028	A	A+	A+	A	A+	A+	A+	A+	A+	A	A+	A+	A+	A+	15	23	220	57	90
over prepared sub-base	830120009	C	A	A+	E	A	A+	A+	A+	A+	D	A	A+	A+	A+	15	42	0	0	90
Proprietary grass concrete paving (120 mm) over prepared sub-base (using suitable on-site available material)	830120011	A	A	E	A+	A+	A+	B	E	B	A+	A	A+	A+	A+	35	60	9.2	2	38
Reclaimed clay pavers (50 mm):																				
over prepared recycled sub-base	830120023	A+	A+	A+	A+	A+	A+	A+	A+	A+	A	A+	A+	A+	A+	50	18	330	74	90
over prepared sub-base	830120022	A+	A+	A+	A	A+	A+	A+	A+	A+	A	A+	A+	A+	A+	50	18	110	25	90
Reinforced concrete laid in situ (100 mm):																				
over prepared recycled sub-base	830120024	A	B	A+	A+	A+	A+	C	B	B	A	A	A+	A+	A+	50	77	224	49	90
over prepared sub-base	830120004	A	B	A+	B	A+	A+	C	B	B	A	A	A+	A+	A+	50	76	4.2	1	90

Surfacing for heavily trafficked areas

	Element number	Summary Rating	Climate change	Water extraction	Mineral resource extraction	Stratospheric ozone depletion	Human toxicity	Ecotoxicity to freshwater	Nuclear waste (higher level)	Ecotoxicity to land	Waste disposal	Fossil fuel depletion	Eutrophication	Photochemical ozone creation	Acidification	Typical replacement interval	Embodied CO₂ (kg CO₂ eq.)	Recycled content (kg)	Recycled content (%)	Recycled currently at EOL (%)
Asphalt (100 mm):																				
over prepared recycled sub-base	822120034	A+	A+	A+	A+	A	A+	A+	A+	A+	B	B	A+	A+	A+	35	61	449	68	61
Asphalt (100 mm) over prepared sub-base	822120001	B	A	A+	B	B	A	A	A	A+	C	E	A	A	A	35	100	18	2	47
Cement mortar wet laid imported Chinese granite setts (100 mm):																				
over prepared recycled sub-base	822120039	C	D	A+	B	C	D	D	B	E	E	D	E	D	E	40	240	679	55	90
over prepared sub-base	822120008	E	D	A+	E	B	D	D	C	E	E	D	E	C	E	40	240	3	0	90
Cement mortar wet laid imported Indian sandstone riven setts (100 mm):																				
over prepared recycled sub-base	822120055	D	E	A+	C	E	D	E	D	E	E	E	E	E	E	40	270	679	66	90
over prepared sub-base	822120054	E	E	A	E	E	D	E	D	E	E	E	E	E	E	40	270	3	0	90
Cement mortar wet laid reclaimed stone setts (100 mm):																				
over prepared recycled sub-base	822120040	B	C	A+	A+	B	A	C	A	C	E	B	B	B	A	40	180	894	72	90
over prepared sub-base	822120013	C	C	A+	B	A	A	C	B	C	E	B	B	A	A	40	170	218	18	90
Cement mortar wet laid UK sandstone setts (100 mm):																				
over prepared recycled sub-base	822120042	C	C	A+	B	A	A	C	B	C	E	B	B	B	A	40	180	679	55	90
over prepared sub-base	822120019	D	C	A+	E	A	A	C	B	C	E	B	B	A	A	40	180	3	0	90
Clay pavers (50 mm):																				
over prepared recycled sub-base	822120035	A	B	A+	A+	A	E	B	B	B	C	B	A	A	A	40	150	595	64	90
over prepared sub-base	822120002	B	B	A+	B	A+	E	B	B	B	C	B	A	A	A	40	150	1.7	0	90
Concrete block pavers (CBP) (80 mm):																				
over prepared recycled sub-base	822120037	A	B	A+	A+	A	A+	B	B	B	C	A	A	A	A	40	150	604	60	90
over prepared sub-base	822120005	B	B	A+	B	A	A+	C	B	C	C	A	A	A	A	40	150	11	1	90
Proprietary grass concrete paving (120 mm) over prepared sub-base (using suitable on-site available material)	822120011	A+	A+	E	A+	A+	A+	A+	B	A	A+	A+	A+	A+	A+	35	68	9.2	2	38

Surfacing for heavily trafficked areas	Element number	Summary Rating	Climate change	Water extraction	Mineral resource extraction	Stratospheric ozone depletion	Human toxicity	Ecotoxicity to freshwater	Nuclear waste (higher level)	Ecotoxicity to land	Waste disposal	Fossil fuel depletion	Eutrophication	Photochemical ozone creation	Acidification	Typical replacement interval	Embodied CO2 (kg CO2 eq.)	Recycled content (kg)	Recycled content (%)	Recycled currently at EOL (%)
Reclaimed clay pavers (50 mm):																				
over prepared recycled sub-base	822120045	A+	A+	A+	A+	A+	A+	A	A+	A	C	A+	A+	A+	A+	40	97	705	76	90
over prepared sub-base	822120044	A	A+	A+	A	A+	A+	A	A+	A	C	A+	A+	A+	A+	40	96	265	28	90
Reinforced concrete laid in situ (200 mm):																				
over prepared recycled sub-base	822120036	A	B	A+	A	A+	A+	C	A	C	C	A	A	A+	A	50	150	447	48	90
over prepared sub-base	822120004	B	B	A+	B	A+	A+	C	A	C	C	A	A	A+	A	50	150	6.9	1	90

Boundary protection

	Element number	Summary Rating	Climate change	Water extraction	Mineral resource extraction	Stratospheric ozone depletion	Human toxicity	Ecotoxicity to freshwater	Nuclear waste (higher level)	Ecotoxicity to land	Waste disposal	Fossil fuel depletion	Eutrophication	Photochemical ozone creation	Acidification	Typical replacement interval	Embodied CO2 (kg CO2 eq.)	Recycled content (kg)	Recycled content (%)	Recycled currently at EOL (%)
Brickwork wall:																				
1 brick thick	827020001	E	E	B	C	E	E	C	D	B	D	E	E	A	E	60	80	0.3	0	90
1/2 brick thick	827020002	B	D	A	A	B	B	A	B	A	B	B	B	A+	B	60	38	0.2	0	90
Concrete post: gravel board close boarded fencing	827020020	A	C	A+	A+	A	A+	A	A	A	A	A	B	A+	A	35	21	0	0	90
Galvanised steel:																				
palisade fencing	827020018	C	D	C	A+	A+	A+	A+	D	C	D	C	B	A+	B	35	57	1.9	15	94
post and wire strung at 1 ft intervals	827020003	A+	B	A+	A+	A+	A+	A+	A+	A+	A+	A+	A+	A+	A+	35	5.9	1.2	60	94
railings	827020004	B	D	A+	A+	A	A+	A+	E	E	B	B	C	A+	A	35	54	12	60	94
welded mesh fencing, metal posts	827020029	A	C	A+	A+	A+	A+	E	A	A	A+	A+	A+	A+	A+	20	14	1.2	44	94
wire chain link fence, metal posts	827020005	A	C	A+	A+	A+	A+	D	A	A	A+	A+	A+	A+	A+	35	14	2.5	60	94
Hedging or any living barrier	827020006	A+	B	A+	A+	A+	A+	A+	A+	A+	A+	A+	A+	A+	A+	25	1.7	0	0	5
Perforated concrete blockwork wall	827020008	A	B	A+	A+	A+	A+	A+	A+	A+	A+	A+	A	A+	A+	60	9.9	0	0	90
Plastic coated:																				
chain link fencing, metal posts	827020009	A	C	A+	A+	A+	A+	D	B	A	A+	A	A	A+	A+	30	16	2.4	55	87
steel palisade fencing	827020017	C	D	E	A+	A+	A+	A+	E	B	D	C	B	A+	B	35	55	1.9	15	94
weld mesh fencing, metal posts	827020016	A	C	A+	A+	A+	A+	D	A	A	A+	A+	A+	A+	A+	30	12	1.6	54	84
Pre-treated timber:																				
close boarded fencing	827020010	A+	A	A+	A+	B	A+	A	A+	A+	B	A+	A	D	A+	30	-14	0	0	17
palisade or picket fencing	827020011	A+	B	A+	A+	A	A+	A+	A+	A+	A	A+	A+	B	A+	30	-8	0	0	17
post and panel fencing	827020012	A+	A	A+	A+	C	A+	A	A	A+	C	A+	A	E	A+	20	-18	0	0	17
post and rail fencing	827020013	A+	B	A+	A+	A	A+	A+	A+	A+	A	A+	A+	C	A+	30	-9	0	0	17
post and trellis fencing	827020014	A+	B	A+	A+	A	A+	A+	A+	A+	A	A+	A+	B	A+	15	-8	0	0	17
Reclaimed brickwork wall:																				
1 brick thick	827020023	B	C	A+	A+	C	A+	A	A	A	E	A	C	A+	A	60	27	264	80	90
1/2 brick thick	827020024	A	C	A+	A+	A	A+	A+	A+	A+	B	A+	A	A+	A+	60	13	126	80	90

Boundary protection	Element number	Summary Rating	Climate change	Water extraction	Mineral resource extraction	Stratospheric ozone depletion	Human toxicity	Ecotoxicity to freshwater	Nuclear waste (higher level)	Ecotoxicity to land	Waste disposal	Fossil fuel depletion	Eutrophication	Photochemical ozone creation	Acidification	Typical replacement interval	Embodied CO2 (kg CO2 eq.)	Recycled content (kg)	Recycled content (%)	Recycled currently at EOL (%)
Reclaimed fencing	827020021	A+	A+	A+	A+	A+	A+	A+	A+	A+	C	A+	A+	A+	A+	10	-57	7.1	100	36
Reclaimed split stone wall:																				
cement mortar	827020032	A	C	A+	A+	B	A+	A+	A+	A+	B	A	B	A+	A+	60	14	149	87	90
lime mortar	827020027	A	C	A+	A+	B	A+	A+	A+	A+	B	A	B	A+	A+	60	14	149	87	90
Reclaimed stone wall:																				
cement mortar	827020025	B	C	A+	A+	D	A+	A+	A+	A+	E	A	C	A+	A	60	21	342	96	90
lime mortar	827020028	B	C	A+	A+	D	A+	A+	A+	A+	E	A	C	A+	A	60	20	342	96	90
Site sourced dry stone wall	827020007	A+	B	A+	A+	A+	A+	A+	A+	A+	A+	A+	A+	A+	A+	60+	0	0	0	90
Split stone wall:																				
cement mortar	827020026	C	C	A+	B	B	A+	A+	A	A+	B	A	B	A+	A	60	16	0.1	0	90
lime mortar	827020031	C	C	A+	B	B	A+	A	A+	A+	B	A	B	A+	A	60	15	0.1	0	90
Stone wall:																				
cement mortar	827020015	E	C	A	E	C	A+	A	B	A	E	B	D	A+	A	60	27	0.1	0	90
lime mortar	827020019	E	C	A	E	C	A+	A	B	A	E	B	D	A+	A	60	27	0.1	0	90

APPENDIX

PROJECT STEERING GROUP AND PEER REVIEW PANELS

The Green Guide to Specification and Environmental Profiles methodology research programme project steering group

- John Bowdidge — LCA Expert (Independent)
- John Burdett — BRE Trust
- Richard Daniels — Department for Children, Schools and Families (DCSF)
- Ken Double — Energy Saving Trust
- Michael Dowds — Post Office (Royal Mail)
- Andrew Eagles — Housing Corporation (now Homes and Communities Agency)
- John Gelder — NBS/RIBA
- David Graham — RBS
- Chris Hargreaves — HSBC
- George Martin — Willmott Dixon
- Brian Millsom — OGC
- David Moon — WRAP
- Jon Muncaster — English Partnerships (now Homes and Communities Agency)
- John Newman — Department for Business, Enterprise and Regulatory Reform (BERR)
- David Shiers — Oxford Brookes University
- Neil Smith — NHBC
- Kristian Steele — BRE Global
- Jane Thornback — Construction Products Association
- James Tinkler — RICS

The Green Guide to Specification and Environmental Profiles methodology critical peer review panel

- John Bowdidge — Independent LCA expert, UK
- Jacques Chevalier — CSTB, France
- Sverre Fossdal — Sintef, Norway
- Rolf Frischknecht — Centre for Life Cycle Inventories, Switzerland
- Tarja Häkkinen — VTT, Finland

Environmental Profiles methodology PCR third-party peer review panel

- John Bowdidge — Independent LCA expert, UK
- Eva Schmincke — Five Winds, Germany
- Wayne Trusty — Athena Sustainable Materials Institute, Canada

CONTACTS AND FURTHER INFORMATION

- For further information on BRE Environmental Profiles, visit www.bre.co.uk/envprofiles

- For further information on BREEAM, visit http://products.bre.co.uk/breeam/default.html

  The BREEAM Office
  Sustainability Group
  BRE Global
  Garston
  Watford
  WD25 9XX
  Tel: 01923 664462
  Fax: 01923 664103
  breeam@bre.co.uk
  www.bre.co.uk
  www.thegreenguide.org.uk

- For further information on the Envest software tool which provides more detailed analysis of building designs, including operational impacts of a building, visit www.bre.co.uk/envest

- For further information on sourcing of reclaimed and recycled materials, visit the Materials Information Exchange at www.bre.co.uk/waste

- For further information on the work of the Oxford Institute of Sustainable Development, contact David Shiers at davidshiers@brookes.ac.uk

REFERENCES

[1] **Shiers D, Howard N & Sinclair M.** The Green Guide to Specification. London, Post Office Property Holdings, 1996

[2] **Howard N, Shiers D & Sinclair M.** The Green Guide to Specification: An environmental profiling system for building materials and components. BR 351. Watford, BRE, 1998

[3] **BREEAM Centre.** BREEAM: BRE Environmental Assessment Method. www.breeam.org

[4] **Rao S, Yates A, Brownhill D & Howard N.** EcoHomes: the environmental rating for homes. BR 389. Bracknell, IHS BRE Press, 2000 (Reprinted 2003 with minor revisions)

[5] **Communities and Local Government (CLG).** The Code for Sustainable Homes. Available from www.communities.gov.uk/thecode or from www.planningportal.gov.uk

[6] **Anderson J & Howard N.** The Green Guide to Housing Specification: An environmental profiling system for building materials and components used in housing. BR 390. Bracknell, IHS BRE Press, 2000

[7] **Anderson J, Shiers D & Sinclair M.** The Green Guide to Specification: An environmental profiling system for building materials and components. 3rd edition. Oxford, Blackwell, 2002

[8] **BRE Global.** The Green Guide to Specification Online. www.thegreenguide.org.uk

[9] **Howard N, Edwards S & Anderson J.** BRE methodology for environmental profiles of construction materials, components and buildings. BR 370. Bracknell, IHS BRE Press, 1999

[10] **Anderson J & Edwards S.** Addendum to BRE methodology for environmental profiles of construction materials, components and buildings. Watford, BRE, 2000

[11] **BRE Global.** BRE Environmental and Sustainability (BES) Standard 6050. Methodology for Environmental Profiles of Construction Products: Product Category Rules for Type III environmental product declaration of construction products. BES 6050: Issue 1.0. 2009. Bracknell, IHS BRE Press, to be published 2009

[12] **British Standards Institution (BSI).** BS EN ISO 14040: 2006 Environmental management – Life cycle assessment – Principles and framework. London, BSI

[13] **British Standards Institution (BSI).** BS EN ISO 14025: 2006 Environmental labels and declarations – Type III environmental declarations – Principles and procedures. London, BSI

[14] **British Standards Institution (BSI).** BS EN ISO 21930: 2007 Sustainability in building construction – Environmental declaration of building products. London, BSI

[15] **Yates A, Baldwin R, Howard N & Rao S.** BREEAM '98 for Offices. Bracknell, IHS BRE Press, 1998

[16] **BRE.** Envest. Available from www.bre.co.uk/envest

[17] **BRE Certification.** www.GreenBookLive.com

[18] **BRE Global.** BRE Environmental and Sustainability (BES) Standard 6001. Framework Standard for Responsible Sourcing of Construction Products. BES 6001: Issue 1.0. 2008. Available as a pdf download from www.bre.co.uk

[19] **Bringezu S & Schütz H.** Total material requirement of the European Union. Technical report Nos 55 & 56. Copenhagen, European Environment Agency, 2001

[20] **Huijbregts MAJ.** Priority assessment of toxic substances in the frame of LCA – The multi-media fate, exposure and effect model USES-LCA. Amsterdam: University of Amsterdam, 1999

[21] **Institute for Environment & Sustainability.** European Union System for the Evaluation of Substances (EUSES). Version 1. Ispra, Italy, Joint Research Centre, European Commission, 1997

[22] **World Nuclear Association (WNA).** www.world-nuclear.org/education/wast.htm

[23] **Bundesamt für Umwelt, Wald und Landschaft (BUWAL: Swiss Agency for the Environment, Forests and Landscape).** Methodik für Oekobilanzen auf der Basis oekologischer Optimierung, Schriftenreihe Umwelt no. 133. Bern, Switzerland, BUWAL, October 1990

[24] **Product Ecology Consultants (PRé).** Eco-indicator 99: life cycle impact assessment and ecodesign method. Available at www.pre.nl/eco-indicator99

[25] **Heijungs R, Guinée JB, Huppes G et al.** Environmental life cycle assessment of products. Guide and background (Part 1). October 1992. Centrum voor Milieukunde (Institute for Environmental Sciences), Leiden University, 1992

[26] **Forster P, Ramaswamy V, Artaxo P, Berntsen T et al.** Changes in atmospheric constituents and in radiative forcing, Table 2.14. In: Solomon S, Qin D, Manning M, Chen Z et al (eds) Climate Change 2007: The physical science basis. Contribution of Working Group I to the Fourth Assessment Report of the Intergovernmental Panel on Climate Change. Cambridge, Cambridge University Press, 2007

[27a] **Derwent RG, Jenkin ME, Saunders SM & Pilling MJ.** Photochemical ozone creation potentials for organic compounds in Northwest Europe calculated with a master chemical mechanism. Atmospheric Environment 32: 2429–2441. 1998

[27b] **Jenkin ME & Hayman GD.** Photochemical ozone creation potentials for oxygenated volatile organic compounds: sensitivity to variations in kinetic and mechanistic parameters. Atmospheric Environment 33: 1775–1293. 1999

[28] **Heijungs R & Huijbregts M.** Threshold-based life cycle impact assessment and marginal change: incompatible? CML-SSP Working Paper 99.002. 1999. Centrum voor Milieukunde (Institute for Environmental Sciences), Leiden University (CML). Available from: www.leidenuniv.nl/CML

[29] **Aizlewood C, Edwards S, Hamilton L, Shiers D & Steele K.** Environmental weightings: their use in the environmental assessment of construction products. Information Paper IP 4/07. Bracknell, IHS BRE Press, 2007

[30] **Hamilton L, Edwards S, Aizlewood C, Shiers D, Thistlethwaite P & Steele K.** Creating environmental weightings for construction products: Results of a study. BR 493. Bracknell, IHS BRE Press, 2007

[31] **Anderson J, Bourke K, Clift M, Lockie S, Steele K & Wilkins A.** Performance and service life in the Environmental Profiles Methodology and Green Guide to Specification. Information Paper IP 1/09. Bracknell, IHS BRE Press, 2009

[32] **VB Johnson & Partners (Eds).** Laxton's Building Price Book 2006: Major and small works. Oxford, Butterworth-Heinemann, 2005

[33] **Construction Audit Limited.** HAPM Component life manual. Abingdon, E & FN Spon, 1992*

[34] **Building Performance Group** (**BPG**). BPGP Building fabric component life manual. Abingdon, E & FN Spon, 1999*

[35] **Building LifePlans** (**BLP**). Building services component life manual: Building LifePlans. Oxford, Wiley-Blackwell, 2000*

[36] **CIBSE.** Guide to ownership, operation and maintenance of building services. London, CIBSE, 2000

[37] **Building Cost Information Service (BCIS).** BMI Life expectancy of building components. London, BCIS, 2001

[38] **Property Services Agency** (**PSA**). Costs-in-use tables. Norwich, The Stationery Office, 1991

---

* The HAPM, BPG and BLP publications have now been updated
  and amalgamated into the BLP Construction Durability Database
  (www.blpinsurance.com: follow links to durability data);
  this was used as a central record).

[39] **WRAP.** Net Waste tool. Available at http://nwtool.wrap.org.uk

[40] **Department for Education and Skills.** Acoustic design of schools: a design guide. Building Bulletin Number 93. London, The Stationery Office, 2003

[41] **Department for Communities and Local Government (CLG).** Approved Document E: Resistance to the passage of sound. (2003 edition). Available as a pdf from www.planningportal.gov.uk

[42] **British Fenestration Rating Council** (**BFRC**). www.bfrc.org

[43] **British Standards Institution (BSI).** BS 5234-2: 1992 Partitions (including matching linings). Specification for performance requirements for strength and robustness including methods of test

[44] **Robust Details Limited.** Robust Details Handbook. 3rd edition (amended 2007). Available from www.robust details.com

[45] **Department for Education and Skills (DfES).** Standard specifications, layouts and dimensions for school buildings. SSLD 1: Partitions in schools. 2007. Available from www.teachernet.gov.uk

[46] **British Standards Institution (BSI).** BS 7533: 2001 Pavements constructed with clay, natural stone or concrete pavers
    Part 1: Guide for the structural design of heavy duty pavements constructed of clay pavers or precast concrete paving blocks
    Part 2: Guide for the structural design of lightly trafficked pavements constructed of clay pavers or precast concrete paving blocks

INDEX